JK
1316
·G22
1965

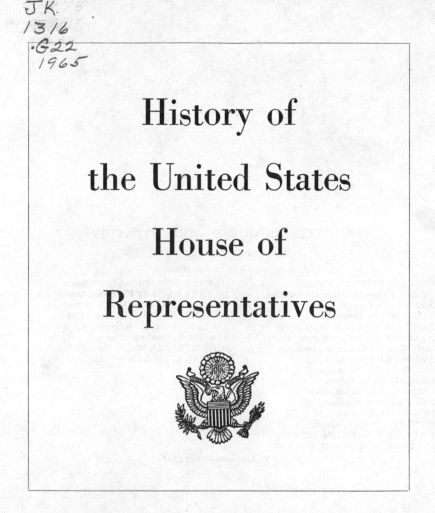

History of

the United States

House of

Representatives

PRINTED UNDER THE SUPERVISION OF THE
COMMITTEE ON HOUSE ADMINISTRATION
OMAR BURLESON, Chairman

U.S. GOVERNMENT PRINTING OFFICE, WASHINGTON : 1965

For sale by the Superintendent of Documents, U.S. Government Printing Office
Washington, D.C., 20402 · Price 60 cents

COMMITTEE ON HOUSE ADMINISTRATION

EIGHTY-NINTH CONGRESS

OMAR BURLESON, Texas, *Chairman*

SAMUEL N. FRIEDEL, Maryland
ROBERT T. ASHMORE, South Carolina
WAYNE L. HAYS, Ohio
PAUL C. JONES, Missouri
FRANK THOMPSON, JR., New Jersey
WATKINS M. ABBITT, Virginia
JOE D. WAGGONNER, JR., Louisiana
CARL D. PERKINS, Kentucky
JOHN H. DENT, Pennsylvania
SAM M. GIBBONS, Florida
LUCIEN N. NEDZI, Michigan
JOHN BRADEMAS, Indiana
JOHN W. DAVIS, Georgia
KENNETH J. GRAY, Illinois
AUGUSTUS F. HAWKINS, California
JONATHAN B. BINGHAM, New York

GLENARD P. LIPSCOMB, California
ROBERT J. CORBETT, Pennsylvania
CHARLES E. CHAMBERLAIN, Michigan
CHARLES E. GOODELL, New York
WILLARD S. CURTIN, Pennsylvania
SAMUEL L. DEVINE, Ohio
JOHN N. ERLENBORN, Illinois
WILLIAM L. DICKINSON, Alabama

JULIAN P. LANGSTON, *Chief Clerk*

II

H. Con. Res. 428   Passed July 7, 1965

(Submitted by Mr. Burleson of Texas)

Eighty-ninth Congress of the United States of America

AT THE FIRST SESSION

Begun and held at the City of Washington on Monday, the fourth day of January, one thousand nine hundred and sixty-five

Concurrent Resolution

Resolved by the House of Representatives (the Senate concurring), That there be printed as a House document a revised edition of the publication entitled "History of the United States House of Representatives", and that there be printed twenty-one thousand nine hundred and fifty additional copies to be prorated to the Members of the House of Representatives for a period of sixty days, after which the unused balance shall revert to the House document room.

Attest:

RALPH R. ROBERTS,
Clerk of the House of Representatives.

Attest:

FELTON M. JOHNSTON,
Secretary of the Senate.

III

PREFACE

In 1962 the "History of the United States House of Representatives" was published as House Document No. 246. The document enjoyed immediate success in filling a real need for a clear and concise history of the House, as well as a detailed explanation of the organization and inside functions of this intricate legislative body. The information in this document should acquaint Members of the House of Representatives and the public with the varied background of the first Chamber and impart a sense of its long and honorable history. It should inspire appreciation of the vitality and genius of our legislative institution.

The supply of House Document No. 246 is exhausted, with interest and demand for this informative work continuing unabated. House Document No. 250 renews the supply of the "History of the United States House of Representatives."

OMAR BURLESON, *Chairman.*

v

ACKNOWLEDGMENTS

The author acknowledges with thanks permission received from the following publishers and authors to quote brief passages from their indicated published works:

Annals of the American Academy of Political and Social Science. Article by Dorothy B. Goebel, September 1953.

The Macmillan Co. Quotations from *The Federalists*, *The Jeffersonians*, *The Jacksonians*, and *The Republican Era*, all by Leonard D. White.

University of Chicago Press. Quotations from *The Philosophy and Policies of Woodrow Wilson*, edited by Earl Latham.

University of Pittsburgh Press. Quotations from *The House of Representatives and Foreign Affairs*, by Holbert N. Carroll.

Floyd M. Riddick. Quotation from *Congressional Procedure*.

CONTENTS

APPENDIXES

HISTORY OF THE UNITED STATES HOUSE OF REPRESENTATIVES

(By George B. Galloway)

CHAPTER I

PLANNING THE HOUSE IN THE CONSTITUTIONAL CONVENTION

During the debates on the framing of the Constitution in the Federal Convention of 1787 a score of questions about the first branch of the National Legislature were discussed and decided. These decisions were derived in large part from the constitutions of the individual States, from the experience of the colonial assemblies, and from the practice of the Continental Congresses and the Congress of the Confederation. According to Farrand, "every provision of the federal constitution can be accounted for in American experience between 1776 and 1787."[1]

Their experience with state legislatures—

writes Binkley—

quite naturally led the framers of the Constitution to believe that the House of Representatives would possess a tremendous vitality as the immediate representative of the people. It would require no such special safeguards for its protection as the other coordinate branches of the government. [2]

After deciding that a National Government ought to be established consisting of a supreme legislative, executive and judiciary, the Federal Convention took up the question: Should the National Legislature be unicameral or bicameral? It was decided, apparently without debate, that it should consist of two branches. Although the Continental Congresses and the Congress of the Confederation had been unicameral, and likewise three State legislatures—Pennsylvania, Georgia, and Vermont—bicameralism was the prevailing form in most of the separate States and in the British Parliament from which the new Republic inherited much of its parliamentary practice. So it was decided, first in Committee of the Whole with Pennsylvania alone dissenting, and finally in the Convention itself by a vote of seven States to three (Maryland divided), that the new Congress should have two branches.

The next question was: Should the members of the first branch of the National Legislature be elected by the people or by the State legislatures? This question was twice debated in Committee of the Whole and twice decided in favor of their election by the people of

---

[1] Max Farrand, *The Framing of the Constitution of the United States* (1913), p. 204.
[2] Wilfred E. Binkley, *President and Congress* (1947), pp. 21-22. Binkley adds, however, that "the framers probably greatly overestimated the inherent strength of the lower house and left it too weak * * *. Is it not possible [he asks] that in their eagerness to establish a strong executive the framers left the lower house an 'incurably deficient and inferior organ of government'?" (pp. 22-23).

1

the several States. Some delegates like Sherman of Connecticut and Gerry of Massachusetts distrusted the people and feared an excess of democracy, but the majority favored popular election. Madison said that he "considered the popular election as essential to every plan of free government. * * *" George Mason of Virginia asserted that the House "was to be the grand depository of the democratic principles of the Government. * * * The requisites in actual representation are that the Representatives should sympathize with their constituents, should think as they think and feel as they feel, and that for these purposes should even be residents among them." When this question came before the Convention for final action, nine States voted for election by the people, two dissented, and one divided.

The third question considered was that of the powers of the National Legislature. Under the Articles of Confederation Congress had been a weak and incompetent creature of sovereign States which retained control over the essential functions of government. To correct this condition, the Convention (by a vote of six States to four), after debate, first conferred a broad grant of power upon Congress in the following terms:

To enjoy the legislative rights vested in Congress by the Confederation, and moreover to legislate in all cases for the general interests of the Union, and also in those to which the States are separately incompetent, or in which the harmony of the United States may be interrupted by the exercise of individual legislation

In the event, however, instead of this broad outline of authority, the Convention enumerated 18 specific powers of Congress, as reported by the Committee of Detail, which are set forth in article I, section 8 of the Constitution.

The next question relating to the first branch of the Legislature considered by the Convention was upon the rule of suffrage in the House. Should the States be equally represented in the first branch or in proportion to their population? After long discussion in Committee of the Whole, it was agreed that Members of the House should be elected in proportion to the population of the respective States, counting the whole number of free citizens and three-fifths of all others (slaves) except Indians not paying taxes. Later, after more than 2 weeks of discussion, this decision against equal representation of the States in the first branch of the Legislature was confirmed by the Convention by a vote of six States to four.

The term of office of Members of the Legislature next came up for discussion. Many Delegates preferred annual elections for the first branch, following colonial practice which was designed as a check on the royal governors. But Madison argued for triennial elections in order to enable Representatives to acquire knowledge of the interests and needs of other States. After debate, the Committee of the Whole decided in favor of a 3-year term for Representatives, but the Convention itself later fixed on biennial elections as a compromise between a 1-year and a 3-year term of office.

A long and hard fight took place in the Convention over the power to originate money bills. Should this power be limited to the popular branch, as most of the State constitutions then provided; or should the second branch have the right to amend them, as it could in three States? On these questions the Convention was deeply divided. Acting on a report from a compromise committee, it was first decided that money bills should originate in the first branch and should not be amended by the second branch. This was part of "the great compromise" of the Convention between the large and small States. After reconsideration and vacillation, however, the Convention finally decided (by a vote of nine States to two) that—

all bills for raising revenue shall originate in the House of Representatives; but the Senate may propose or concur with amendments as on other bills—

the latter being the language of the Massachusetts State Constitution.

A group of related questions now gave rise to a long and spirited debate: How many Members should the lower House of the First Congress have? How should they be distributed among the original States? Should Congress have power to regulate the representation of all the States in the future? Should the representation of the States in the first branch of the Legislature be based upon their wealth and number of inhabitants? After much disagreement, it was finally decided that the first House should have 65 Members, divided among the Thirteen Original States in the numbers prescribed in article I, section 2 of the Constitution; and that Congress should itself determine future apportionments of Representatives and direct taxes on the basis of the population of the States, counting three-fifths of the slaves and excluding Indians not taxed. Thus, the principle that taxation and representation should be linked together was inserted in the Constitution. Lest Congress have the power of making future changes in the representation of the States, Randolph's motion for a decennial census of inhabitants was adopted so as to provide a basis for a reapportionment of Representatives every 10 years. Both wealth and population were at first accepted as bases of representation, but after strong opposition was voiced to the use of property as a basis, the word "wealth" was stricken. On the eve of final adoption of the Constitution, after George Washington had spoken in its favor, the Convention unanimously agreed to change the ratio of representation in the lower House from 1 for every 40,000 inhabitants to 1 for every 30,000.

What qualifications should be required of those who were to elect the Congress? The population at that time comprised some seven classes:

first, the farmers, frontiersmen, and planters who formed the greatest single class, but almost all of whom owned land, even if they had no other property; second, the craftsmen and mechanics who largely worked on their own business; third, the mercantile interest composed of shopkeepers and their clerks; fourth, the commercial interest, most of whom were shipowners or importers or exporters; fifth, the shipbuilding interest; sixth, apprentices, domestic servants, and farm laborers; seventh, the lawyers, doctors, and clergymen.[3]

Property qualifications for voting varied so greatly among the States that it would have been difficult to devise any uniform rule for all the States. After debate, it was decided, therefore, to leave the qualifications of voters to regulation by the several States so as to avoid discriminating for or against any particular class of property owner. This the Convention did by adopting without dissent the proposal of its Committee of Detail stating that the qualifications of electors for the House of Representatives "shall be the same * * * as those of the electors in the several states, of the most numerous branch of their own legislatures."

---

[3] Charles Warren, *The Making of the Constitution* (1937), p. 400.

As regards the mode of congressional elections, the Convention, after little debate, adopted the provision contained in article I, section 4 of the Constitution that:

The times, places and manner of holding elections for Senators and Representatives, shall be prescribed in each State by the legislature thereof; but the Congress may at any time by law make or alter such regulations, except as to the places of choosing Senators.

What qualifications should Members of Congress have? Each of the State constitutions at that time contained provisions establishing various qualifications for members of the State legislatures as to residence, age, property, religion, etc. Almost all the State constitutions contained property qualifications for members of their legislatures. The Convention declined after debate, by a vote of seven States to three, to require Members of Congress to possess property. As to residence, proposals for 1, 3, and 7 years within the State were rejected and the provision was finally approved that "no person shall be a Representative * * * who shall not, when elected, be an inhabitant of that state in which he shall be chosen." Residence in the congressional district was not required. After much disagreement, it was finally decided to require a Member of the House of Representatives to be 25 years of age and 7 years a citizen of the United States. Thus, the qualifications of Members of Congress were much more democratic and liberal than those in the State constitutions of the period for members of their own legislatures.

Meanwhile, the Convention without debate or dissent agreed to the provision that "Each House shall be the judge of the elections, returns and qualifications of its own members"—a provision found in eight of the State constitutions at that time. A provision that "Each House may determine the rules of its proceedings, punish its members for disorderly behavior, and, with the concurrence of two thirds, expel a Member" was also approved. And Members of Congress, as well as all public officers of the United States, were exempted from any religious qualifications by the pronouncement that "no religious test shall ever be required as a qualification to any office or public trust under the authority of the United States."

On the adjournments of Congress and its place of sitting, the Convention accepted the report of its Committee of Detail. Power to prorogue or dissolve the colonial assemblies had often been a bone of contention between them and the royal governors. Hence, the new State constitutions reserved control over their own sessions and adjournments to the legislatures themselves. And these provisions were copied in the Federal Constitution, the final version of the pertinent subsection reading as follows:

Neither House, during the Session of Congress, shall, without the Consent of the other, adjourn for more than three days, nor to any other Place than that in which the two Houses shall be sitting.

The privileges of freedom from arrest and freedom of speech and debate, which are of great antiquity, dating far back in the practice of the English Parliament, and which were reaffirmed in the Articles of Confederation, were adopted by the Convention without debate and appear in the Constitution as follows:

The Senators and Representatives * * * shall in all Cases, except Treason, Felony and Breach of the Peace, be privileged from Arrest during their Attendance at the Session of their respective Houses, and in going to and returning from the same; and for any Speech or Debate in either House, they shall not be questioned in any other Place.

On the question whether legislative proceedings should be published or kept secret, there was considerable debate about the people's "right to know." Finally, the Convention approved of the requirement that:

Each House shall keep a Journal of its Proceedings, and from time to time publish the same, excepting such Parts as may in their Judgment require Secrecy; and the Yeas and Nays of the Members of either House on any question shall, at the Desire of one fifth of those Present, be entered on the Journal.

On the compensation of Members of Congress two questions gave rise to diverse views: Should Members of Congress be paid by the States or out of the National Treasury? And should the amount of their salaries be fixed in the Constitution or left to the discretion of Congress? Adherents of States' rights favored payment by the States, while the Nationalists argued that Congressmen were to be National, not State, officers and should be paid out of the Federal Exchequer. Evidently the majority of delegates "were convinced of the necessity," as Dickinson expressed it, "of making the general government independent of the prejudices, passions and improper views of the state legislatures," for the Convention finally decided by a vote of nine to two to pay congressional salaries out of the National Treasury in amounts "to be ascertained by law."

Two related questions provoked prolonged debate in the Convention: Should Members of Congress be ineligible to hold office under the State and National Governments? And should they be ineligible to reelection? Great importance was attached to the first question by "the resentment of the delegates towards some of the appointments which had been made by the Congress under the Confederation" of its own members to diplomatic and executive posts: "but it was chiefly due to the fear lest the President should combine with the Congress in corrupt bargains as to his appointments." [4] Those opposed to a ban on such appointments argued that it would degrade the legislature and impair the caliber of its membership. The impasse was finally broken by a vote of five States to four when the Convention adopted the following provision:

No Senator or Representative shall, during the Time for which he was elected, be appointed to any civil Office under the Authority of the United States, which shall have been created, or the Emoluments whereof shall have been increased during such time; and no Person holding any Office under the United States, shall be a Member of either House during his Continuance in Office.

The proposal to make Members of Congress ineligible for reelection, at least for a period of time, which was incorporated in the Articles of Confederation, was favored by those who believed in the theory of rotation in office. But it had operated to deprive the Congress of the Confederation of the continued and valuable services of such delegates as James Madison, and it was rejected by the Committee of the Whole without debate or dissent.

During the debates in the Convention several proposals were made by individual delegates, and later in the report of the Committee of Detail, to restrict the powers of Congress in various respects. Eight

[4] *Ibid.*, p. 618.

of these restraints were ultimately approved and embodied in article I, section 9 of the Constitution.

Two other decisions of the Convention affected the role of the House of Representatives. One concerned election of the President. Here it was finally agreed that, if no person received a majority of votes for President in the electoral college, the eventual election should be by the House instead of the Senate, each State to have one vote. The Convention assumed that this would happen in most cases, but it has actually occurred only twice in American history: in 1801 when the House chose Jefferson over Burr, and in 1825 when the House elected John Quincy Adams over Andrew Jackson.

The other decision affecting the House concerned the removal of the President. In all the State constitutions then in force the lower branch of the legislature was empowered to impeach. This precedent was followed by the Convention and the House of Representatives was assigned "the sole power of impeachment."

Such were the momentous decisions relating to the House of Representatives that were made by the framers in Philadelphia in 1787.

CHAPTER 2

PRECEDENTS ESTABLISHED IN FIRST CONGRESS

The first session of Congress under the new Constitution was scheduled to meet in New York City on March 4, 1789. But only 13 Members of the House of Representatives, from 5 of the 11 States that had ratified the Constitution up to that time, appeared and took their seats on that day. So the House met and adjourned from day to day until a quorum finally appeared on April 1. They came by ship, wagon, and stagecoach; some were delayed by bad roads, others by storms and shipwreck.

In its composition the first House of Representatives resembled the membership of the State legislatures of that period. "The members were good eighteenth century Americans," as one writer remarks, "average representatives of the ruling class of the time." [1] Mostly men of moderate views, the first Congress "contained many men of talent, character, and wide legislative experience." [2]

We are indebted to Fisher Ames, a Federalist member of the first four Congresses from Massachusetts, for a contemporaneous description of his colleagues. An impulsive and prolific letter writer, Ames said of the first House:

> The House is composed of sober, solid, old-charter folks * * *. There are few shining geniuses; there are many who have experience, the virtues of the heart, and the habits of business. It will be quite a republican assembly. * * * [3]

After 2 months in the House we find Ames writing to a friend as follows:

> I felt chagrined at the yawning listlessness of many here, in regard to the great objects of the government; their liableness to the impression of arguments *ad populum;* their State prejudices; their overrefining spirit in relation to trifles; their attachment to some very distressing formalities in doing business, and which will be a curse to all despatch and spirit in transacting it. I compared these with the idea I had brought here, of demigods and Roman senators, or at least, of the first Congress [meaning the Congress of the Confederation]. The objects now before us require more information, though less of the heroic qualities, than those of the first Congress. * * * But since, I have reflected coolly, that in all public bodies, the majority will be such as I have described—I may add, ought to be such; and if a few understand business, and have, as they will, the confidence of those who do not, it is better than for all to be such knowing ones; for they would contend for supremacy; there would not be a sufficient principle of cohesion. The love of ease makes many, who are knowing, submit to the judgment of others, more industrious, though not more knowing, than themselves, and this cements the mass. It produces artificial ignorance, which, joined with real ignorance, has been found, in fact, to furnish mortar enough for all public assemblies. The House is composed of very good men, not shining, but honest and reasonably well-informed, and in time they will be found to improve, and not to be much inferior in eloquence, science, and dignity, to the British Commons. [4]

---

[1] Ralph V. Harlow, *The History of Legislative Methods Before 1825* (1917), p. 123.
[2] Charles O. Paullin, "The First Elections Under the Constitution," *Iowa Journal of History and Politics,* January 1904, p. 28.
[3] Fisher Ames, *Works* (1854), vol. 1, p. 33.
[4] *Ibid.,* pp. 44-45.

Writing to the same friend 6 weeks later, Ames said:

There is the most punctual attendance of the members at the hour of meeting. Three or four have had leave of absence, but every other member actually attends daily, till the hour of adjourning. There is less party spirit, less of the acrimony of pride when disappointed of success, less personality, less intrigue, cabal, management, or cunning than I ever saw in a public assembly.[5]

The first House of Representatives contained 55 Federalists and 10 Anti-Federalists. The South accounted for half the seats in the House; New England and the Middle Atlantic States for one-quarter each. In the first Congress 9 Representatives had been members of the Constitutional Convention and 36 of the Continental Congress. Thirty-nine Representatives had served in State legislatures and 52 had been Members of either a State legislature, the Continental Congress, or the Federal Convention. Nineteen members of the first House were college graduates and 19 others had some academic training. Twenty-four were lawyers. Their median age was 44.

Popular interest in the first congressional elections was slight and only a small minority of interested property holders voted. One historian estimates the total vote in the first congressional elections at from 75,000 to 125,000, or from 3 to 3½ percent of the free population (3,200,000).[6]

Among the outstanding members of the first House were Frederick A. C. Muhlenberg, of Pennsylvania, the first Speaker; the studious James Madison of Virginia who was regarded as the "first man" in the House; and the vigorous Fisher Ames of Massachusetts who was often critical of the slow pace of the legislative process. The others spent their day on the legislative stage, played their parts, and then disappeared in the wings of oblivion.

ORGANIZATION OF THE HOUSE

The Constitution was silent on the organization and structure of the House beyond saying that it should choose its Speaker and other officers, that it could determine the rules of its proceedings, and that it should keep and publish a Journal of its business. But once a quorum appeared the House lost little time in organizing itself for the tasks ahead of the new Republic. This involved four steps: election of officers, adoption of rules, appointment of committees, and the acceptance of credentials.

On April 1, 1789, the first day a quorum was present, the House chose Frederick A. C. Muhlenberg, a Representative from Pennsylvania, as its Speaker by ballot by majority vote. A Clerk of the House (John Beckley) was then elected in the same manner on the same day. On April 4 a Doorkeeper and Assistant Doorkeeper were likewise appointed. A House Chaplin, Rev. William Linn, was elected by ballot on May 1. And a Sergeant at Arms (Joseph Wheaton) was elected on May 12. Meanwhile, the House approved the form of oath to be taken by Members and the chief justice of New York State, on request, administered the oath of office to the Speaker and other Representatives.

On April 2 a committee of 11 members was appointed, by order of the House, to prepare and report standing rules and orders of

---

[5] *Ibid.*, p. 61.
[6] Paullin, *loc. cit.*, p. 31.

proceeding. Five days later the report of this committee was submitted by Mr. Boudinot, read at the Clerk's table, and agreed to by the House. The simple code of initial rules then adopted dealt with four topics: the duties of the Speaker, decorum and debate, bill procedure, and Committees of the Whole House. On April 13 the House debated and adopted additional rules, as reported by the same committee, relating to committee service, leaves of absence, and appointment of a standing Committee of Elections. A resolution relating to joint rules with the Senate was laid on the table. And the next day the House agreed to an additional rule concerning its Sergeant at Arms: his appointment, symbol of office, and fees.

As noted above, a select Committee on Rules was appointed on April 2. And a standing Committee of Elections, composed of seven members, was elected by ballot on April 13 to examine and report upon Members' certificates of election which the House had ordered to be "delivered in" at the Clerk's table. On April 18 the House received and agreed to a report from its Committee on Elections accepting the credentials of 49 Members from nine States. And on April 29 the House agreed to the procedure to be followed by its Elections Committee in handling contested election cases which arose in South Carolina and New Jersey. Thus the first House expeditiously completed its organization.

EARLY HOUSE PROCEDURE

Compared with today's intricate, complex code, the parliamentary practice of the first House was simple indeed. Many of its Members had previous legislative experience and were presumably familar with the precedents in contemporary State legislative practice. Yet they preferred at the outset to adopt a few simple rules and let experience guide them in making additions to the rule book.

Fisher Ames complained of the slow progress of business in the early days. "As we manage our time," he wrote, "I think we shall never get out of employment." [7] After 2 months Madison wrote that—

in every step the difficulties arising from novelty are severely experienced, and are an ample as well as just source of apology. Scarcely a day passes without some striking evidence of the delays and perplexities springing merely from the want of precedents. Time will be a full remedy for this evil; and will, I am persuaded, evince a greater facility in legislating uniformly for all the States than has been supposed by some of the best friends of the Union.[8]

The duties assigned to the Speaker of the House by the first standing rule were modeled on those of the Speaker of the English House of Commons. He was to preside at sessions of the House, preserve decorum and order, put questions, decide points of order, announce the result of divisions and teller votes, appoint committees of not more than three members, and vote in all cases of ballot by the House.

Decorum and debate, motions and balloting, were governed by the second standing rule. No Member could speak more than twice to the same question without leave of the House. No Member could vote on any question in the result of which he was immediately and particularly interested; or in any other case where he was not present when

7 Fisher Ames, op. cit., p. 126.
8 Madison, Writings, V, p. 373.

the question was put. Every Member present in the House when a question was put was required to vote for or against it, unless excused. The previous question was to be admitted upon demand of five Members and its form was defined. Committees of more than three Members were to be chosen by ballot. And any 15 Members could compel the attendance of absentees.

According to the third rule, a committee was to be appointed to prepare every bill which should receive three readings but no bill could be read twice on the same day without special order of the House. After second reading a bill was to be engrossed or committed either to a select committee or to a Committee of the Whole House. After commitment and report, a bill could be recommitted at any time before its passage. But no bill amended by the Senate could be committed.

The fourth rule adopted on April 7, 1789, prescribed the procedure of Committees of the Whole House in which bills were to be twice read, debated by clauses, and subjected to amendment.

Several features of early parliamentary practice are interesting to recall. Conspicuous reliance was placed by the House, then as now, on the Committee of the Whole. The guiding principles of all the major measures of the first five Congresses, such as the first tariff bill and the acts organizing the executive departments, were formulated first in Committee of the Whole and were then referred to select committees to work out the details and draft the bills. A Committee of the Whole was the House itself under another name and in those days the House was small enough (65 Members) to function as a genuine deliberative assembly and to stage great debates on national questions.

After a problem such as the location of the permanent seat of the Federal Government had been discussed from every angle, in Committee of the Whole House on the State of the Union, it would be referred by House resolution to an *ad hoc* select committee with instructions to prepare and report a bill on the subject. Some days later the select committee would present its bill to the House, according to order, and after second reading the bill would be ordered committed to a Committee of the Whole House. The House would then resolve itself into a Committee of the Whole House, the Speaker would leave the chair, another Member would take the chair and the Committee of the Whole House would consider and probably adopt amendments to the bill. Then the Speaker would resume the chair and the chairman of the Committee of the Whole would report its action to the House and deliver the proposed amendments at the Clerk's table where they would be read twice and usually agreed to by the House. The House would then order the bill, with the amendments, to be engrossed and read the third time the next day. After third reading, the House would adopt a resolution that the bill pass and be entitled. Finally, the Clerk of the House would be directed to carry the bill to the Senate and request their concurrence.

The quality of the debates in Committee of the Whole varied, of course, for not all the Members were competent to elucidate general principles and some of the more brilliant Members were impatient at this time-consuming procedure. Fisher Ames, to quote him again, thought it was "certainly a bad method of doing business. Too little use is made of special committees." [9]

---

[9] Ames, *Works*, vol. 1, p. 64.

Writing to a friend in July 1789 about a revenue collection bill, Ames described the procedure as follows:

The bill was at first very imperfect. We labored upon it for some time, settled some principles, and referred it to a large and very good committee. They met, agreed upon principles, and the clerk drew the bill which they reported. We consider it in committee of the whole, and we indulge a very minute criticism upon its style. We correct spelling, or erase *may* and insert *shall*, and quiddle in a manner which provokes me. A select committee would soon correct little improprieties. Our great committee is too unwieldy for this operation. A great, clumsy machine is applied to the slightest and most delicate operations—the hoof of an elephant to the strokes of mezzotinto. * * * [10]

Another feature of early procedure was the election of House committees to confer with Senate committees on matters of mutual interest, such as the use of titles, if any, to be given to the President and Vice President; the enrollment of bills; the presentation of bills to the President for his approval; and to consider the remaining business of the session and the prospects of adjournment. In a bicameral legislature conference committees were from the start an essential feature.

Four instances of the use of the previous question are found in the *House Journal* of the first session of the First Congress. On the demand of five members that "the main question be now put," it was twice resolved in the negative and twice in the affirmative.[11]

The standing rules of the House were twice amended during the First Congress: first, on June 9, 1789, by changing the procedure when a division was called for; and, second, on January 12, 1791, by rescinding the rule that no bill amended by the Senate should be committed.

Only one instance is recorded during the first session of an appeal from a decision of the Chair. On September 11, 1789, an appeal was taken from a decision of the Chair that a motion to reconsider the proceedings of the previous day on the congressional salary bill was in order. After debate, the Speaker's ruling was upheld.[12]

The annals also disclose that the first election contest arose during the first session of Congress. The question was whether William Smith of South Carolina has been 7 years a citizen of the United States at the time of his election. After due consideration, the House resolved the question in his favor.[13]

COMMITTEES IN THE FIRST CONGRESS

In the light of recent criticisms that the modern Congress has lost control of its autonomous standing committees, it is interesting to recall that the early practice of the House of Representatives was to set up a select committee on every bill. Whether it was to provide for the first census or to regulate the importation of slaves prior to 1808, or whatever the subject matter, Congress retained control of its committees by giving them specific instructions as to their authority and duties.

The First Congress relied, as we have seen, on Committees of the Whole House for developing the general principles of legislation, and upon numerous select committees to perfect the details of bills.

10 *Ibid.*, p. 61.
11 *House Journal*, vol. 1, May 11, 16, Aug. 18, 1789, and Apr. 26, 1790.
12 *Ibid.*, Sept. 11, 1789.
13 *Ibid.*, May 22, 1789.

Thus, on April 11, 1789, the House elected by ballot a select committee of nine to draft a bill to regulate import duties. On April 29 it ordered the appointment of a committee to report on the supplies needed for the current year. A select committee to consider and report on the state of unappropriated lands in the Western territory was set up on May 28, 1789. A select committee of 11—1 from each State—was elected to consider amendments to the Constitution on July 21. And at the opening of the second session of the First Congress the House appointed four select committees to consider as many matters mentioned in the President's state-of-the-Union message; it amended its rules at the same time by providing that all committees should be appointed by the Speaker, unless otherwise directed by the House in which event they were to be appointed by ballot.

Only one standing committee dates from the First Congress, the Committee of Elections, whose seven members were elected by ballot on April 13, 1789, to examine and report upon the certificates of election and to investigate election contests. On February 1, 1790, after the opening of the second session, this committee was reappointed with three of its original members and four new ones.

In approving joint rules between the two Houses on July 27, 1789, the House authorized the creation of a joint standing Committee on Enrolled Bills to be composed of one Senator and two Representatives who were named a few days later. This committee was reappointed on February 2, 1790. Joint select committees were set up during the First Congress to consider furnishing newspapers to Members of Congress at public expense, to receive proposals for printing the acts and proceedings of Congress, to request the President to establish a day of public thanksgiving, and to consider the time for the commencement of the next Congress.[14]

During debate on the bill to establish a Treasury Department, the question of creating a Committee of Ways and Means arose. Several of the State legislatures had finance committees and many Members felt that Congress should have a committee to advise it on fiscal matters. The House agreed and ordered the appointment of a Committee of Ways and Means, consisting of a member from each State who were named on July 24, 1789. But on September 17 this committee was "discharged from further proceeding on the business referred to them" and it was "referred to the Secretary of the Treasury, to report thereon." [15] Evidently the House, or at least the Federalists, had more confidence at that time in Alexander Hamilton, who had just become Secretary of the Treasury, than in its own committee. Not until 1795 was a permanent standing Committee on Ways and Means created.

RELATIONS WITH THE SENATE

By the great compromise of 1787 the Constitution created a bicameral legislature in which the House was to represent the people of the several States and the Senate, whose Members were to be elected by the State legislatures, was to represent the "sovereign states" themselves. Since all legislative powers "herein granted" had been vested in a Congress composed of two Houses, it was

14 *House Journal*, May 15, and Sept. 25, 1789, and Jan. 20, 1791.
15 *Annals*, 1st Cong., vol. 1, p. 929.

obviously necessary for them to devise methods of communication and cooperation with each other in order to carry out their concurrent functions. Relations between the Houses were destined to be different from those between the House of Commons and the House of Lords in the English Parliament, and those between the councils and assemblies in the colonial legislatures, because of the differences in their powers, their representative character, and their constitutional functions.

Important precedents were established during the First Congress regarding the forms of joint action between the two bodies. Within the first 6 weeks of their organization the two Houses had met in joint sessions, had set up several joint committees, and had adopted joint rules.

The first communication between them took place on April 6, 1789, the day on which the Senate organized, when the House received a message from the Senate, delivered by Mr. Ellsworth of Connecticut, that a quorum of that body had formed and was now ready in the Senate Chamber to proceed, in the presence of the House, to count the votes of the electors for President and Vice President. Whereupon the House resolved to proceed to the Senate Chamber for this purpose and appointed two of its Members to make a list of the votes in cooperation with a Member of the Senate. Accordingly, the two Houses held their first joint session in the Senate Chamber and canvassed the votes of the electors. After the House had withdrawn, Mr. Madison conveyed a message to the Senate saying that it was the desire of the House that the notifications of the election of the President and Vice President of the United States should be made by such persons and in such manner as the Senate should be pleased to direct.

Congress met again in joint session on April 30 in the Senate Chamber to hear the inaugural address of President Washington and then the Members of both Houses accompanied the President and Vice President for divine services at St. Paul's Chapel, performed by the Chaplain of Congress.

The House resolved on June 16, 1789, that seats be provided, "within the bar," for the accommodation of the President and Members of the Senate, presumably in order to facilitate joint sessions. The first joint committee was set up, at the initiative of the Senate, to prepare a system of rules to govern the two Houses in cases of conference and to regulate the appointment of Chaplains. Upon receipt of a letter from Senator Ellsworth stating that the Senate had appointed its members of this committee, the House on April 9 elected a committee of five for these purposes. The joint committee's report was agreed to by the House on April 17. In seven lines it stated the rule for a free conference between committees of the two Houses in cases of disagreement on amendments to bills, the law and practice of which now occupy 16 pages in the *Senate Manual*. Each House was also to appoint a Chaplain and they were to "interchange weekley."

Subsequently, joint committees were frequently set up for both ceremonial and legislative purposes. During the first session of the First Congress such groups were created to consider the titles to be used in addressing the President and Vice President, the administration of the Presidential oath, the ceremonial of receiving the President and the arrangements for reception of the Vice President, the proper mode of communicating papers, bills, and messages between the Houses, the disposition of certain executive papers, the preparation of joint rules, the mode of presenting addresses, bills, etc. to the President, certain amendments of the tariff bill, and the unfinished business of the Congress.

Almost 3 months elapsed between the appointment and report of the committee set up to prepare joint rules. Its report, accepted by the House on July 27, 1789, established joint rules relating to the enrollment, examination, and signature of bills, orders, resolutions and votes and to the presentment of joint addresses to the President.

Several weeks also passed before the two Houses reached an agreement on the formalities of intercommunications. At first it was proposed that messengers from either House should make "obeisances" at the door of the other Chamber upon entering and leaving it, during which ceremony the Members were to rise and remain standing. But a simpler ritual was finally agreed upon, requiring merely that a message sent from one House to the other be announced at the door by the doorkeeper and be respectfully communicated to the Presiding Officer by the messenger. It was further provided that "Messages shall be sent by such persons as a sense of propriety in each House may determine to be proper." [16] The first communications between the two Houses were conveyed by Members thereof. After John Adams assumed the duties of the Vice Presidency, he wrote several letters to the Speaker of the House about titles and ceremonies in which he was greatly interested. It was not long, however, before the journals showed messages and bills being transmitted between the Houses by the Secretary of the Senate and the Clerk of the House.

Later, after a year's experience, supplementary rules were adopted on the recommendation of a joint committee appointed to consider what additional regulations were necessary for conducting the business between the Houses. These rules prescribed that when a bill, passed by one House, was rejected by the other, notice of such rejection should be given to the House which had approved, and that a bill thus rejected should not be brought in during the same session, without 10 days notice and leave of two-thirds of that House in which it should be renewed. It was also provided that each House should transmit to the other the papers pertinent to any pending bill or resolution, and that after each House should have adhered to its disagreement, a bill or resolution should be lost. [17]

LEGISLATIVE OUTPUT

The First Congress enacted many important and useful laws. It met for three sessions lasting a total of 519 days. It had not only to organize itself and to establish the basic institutions of the new government, but also to lay the foundations of the American economy. More than threescore major statutes were the legislative fruit of its efforts. It created the War, Treasury, and Foreign Affairs (State) Departments. It established the judicial courts of the United States, a Land Office, and a government for the Northwest Territory. It passed a tariff bill, an invalid pensions measure, and a bill for the regulation of the coastal trade. It established the permanent seat of the National Government and fixed the compensation of executive and judicial officers and employees. It enacted the first annual

16 *House Journal*, Apr. 28, 1789.
17 *Annals of Congress*, vol. 1, p. 987.

appropriations acts, passed several relief bills, and submitted the first 10 amendments to the Constitution. It considered scores of memorials and petitions as well as laws regulating patents and copyrights, bankruptcies, harbors, the punishment of crimes, naturalization, the importation of slaves, and intercourse with the Indian tribes. It also considered bills for the establishment of lighthouses and hospitals, the encouragement of commerce and navigation, the establishment of a uniform militia, conveyance of the mails, claims against the United States, the remission of fines, the encouragement of learning, progress of the useful arts, succession to the Presidency, reduction of the public debt, rates of foreign exchange, and the admission of Kentucky and Vermont into the Union.

The House and the Senate divided the honors in originating this vast legislative output. The bills creating the new departments, the financial measures, the tariff bill, and the bill for the assumption of the State debts started in the House of Representatives. On the other hand, the Senate took the initiative in the act establishing the temporary and permanent seat of the Government, it started the bill for incorporating the first bank of the United States, and it originated the procedure for the organization of new States and territories. The Senate also took the lead in the measures establishing the judicial courts of the United States, regulating their procedure, and providing for the punishment of crimes against the United States. From the earliest days the Senate functioned not only as a chamber of revision but also exercised its right to originate legislation. However, its sessions were held in secret while those of the House were open to the public which thronged its galleries.

RELATIONS WITH THE PRESIDENT

During the first decade of the new Republic, when the sessions of Congress were held in New York City and Philadelphia, the office of the President was located in the same building where Congress met. This physical propinquity combined with the need of collaboration in organizing the new Government to make for closer relations between Congress and the Executive than obtained after the seat of the Government was transferred to the District of Columbia.

The first contact occurred on April 23, 1789, when a joint committee composed of five Representatives and three Senators, appointed for the purpose, met President Washington at Elizabethtown, N.J., and escorted him by vessel to New York and to the house selected for his residence. Meanwhile, a joint committee of three Representatives and two Senators waited upon Vice President Adams and congratulated him upon his arrival in the city.

One week later, in accordance with a ceremonial arranged by another joint committee, the oath of office was administered to the new President in the Representatives' Chamber by the Chancellor of New York State in the presence of both Houses. George Washington then delivered his first inaugural address in person to a joint session of Congress held in the Senate Chamber, whereupon the President, Vice President, and all the Members of both Houses proceeded to St. Paul's Chapel to hear divine service.

The next day the Speaker laid a copy of the President's address before the House which considered it in Committee of the Whole and then appointed a committee of five members, chaired by James Madison, to prepare a reply. The Madison committee prepared an eloquent reply, congratulating the First Magistrate upon his election to the highest honor in the land and expressing sentiments of affection and esteem, which was read to the House on May 5 and unanimously approved. On May 8 the Speaker, attended by the Members of the House, presented their reply to the President in a room adjoining the House Chamber.

Some other matters affecting legislative-executive relations were disposed of during the first session. The House agreed to a report of a joint committee regarding the impropriety of using any supplementary titles of the offices of President and Vice President other than those given in the Constitution. The House also accepted the report of another joint committee concerning the proper mode of communications from the President which were to be directed to the President of the Senate or the Speaker of the House, as the case might be.

On January 8, 1790, President Washington delivered his state of the Union message in person to a joint session of Congress in the Senate chamber. After considering his address in Committee of the Whole on the following day, the House appointed a committee of three to prepare a reply "with assurances that this House will, without delay, proceed to take into their serious consideration the various and important matters recommended to their attention." [18] And when on January 14 the entire House presented their reply to the President at his residence, he said to them: "I have full confidence that your deliberations will continue to be directed by an enlightened and virtuous zeal for the happiness of our country." [19] When the same ritual was repeated the following December, Fisher Ames confided to a friend: "We have had the speech from the throne, have answered it, and tomorrow we are to present our answer. Both contain some divine molasses." [20]

RELATIONS WITH THE DEPARTMENTS

The First Congress, as we have seen, established three executive departments: of Foreign Affairs (State), of War, and a Treasury Department, each headed by a Secretary removable by the President. It also passed an act for the temporary establishment of the Post Office.

While these new department heads were executive officials and were designed to be instruments of the President, and while the statutes creating them did not authorize the Congress to give them orders, nevertheless we find the First Congress soon issuing them a series of directives. Thus, the Secretary of State, Thomas Jefferson, was "ordered" by the House on January 15, 1790, to prepare and report "a proper plan or plans for establishing uniformity in the currency, weights, and measures of the United States." [21] And on February 23, 1791, the House "ordered" the Secretary of State to report to Congress the nature and extent of the privileges and restrictions of the commercial intercourse of the United States with foreign nations

[18] House Journal, Jan. 9, 1790.
[19] Ibid., Jan. 14, 1790.
[20] Fisher Ames, Works, I, p. 89.
[21] House Journal, Jan. 15, 1790.

and measures for the improvement of our commerce and navigation.[22] Again, on April 23, 1790, the House directed the Secretary of War, Mr. Knox, to submit an account of the troops and ordnance stores furnished by the several States toward the support of the late war.[23]

These early precedents were overshadowed, however, by the relations between the First Congress and the Secretary of the Treasury, Alexander Hamilton. As noted above, the House of Representatives set up a Committee of Ways and Means on July 24, 1789, to advise it on fiscal matters, but 8 weeks later the House discharged this committee and referred its business to the Secretary of the Treasury "to consider and report thereupon." [24] Simultaneously it ordered him to report an estimate of the sums required to defray the expenses of the civil list and the War Department for the current year. This precedent was followed by a long series of House directives to Mr. Hamilton which made it evident that Congress regarded him as its agent and adviser in matters of public finance and the national economy. Among the matters that the Secretary was directed to report upon to the House during his first 16 months in office were the following: [25]

A plan for the support of the public credit.

The public debts of the several states.

Statement of warrants issued by Superintendent of Finance and the Board of Treasury.

A plan for the promotion of manufactures.

Difficulties encountered in collecting duties and regulating the coastal trade.

Payment of interest in State debts.

Collection of import and tonnage duties.

A plan for establishing a National Mint.

Receipts from and payments to the several States.

Compensation of collectors of internal revenue.

Such heavy congressional reliance upon the Secretary of the Treasury, in lieu of its own Ways and Means Committee, reflects the intimate relationship that existed between Alexander Hamilton and the first Congresses. The statute creating his Department evidently permitted a closer relationship between Congress and the Treasury than with the State and War Departments, for it required the Secretary of the Treasury—

to digest and prepare plans for the improvement and management of the revenue, and for the support of the public credit; to prepare and report estimates of the public revenue, and the public expenditures; * * * to make report, and give information to either branch of the legislature, in person or in writing * * * respecting all matters referred to him by the Senate or House of Representatives, or which shall appertain to his office; and generally to perform all such services relative to the finances, as he shall be directed to perform.[26]

The absence of similar language in the laws creating the State and War Departments, and the failure of this statute to authorize the President to assign duties to the Secretary of the Treasury, seems to signify a congressional intent to give this official a unique status.

[22] Ibid., Feb. 23, 1791.
[23] Ibid., Apr. 23, 1790.
[24] Ibid., Sept. 17, 1789.
[25] Ibid., Sept. 21, 23, 1789; Jan. 9, 15, 19, Mar. 2, Apr. 15, 23, 1790; Jan. 18, 1791.
[26] Statutes at Large, vol. I, pp. 65-67.

Hamilton's successful influence with the first Congresses and their early use of the department heads to prepare plans, draft bills, handle petitions, etc., explain perhaps why the system of standing committees did not develop until later years. It appears that the early Federalists may have conceived of the heads of departments as constituting a ministry in the British sense of the term. Under this concept it was the proper function of a finance minister to take the initiative in fiscal policy formation, to supervise the legislative process, and to promote the adoption of his policies.

Be this as it may, Hamilton's power in Congress caused deep distress among some Republican Members. Thus Senator Maclay confided to his diary:

Were Eloquence personified and reason flowed from her tongue, her talents would be in vain in our assembly; * * * Congress may go home. Mr. Hamilton is all-powerful, and fails in nothing he attempts.[27]

Maclay goes on to cite four measures: the assumption, bank, and excise bills, and a resolution regarding the mint, all of which, despite opposition, were passed largely as a result of Hamilton's personal efforts and influence.[28] One historian concludes his description of these events by saying that "the Secretary of the Treasury was the most important factor in Congress during its first session." [29]

RELATIONS WITH THE STATES

Official relations with the governments of the States were rare during the first session. In May 1789, applications were received by the Congress from the Legislatures of Virginia and New York for the calling of a convention to consider the "defects" of the Federal Constitution and to report amendments thereof designed to secure "the great and unalienable rights of mankind." In the same month the House received an offer from the Legislature of Virginia of 10 square miles of territory anywhere in the State for use as the seat of the Federal Government. A similar offer was received from the Maryland Legislature. On June 5, 1789, the House concurred with a Senate resolution requesting the President to transmit two copies of every act of Congress to the Governors of each of the States.

EVOLUTION OF PARTY ORGANIZATION

The early months of the First Congress were marked by a notable absence of party spirit. Peace and brotherly love prevailed at the outset, induced perhaps by a sense of historic responsibility for launching the new regime. It was not long, however, before controversies arose, inspired by underlying sectional and philosophical differences among the members. These were reflected in the arguments over legislative proposals to regulate the slave trade and in the debates over the location of the permanent seat of the Federal Government.

These disputes gave rise, in turn, to the first meeting of like-minded Members of the Legislature which gradually evolved into party organizations of Federalists and Republicans. At these meeting party policies on current issues were discussed, crystallized, and embodied in drafts of bills which were subsequently introduced in Congress.

---

[27] Maclay, *Journal*, p. 387.
[28] *Ibid.*, pp. 209, 355, 385, 409.
[29] Harlow, *op. cit.*, p. 143.

Thus, the actual initiative in legislation came to be transferred from the Committee of the Whole to the party caucus.

The Federalists were the first to develop a parliamentary party in Congress because they were in the majority in the early years and because they also had the advantage of the superlative leadership of Alexander Hamilton who was a master of the arts of political organization. As Secretary of the Treasury he was in close touch with the Congress and, according to contemporary observers, he dominated it behind the scenes through what were, in effect, party caucuses. Thus Maclay speaks of "the rendezvousing of the crew of the Hamilton galley," and to a "call of the gladiators this morning," and to the statement of Speaker Muhlenberg that "there had been a call of the Secretary's party last night." [30]

The gap between the Legislature and the Executive, created by the constitutional system of separated powers, was thus bridged by the Hamiltonian or Federalist Party organization before the First Congress ended.

Instead of being a forum, where every member was a peer and no man led, where great principles of government were evolved through the give and take of unrestricted discussion, Congress as such had become in effect a mere ratifying body. The real work of legislation was put in shape, not in the legislature, but in secret session of the majority party. In this organization, unknown to the Constitution and beyond the reach of the rules of either chamber, the executive could work with the party-following in Congress, and secure the adoption of a prearranged program.[31]

Thus the first manifestation of party tactics made an early appearance, although the State legislatures were already familiar with them. They attained their peak of perfection a century later under the astute leadership of Speakers Reed and Cannon.

---

[30] Maclay, *Journal*, pp. 208, 227, 235.
[31] Harlow, *op. cit.*, p. 145.

CHAPTER 3

THE COMPOSITION OF CONGRESS

As the young Nation grew in population and expanded westward toward the Pacific, the size of the House of Representatives increased, although not at a corresponding pace. During the first half century the population quadrupled in number, growing from some 3.9 million in 1790 to 17 million in 1840, while their Representatives in Congress were increasing from 65 to 232 Members. By 1890 the population had almost quadrupled again, rising to 63 million persons who were represented at Washington by 357 Congressmen. And after another half century of amazing expansion, the Nation had 132 million inhabitants in 1940 while the House of Representatives had limited its size since 1913 to 435 Members. By 1960 the population had reached 180 million.

Since population grew more rapidly than the membership of the House of Representatives, the effect of these changes was gradually to increase the average number of inhabitants represented by each Member. Thus during the First Congress the constituencies averaged about 33,000 persons compared with an average of 71,000 in 1840, 176,000 in 1890, 303,000 in 1940, and 390,000 in 1957. In other words, a Member of the House today has almost 12 times as many constituents on the average as he had in 1790.

It is also interesting to note the effect of these changes upon the distribution of seats in the House of Representatives among the principal geographical regions of the country. The South controlled half the seats in the House in the First Congress and accounts with 134 seats for 31 percent of the total today. New England, which had about one-quarter of the seats in 1790, now has only 6 percent of the total. The Middle Atlantic States, which were on a par with New England in the beginning, now have 20 percent, or more than three times as many Representatives as New England. The North Central region, whose 12 stars did not appear upon the flag until the 19th century, now controls 129 seats (30 percent) in the House—the second largest single regional bloc. And the 11 Western States, last to be admitted to the Union, prior to Alaska and Hawaii, account for 13 percent of the present membership with 57 Members.

HISTORY OF APPORTIONMENT

Recalling the old system of "rotten" or "pocket" boroughs represented in the British House of Commons, the Founding Fathers provided in the Constitution of the new Republic that Representatives in Congress should be apportioned among the several States according to their respective numbers and that the actual enumeration should be made within 3 years after the first meeting of the Congress, and within every 10 years thereafter "in such manner as they shall by law direct." Article I, section 2, further provided that "the number of

20

Representatives shall not exceed one for every thirty thousand, but each state shall have at least one Representative." In the event of vacancies in the representation from any State, the Governor thereof was to issue writs of election to fill them. The growth in the size of the House since 1789 is shown in the table below.

Growth in size of House, 1789–1960

Year	Number of Representatives [1]	Year	Number of Representatives [1]
1789	65	1870	293
1790	106	1880	332
1800	142	1890	357
1810	186	1900	391
1820	213	1910	435
1830	242	1930	435
1840	232	1940	435
1850	237	1950	435
1860	243	1960	437

[1] No apportionment was made in 1920.

As the 19th century advanced and the country grew, the question of the formula to be employed in distributing representation among the States provoked bitter arguments on the House floor between spokesmen for the slow-growing and fast-growing commonwealths. Whether or not one Representative should be added for each major fraction over the ratio was a particular bone of contention. The disuse of fractions in some of the early apportionment acts deprived some States of full representation in the House, notably the New England States. In 1832, for example, John Quincy Adams confided to his diary:

I passed an entirely sleepless night. The iniquity of the bill and the disreputable means by which so partial and unjust a distribution of the representation had been effected, agitated me so that I could not close my eyes. I was all night meditating in search of some device, if it were possible, to avert the heavy blow from Massachusetts and from New England.[1]

Advocates of a small body argued, meanwhile, that it would result in economy and less confusion on the floor, more efficient transaction of business and greater opportunity for the individual Member, reduced power of committees and less rigid rules. James Bryce suggested that it would also spare the House the hazards of a crowd psychology.[2]

There has been a readjustment of House representation every decade except during the period 1911 to 1929. The present total membership of 435 was first attained in 1913 and has not been changed since then. Congress has by law provided for the automatic apportionment of the 435 Representatives among the States according to each census including and after that of 1950. After the admission of Alaska and Hawaii as States during the 86th Congress, the size of the House temporarily increased to 437 Members. The apportionment acts formerly provided that the districts in a State should equal the number of its Representatives, with no district electing more than one Member, and that the districts were to be composed of contiguous and compact territory containing as nearly as practicable an equal number of inhabitants; but the acts of 1929 and 1941 omitted such

[1] John Quincy Adams, *Diary*, vol. VIII, pp. 471–472.
[2] De Alva S. Alexander, *History and Procedure of the House of Representatives* (1916), p. 8.

provisions. After any apportionment, until a State is redistricted in a manner provided by its own law, the question whether its Representatives shall be elected by districts, at large, or by a combination of both methods, is determined by the Apportionment Act of 1941. The House has always seated Members elected at large in the States, although the law required election by districts. Questions have arisen from time to time, when a vacancy has occurred soon after a change in districts, whether the vacancy should be filled by election in the old or new district. The House has declined to interfere with the act of a State in changing the boundaries of a district after the apportionment has been made.

LEGISLATIVE APPORTIONMENT PROCEDURE

The Apportionment Act of November 15, 1941, makes the procedure for apportioning Representatives entirely automatic, requiring no action by Congress other than review. The right of Congress to change the procedure whenever it deems such action advisable has in no way been relinquished. As the first step in the procedure of apportionment the Bureau of the Census enumerates the population and tabulates State totals within 8 months after the start of the enumeration. As part of the report to accompany these population figures, a table shows the distribution of the existing number of Representatives among the States, using the method of equal proportions. The report containing this information is transmitted to the Congress by the President within the first week of the next session of that body. In 15 days the Clerk of the House of Representatives informs the Executive of each State of the number of Members of the House of Representatives to which his State will be entitled in the following Congress, to meet about 2 years hence. Thus, Congress has eliminated the possiblity of a decade passing without a redistribution of seats, such as occurred during the decade 1920 to 1930. The use of a method based upon sound mathematical principles has been combined with an automatic procedure for putting the results of this method into effect.

The need for an automatic procedure that would assure a reapportionment after each decennial census was apparently felt at an early date, as the legislation for the seventh (1850) decennial census contained such a provision. The method specified by this act was the "Vinton Method." However, when a new census act was passed in 1870, no mention was made of any reapportionment procedure, automatic or otherwise. Apparently the apportionments of both 1850 and 1860 as calculated under the procedures set up by the act of 1850 were not satisfactory, for in both years changes in assignments to certain States were made by supplementary legislation.

An automatic procedure was not discussed again to any extent until late in the decade 1920 to 1930. At that time a great many persons were disturbed by the failure of Congress to redistribute seats on the basis of the 1920 census, for it was felt that many States were not properly represented. Until the 73d Congress, which convened in 1933, the number of Representatives from each State remained as assigned on the basis of the census of 1910. Because of different rates of growth of the various States and because of the large migrations of people from one State to another during and after

World War I, major injustices occurred. For example, one such injustice was corrected when the apportionment based on the census of 1930 went into effect and the State of California gained 9 members, increasing its representation from 11 to 20, although the size of the House did not change.

MAJOR FRACTIONS VERSUS EQUAL PROPORTIONS

As a result of feeling aroused by inequalities in apportionment, Congress took steps to prevent a repetition of such injustices and inserted an apportionment section in the act for the taking of the 15th (1930) and subsequent decennial censuses. The procedure adopted called for a report that included calculations by two methods, major fractions and equal proportions. If Congress did not act on this report within a year, an apportionment by the method last used went into effect automatically. When the 15th Decennial Census Act was passed on June 18, 1929, the proponents of the methods of major fractions and of equal proportions were unable to come to an agreement. It was decided to require computations by both methods and then permit a period for debate after which a decision could be made between the two. When the computations based on the census of 1930 were made, however, they showed no difference between the results of the two methods. Thus, the need for a decision did not arise, and an apportionment was effected without further action by Congress.

In the computations based upon the census of 1940, however, a difference between the methods in the allocation of one Representative did occur. If the method of major fractions had been used, the number of Representatives from the State of Arkansas would have decreased from 7 to 6, while an additional Representative would have been added to the 17 for the State of Michigan. By the method of equal proportions the representations from Arkansas and Michigan remained at 7 and 17, respectively. The volume of other legislation in Congress caused a delay in the consideration of this topic until after the period of debate had expired, but Congress wished to consider further the issues raised by the apportionment report. The primary issue in this instance appears to have been the question of which method of apportionment was to be used. After extensive debate Congress decided that the method of equal proportions was the more desirable, and the present procedure was established. Thus, after 150 years of discussion and debate the procedure for reapportioning Representatives in Congress has developed until now a reapportionment based on a sound statistical approach is assured after each decennial census. Through the cooperation of legislator and technician the fundamental adjustment of representation to population has been made the subject of a scientific procedure, thereby eliminating an important source of possible discontent with the workings of our Government.

REAPPORTIONMENT AFTER 1960

The procedure described above was followed after the 1960 census. As a result of the reapportionment, following the population shifts of the previous decade, 9 States gained 19 seats in the House of Representatives and 16 States lost 21 seats. From a regional viewpoint gains were registered by the East North Central (1), South Atlantic (3), Pacific (9), and Mountain (1), States; losses were sustained by the New England (3), Middle Atlantic (4), East South Central (3), West South Central (1), and West North Central (5) States. The following table shows the shifts in the regional distribution of seats in the House of Representatives at intervals from 1789 to 1960.

Regional apportionment of seats in the House of Representatives based on selected censuses

	1789 (constitutional apportionment)	1840 (6th census)	1890 (11th census)	1940 (16th census)	1960 (18th census)
New England	17	31	27	28	25
Middle Atlantic	18	63	72	92	83
North Central	0	50	128	131	125
South Atlantic	30	47	50	56	63
South Central	0	39	62	79	70
Mountain	0	0	7	16	17
Pacific	0	2	11	33	52
Total	65	232	357	435	435

The post-1960 reapportionment meant an increase in western voting strength and a decrease in New England and Middle Atlantic voting power in the House. Increased voting power for the West, whose Representatives usually vote alike on regional issues regardless of party, strengthened support for reclamation, public power, silver and wool interests, and mineral subsidies. The Pacific and Mountain States combined now have 69 seats in the House, or 16 percent of the total number. In the reapportionment after the 1960 census the largest gains were achieved by California, eight seats, and Florida, four seats.

DISPARITIES WITHIN STATES

Although Congress determines the number of Representatives, the State legislatures determine the boundaries of congressional districts. The long domination of these bodies by their rural members, party considerations, deadlocks following reapportionments, etc., have often resulted in some disparities in the population of congressional districts within States, as well as some rural-urban discrepancies, some gerrymandering, and on occasion selection of Members at Large. These conditions have been reflected in some rural overrepresentation, or urban underrepresentation, in Congress. During the decade 1940–50, for example, rural districts were overrepresented in Congress by a margin of 12 Members, and urban districts were underrepresented by 14, or 17 if the District of Columbia is included. A prime example of rural-urban discrepancies was in Illinois where no redistricting occurred between 1901 and 1948. The Chicago area, with more than half the State's population, elected 10 Representatives; the remainder of the State 15. Congressmen added through Federal reapportionment were elected at large.[3]

From time to time Congress has set up Federal standards for the drawing of district lines by State legislatures. In 1842, when the

[3] For a detailed description of disparities in the size of congressional districts, see *Congressional Record*, Mar. 26, 1956, pp. 5543–5548.

practice of electing representatives by districts had become well established, the Apportionment Act of that year provided that representatives—

should be elected by districts composed of contiguous territory equal in number to the representatives to which said state may be entitled, no one district electing more than one representative.

The Apportionment Act passed after the census of 1850 contained no provision regarding districts.   The requirement of 1842 was revived in 1862 and repeated in the act of 1872 with the added requirement that the districts should contain "as nearly as practicable an equal number of inhabitants."   The 1872 act provided that if there were an increase in the quota of any State the additional Members might be elected at large.   These provisions were repeated after the census of 1880 and in 1891.   In 1901 an act added the words "compact territory" and the clause read "contiguous and compact territory and containing as nearly as practicable an equal number of inhabitants." The act of 1911 repeated the 1901 requirement.   Congress passed no apportionment act after the census of 1920 and the permanent act of June 18, 1929, contained no provision for compactness, contiguity, or equality in population.   In 1932 the Supreme Court held, in the case of *Wood* v. *Broom*, that these requirements "did not outlast the apportionment to which they related," namely, the one made after the census of 1910.   The act of 1940, which amended the act of 1929, likewise contained no such requirements.   Therefore, there is at present no Federal law applying to the population or form of congressional districts.

In a special message to Congress on January 9, 1951, President Truman transmitted the results of the 1950 census of population by States and the number of Representatives to which each State was entitled.   He said that widespread discrepancies had grown up between the populations of the various congressional districts that should be corrected, and that several States had added Congressmen at large instead of redistricting as they should.   From 1842 through 1911, said the President, the apportionment statutes had usually required the States to divide themselves into single-member districts composed of contiguous and compact territory and containing as nearly as practicable an equal number of inhabitants.   He recommended that Congress promptly enact legislation reaffirming these basic standards and that it consider establishing limits of permissible deviation in population between districts of about 50,000 above and below the average size of about 350,000.   Congress should also take steps, he said, to see that these standards were complied with.

President Truman's suggestions closely resembled recommendations made on December 22, 1950, by the Committee on Reapportionment of Congress of the American Political Science Association, under the chairmanship of Prof. Arthur N. Holcombe of Harvard University. The APSA committee recommended that the size of the House should not be changed; that the method of equal proportions be retained; that all Members of Congress be elected by single-Member districts rather than at large; that new legislation should contain express standards of equality and fairness in redistricting; that the deviation in size of congressional districts from the State average should preferably be kept within a limit of 10 percent and should never exceed 15 percent; and that the standards of approximate equality should be enforcible through an express sanction administered by Congress. The committee rejected suggestions that States maintaining unequal districts should be sued in the Federal courts, deprived of their representation in the House, or compelled to elect their Congressmen at large. Instead, it urged that if the States do not create satisfactory districts for themselves, Congress should do it for them.

Following these political science and presidential recommendations, Representative Celler, chairman of the House Judiciary Committee, introduced a bill (H.R. 2648) to amend the Apportionment Act of 1929 so as to require the States to establish congressional districts composed of contiguous and compact territories that should not vary by more than 15 percent from the average size of districts in each State. The Celler bill also provided that—

any Representative elected from a district which did not conform to these requirements should be denied his seat in the House of Representatives, and the Clerk of the House should refuse his credentials.

The Judiciary Committee held hearings on the Celler bill during 1951, but it was not reported. It also held hearings in 1959 on four similar bills establishing standards for congressional districts, but none of them went beyond the committee stage.

QUALIFICATIONS FOR ELECTION

The Constitution requires that [a Member of the House of Representatives must have attained the age of 25, have been a citizen of the United States for 7 years, and be an inhabitant of the State in which he is elected. In practice he is usually a resident of the district that he represents, but that is not a constitutional requirement. The American "locality rule," as it is called, reflects and supports the prevalent belief that a Congressman's primary obligation is to his own district rather than to the country as a whole. He is responsible to a local, not a national, electorate. His chief objective is reelection so as to gain influence and political advancement. To this end, he must spend much of his time promoting the interests of his district and running errands for the folks back home.

The restriction of seats in Congress to local residents—

writes Horwill—

is the oldest of all the usages of the American Constitution. It antedates even the Fundamental Law itself. It is a survival of the intense localism of colonial days, which persisted in America after it had been abandoned in the mother country.[4]

No one has compiled a catalog of exceptions to this rule which have been very rare. There have been a few such cases, particularly in New York City, where residents of uptown districts have occasionally sat for downtown districts. In the 70th Congress Representative James M. Beck of Pennsylvania's First District was charged with not being a *bona fide* inhabitant of Philadelphia. He claimed residence in Pennsylvania and was seated. Champ Clark refers in his autobiography to the Honorable Leonidas F. Livingston of Georgia, namesake of the hero of Thermopylae, who represented the Atlanta district but did not live there.[5]

---

4 Herbert W. Horwill, *The Usages of the American Constitution* (1925), p. 174.
5 Champ Clark, *My Quarter Century of American Politics* (1920), vol. 2, p. 294.

In discussing the residency custom in his *Modern Democracies*, Lord Bryce remarked that:

Europeans are surprised at the strength of this habit, and Englishmen especially, for they remember that nearly all the most brilliant members of the House of Commons during the last two centuries had no connection of residence, perhaps not even of family or previous personal acquaintanceship, with the constituencies they represented, and they know also that even where local interests are concerned—little as these come up in British parliamentary life—a capable man residing elsewhere is quite as fit to understand and advocate such interests as a resident can be.[6]

QUALIFICATIONS FOR VOTERS

Members of Congress are elected by popular vote. The qualifications of voters in congressional elections, which are the same as for the electors of the most numerous branch of the State legislature, have changed over the years. After the Revolutionary War property qualifications for voting existed in each of the Thirteen States. Five States required the ownership of real estate, five States required either real estate or other property, while three States required no real estate but the possession of £50 in money (New Jersey) or property of £10 value (Georgia) or the payment of public taxes (Pennsylvania). The Revolution coincided with a gradual transition that was taking place from the ownership of real estate to taxpaying as a qualification for voting in the States.[7] It is estimated that between one-fifth and one-third of the adult white males were disfranchised by State law at the time of the adoption of the Constitution and that not more than 25 percent of them voted on the ratification of that document.

The last decade of the 18th century witnessed further progress in the democratization of the franchise as four States: Georgia, South Carolina, Delaware, and New Jersey adopted the taxpaying qualification; and four other States: New Hampshire, Kentucky, Maryland, and Vermont provided for manhood suffrage.[8] Property qualifications for voting were dropped by South Carolina in 1778, New Hampshire in 1784, Georgia in 1789, and Delaware in 1792. Taxpaying qualifications expired in New Hampshire in 1792, in Georgia in 1798, and in South Carolina in 1810.

After 1800 party rivalry and the need of immigrants to settle the new States west of the Alleghenies led to the gradual extension of the franchise and the eclipse of the Federalist Party which favored a limited suffrage. Ohio came into the Union in 1803, Louisiana in 1812, and Mississippi in 1817 without property qualifications. Thereafter, no State entered the Union with either a property or taxpaying qualification. Maryland dropped its property requirement in 1810 and Connecticut in 1818; Massachusetts and New York followed suit in 1821.

By the 1830's practically all the Original Thirteen States had acquired a wide, if not universal, suffrage, and by the end of the Civil War practically universal, manhood suffrage had been established for all whites. In the 34 States of the Union in 1860, the essential voting requirement was residence which ranged from 6 months to 2 years and was typically 1 year in the State and from 1 to 6 months in the county. Free Negroes were allowed to vote in six States in 1860 and

6 James Bryce, *Modern Democracies* (1921), vol. 2, pp. 53-54.
7 Kirk H. Porter, *History of Suffrage in the United States* (1918), pp. 11-14.
8 Charles Seymour and Donald P. Frary, *How the World Votes* (1918), vol. 1, p. 232.

aliens in five States.[9] Meanwhile, the taxpaying test had almost disappeared. Of the four States in which it survived, North Carolina abolished hers in 1868 and Delaware gave it up in 1897. Pennsylvania and Rhode Island abandoned theirs, which was only a registry fee, in 1933 and 1950, respectively. By the time of the Civil War all the new States either had been admitted with white male suffrage or had achieved it under the influence of the Jacksonian philosophy.

Under the 15th amendment to the Constitution, adopted in 1870, "the right of citizens of the United States to vote shall not be denied or abridged by any State on account of race, color, or previous condition of servitude." Despite this provision, Negroes have long been systematically disfranchised in various States and it was not until the Civil Rights Acts of 1957 and 1960 that Congress began to implement this article by legislation. Meanwhile, after long agitation, suffrage for women was achieved by adoption of the 19th amendment in 1920.

Today the qualifications for voting in the States are briefly as follows: *Age*—21 years, except in Georgia and Kentucky which allow voting at 18 years, Alaska at 19 years, and Hawaii at 20 years. *Citizenship*—all States require voters to be citizens of the United States. *Residence*—12 States require a residence of 6 months in the State, 35 States require 1 year, and 3 States require 2 years. *Literacy*—18 States now have some form of literacy test. *Poll tax*—five States provide for payment of a poll tax as a prerequisite to voting: Alabama, Arkansas, Mississippi, Texas, and Virginia.[10]

ELECTION CONTESTS

Under Article I, Section 5, of the Constitution "each House shall be the judge of the elections, returns, and qualifications of its own members." Both Houses may exclude Members-elect by majority vote and may expel sitting Members by a two-thirds vote. In practice, they have done so not only for failure to satisfy the constitutional requirements for membership, but also for other reasons. The Supreme Court has ruled that the power to expel a Member after he has been seated extends to all cases where the offense is such, in the judgment of the House or Senate, as to be inconsistent with the trust and duty of a Member.

The procedure with regard to contested elections for seats in the House of Representatives is prescribed by law and practice.[11] From 1789 down through 1951 some 541 election contests were decided by the House, an average of almost 7 cases per Congress. The 6th and 20th Congresses alone were barren of such contests. Their number reached a peak during the Civil War sessions (1861–65), when 36 House contests were instituted, and a record high during the 54th Congress (1895–97), when there were 38 election contests. The House decided 126 contested election cases from the 60th Congress (1908) through the 1st session of the 82d Congress (1951); but only 13 contestants were seated. In two of these instances the election out of which the contest arose was declared null and void or the seat vacant.

The Committee on Elections, which was the first standing committee appointed by the House in 1789 and which had a continuous history

---

[9] Porter, *op. cit.*, p. 148.
[10] *Book of the States:* 1960–61, p. 20.
[11] See United States Code, title 2, ch. 7.

down to 1947 when it became a standing subcommittee of the Committee on House Administration, has jurisdiction over election contests and expulsions. Its reports and the action of the House upon them over more than a century and a half have developed a fairly coherent body of the law and practice of congressional contested election cases, which have been compiled and digested by Rowell and Moores for the first 64 Congresses.[12]

For many years Members of Congress have criticized existing methods of handling election contests, especially in the House of Representatives, as slow, expensive, and unfair. Speaker Thomas B. Reed wrote in 1890 that: [13]

Our present method of determining election cases is unsatisfactory in results, unjust to Members and contestants, and fails to secure the representation which the people have chosen. In addition, it is costly to both the parties interested and to the people of the country, and is costly not only in money, but in time of the legislative body. [He summarizes the changing methods by which elections to the House of Commons have been determined, but concludes:] We could not divest ourselves of our right to be the judges of elections even if we would, nor would any statute enacted by both houses serve the purpose. The election laws which we now have do not bind us except by our own consent. Yet in practice they do bind us; and here may be the solution of our difficulties. There is probably no doubt that, if some tribunal were selected by Congress and its decisions were acquiesced in for a few years, there would spring up such a consensus of opinion that ever afterwards the House would cease to do more than record the decisions established in part by itself, or, to speak more accurately, by its predecessor and by Congress. Any law which made the decision *prima facie* would certainly be respected and would certainly work the cure.

More recently Congressmen who have served on House Elections Committees have proposed that the decision of election cases be referred, at least for preliminary determination, to the Court of Appeals for the District of Columbia, following the English practice; but nothing has come of these suggestions.[14]

EXCLUSION, EXPULSION, AND CENSURE

On various occasions the House has exercised its power to exclude Members-elect, to expel Members, or to censure them.

In 1870, for example, one B. F. Whittemore resigned from the House to escape expulsion for the sale of appointments at the Military Academy, but when he was promptly reelected to the same House, it declined to let him take his seat. In 1882 the House excluded a Delegate-elect from the Territory of Utah for the disqualification of polygamy.[15] In 1900 Brigham H. Roberts, Representative-elect from Utah, was denied his seat in the House for the same reason. In the cases of Baker and Yell, in the 29th Congress, the Elections Committee concluded that the acceptance of a commission as an officer of volunteers in the National Army vacated the seat of a Member, and in another similar case in the 37th Congress, a Member was held to have forfeited his right to a seat. In 1792 Joshua Seney, a Member from Maryland, informed the Speaker of the House by letter that he

---

[12] Chester H. Rowell, *A Historical and Legal Digest of All the Contested Election Cases in the House of Representatives. 1789–1901* (Government Printing Office, 1901); and Merrill Moores, *A Historical and Legal Digest of all the Contested Election Cases in the House of Representatives, 1901–1917* (H. Doc. No. 2052, 64th Cong., 2d sess.).

[13] T. B. Reed, "Contested Elections," *North American Review*, July 1890, pp. 112–120.

[14] Robert Luce, *Legislative Assemblies* (1924), p. 204.

[15] Territorial Delegates are persons whom the House by law admits to its floor and allows to speak, but who have no right to vote. A Territory is a possession of the United States that has not yet been admitted into the Union as a State.

had accepted an appointment in the judiciary department of that State, which disqualified him for a seat in the House. In 1909, when Rep. George L. Lilley, of Connecticut, resigned his seat in the House to become Governor of his State, the House declared his seat vacant because he had accepted an incompatible office.[16]

The power of expulsion has frequently been discussed but seldom exercised by the House, especially in relation to offenses committed before election. In 1861 John B. Clark, a Member-elect from Missouri who had not appeared or taken the oath, was expelled for treason. Later in the same year Representative John W. Reid, of Missouri, and Representative Henry C. Burnett, of Kentucky, were expelled for treason. In general, the House has been dubious of its power to punish Members for offenses committed before their election. In the South Carolina election case of Richard S. Whaley in 1913, it was held that the power of the House to expel one of its Members is unlimited, a matter purely of discretion to be exercised by a two-thirds vote, from which there is no appeal. But the charges against Whaley were dismissed. The resignation of an accused Member has always caused a suspension of expulsion proceedings. No cases of expulsion from the House since Civil War days are reported in *Hinds' and Cannon's Precedents.*[17]

While the composition of the House is not affected by the censure of Members, this subject is worthy of our attention. Under rule XIV—

if any Member, in speaking or otherwise, transgress the rules of the House, and, if the case require it, he shall be liable to censure or such punishment as the House may deem proper.

The annals of Congress disclose only 16 cases in which Members have been censured by the House. All but one of them occurred during the 19th century and 12 of them between 1864 and 1875. In six cases the offense was the use of unparliamentary language against another Member or the Speaker or the House itself. In three cases the offense was the sale of appointments to the Military or Naval Academies. Two were for treasonable words spoken during the Civil War. And two cases of censure (Oakes Ames and James Brooks) were for bribery in connection with the Credit Mobilier scandal. The last recorded censure case occurred in October 1921, and involved Representative Thomas L. Blanton, of Texas.[18]

TERM OF OFFICE

Representatives are elected for 2-year terms in general elections held in the fall of the even-numbered years and take office the following January 3d. Before the ratification of the 20th amendment, the terms of Representatives began on the 4th of March and terminated on the 3d of March. This resulted from the action of the Continental Congress on September 13, 1788, in declaring, on authority conferred by the Federal Convention, "the first Wednesday in March next" to be "the time for commencing proceedings under the said Constitution." Every Congress formerly had a long and a short session. The long session began early in December after the November elections and continued, with a Christmas recess, until the following

---

[16] *Hinds' Precedents of the House of Representatives*, vol. I, chs. 15 and 16.
[17] *Ibid.*, vol. 2, ch. XLII.
[18] *Ibid.*, vol. 6, sec. 236.

summer. The short session began in December after the summer recess and lasted until the 4th of the following March. This schedule meant that the business of the short session was often greatly congested and that it contained numerous "lame duck" Representatives who had lost their seats but continued to legislate for 3 months. It was not until 1932 that the House reluctantly joined the Senate in proposing a constitutional amendment abolishing the short session of Congress. As ratified in 1933, the 20th amendment changed the congressional calendar by providing that the annual sessions shall begin on January 3.

POLITICAL BACKGROUND OF MEMBERS

Many Members of the House of Representatives down through the years have had previous political experience. Perhaps one-third served in the State legislatures before coming to Congress. At least 17 were former Governors of their States.[19] Chester Bowles of Connecticut was a recent addition to this group. At least 50 Representatives formerly sat in the U.S. Senate, including such distinguished men as John Quincy Adams, Henry Clay, Matthew M. Neely, and James W. Wadsworth, Jr.[20] One ex-President of the United States crowned his career by service in the House of Representatives. That was John Quincy Adams—"Old Man Eloquent"—who said of his election by the people of Quincy, Mass.: "My election as President of the United States was not half so gratifying to my inmost soul." He spent 17 years in the House where he achieved fame for his long, dramatic, and finally triumphant fight for the right of petition.[21]

When the first session of the 85th Congress convened in Washington on January 3, 1957, the records showed that, in the entire history of the Nation, 35 Representatives had served 30 years or longer in the House. The record was held by Representative Joseph G. Cannon of Illinois whose total service covered exactly 50 years. The record for continuous House service—45 years and 8 months—was held by Representative Adolph J. Sabath of Illinois. And the record for continuous service of contemporary Members whose entire legislative service has been in the House was held by Representative Sam Rayburn—43 years and 10 months.[22] Mr. Rayburn entered the House on March 4, 1913, and has now served for more than 47 years.

SERVICE AND SENIORITY

The continuity of service of Members of the House has a significant effect upon the relative influence of various States and regions in the legislative process. Continuity of personnel in Congress goes back in an unbroken line to Revolutionary days. Fifty-two Members of the First Congress had been Members of the Continental Congress. There has been no Congress since the first in which men did not sit who had sat in the previous one. The biographical annals show the links of the legislative bond running from sire to son throughout American history.

Of the 391 Members of the House in 1900, 36 had served five or more consecutive terms. Three had served 10 or more consecutive terms

---

[19] *Congressional Record*, Feb. 23, 1953, pp. 1347–1348.
[20] *Ibid.*, June 27, 1952, p. A4275.
[21] Edward Boykin, *Congress and the Civil War* (1955), ch. 13.
[22] *Congressional Record*, Jan. 17, 1957, pp. A267–A269.

and 2 had been in the House for 30 years or longer. Representative J. H. Ketcham of New York had been a Member since March 4, 1865, and Representative Galusha Aaron Grow of Pennsylvania had served at intervals since March 4, 1851. He retired on March 3, 1903, after more than half a century of service. Another veteran of that era was Representative Joseph G. Cannon of Illinois who entered the House on March 4, 1873, and remained until March 3, 1923, missing only the 52d and 63d Congresses.

Long service in the First Chamber was exceptional, however, in earlier days. Writing in 1916, Alexander remarked that: [23]

There is little to be feared * * * from longevity in the House, since each biennial election is the curfew of one fourth of its members. Thus the House, like the heathen goddess, devours its own children. But the rapidity with which the process goes on is a bit startling. Of the three hundred and ninety-one members who appeared in March, 1911, at the first session of the Sixty-second Congress, only four belonged to the House in 1891. This represents the havoc usually made every twenty years by death, defeat, and other circumstances. The average length of a member's service is less than six years.

Of the 435 Members of the House in 1957, 196 had served five or more consecutive terms, 62 had served ten or more such terms, and 16 had been in Congress for 30 years or longer. The House is increasingly composed of Members with long service in that body. Sam Rayburn, dean and Speaker of the House, was first elected in 1913 and was serving his 25th consecutive term in 1961. Carl Vinson of Georgia, chairman of the Armed Services Committee, was first elected in 1914 and was likewise serving his 25th consecutive term. Thanks to its habit of reelecting the same legislators term after term, the South has long occupied a leading place in congressional councils. During the 85th Congress continuity of service reaped its reward in the 12 chairmanships out of the 19 standing committees of the House that were held by Southerners, including such great committees as Agriculture, Armed Services, Banking and Currency, Interstate and Foreign Commerce, Rules, and Ways and Means.

The rule of seniority is a factor not only in the choice of committee chairmen, but also in the distribution of office suites in the House Office Buildings, in committee assignments, in the appointment of Members of the influential conference committees, and even in the protocol of social life in the Nation's Capital. Seniority in the House of Representatives is a major factor in giving a Member position and influence in the Congress and in Washington.

Speaking to the "Baby Congressmen" on "The Making of a Representative," Speaker Clark once said: "A man has to learn to be a Representative just as he must learn to be a blacksmith, a carpenter, a farmer, an engineer, a lawyer, or a doctor." And "as a rule," he continued, "the big places go to old and experienced members" of the House.

---

[23] D. S. Alexander, *op. cit.*, p. 30.

MEMBERSHIP CHARACTERISTICS

Some impression of the character of Congress in the early part of the 19th century is gained from the letters of contemporaries. In a letter to his son dated December 30, 1805, Senator William Plumer of New Hampshire described his mess mates as follows: [24]

At my lodgings there are 16 of us—a numerous family and of course rather more noise than I could wish. However, my chamber is a retreat I often take from the bustle of the dining hall. A better collection or more agreeable society cannot be found in this wilderness city than at Coyle's. There you will find in Pick the stern severity of a Roman Cato; in Tracy genius, wit, poetry, and eloquence; in Dana extensive information, deep erudition and the correct scholar united with an inexhaustible fund of wit and pleasantry; in Hillhouse a sample of court cunning mingled with the manners of low life; in Mosely a chesterfield in dress and address with a tincture of true attic salt; in Pitkin application and shew united; in Davenport the manners of a blunt unpolished countryman—the zeal and bigotry of blind superstition; in Smith manners more polished, some knowledge of the world, and much of that which floats on the surface; in Talmadge much of that plain sound sense which is so necessary to render any man what he is, a man of business and honesty; in Stedman wit, shrewdness, good sense, and prudence; in Chittenden good sense and frankness who directly pursues the object; in Ellis information, caution, and reserve with the timidity and taciturnity of an old bachelor; in Sturgis plain unaspiring common sense; and of Betton you know what.

In the same year Augustus Foster, Secretary of the British Legation, sent his mother, the Dutchess of Devonshire, the following impressions of Washington and Congress: [25]

This undoubtedly is a miserable place, but the elect of all the states are assembled in it, and really such a gang to have the affairs of an empire wanting little of the size of Russia entrusted to them, makes one shudder. Imagination is dead in this country. Wit is neither to be found nor is it understood among them. All the arts seem to shrink from it, and you hear of nothing but calculation and speculation in money or in politics. * * * People's depth of reading goes no farther than Tom Paine's muddy pamphlets or their muddier political newspapers. In Congress there are about five persons who look like gentlemen. All the rest come in the filthiest dresses and are well indeed if they look like farmers—but most seem apothecaries and attorneys. * * * Randolph alone speaks well; strangest looking demagog you ever set eyes on, but gentlemanlike and for this country a prodigy * * *.

Occupationally, the House of Representatives, like the House of Commons, has never been a mirror of the Nation. Some occupations are greatly overrepresented in Congress, notably the legal profession which accounted for 37 percent of the membership of the House in 1790, 70 percent in 1840, 67 percent in 1890, and 54 percent in 1957. Other occupational groups such as workers in manufacturing and farming, persons employed in the service trades, and domestic servants have been greatly underrepresented in Congress or not directly represented at all. The following table shows the occupations and professions of the Members of the 72d and 85th Houses.

---

[24] Plumer Letter Book, IV, 507. All but three of those mentioned in this letter were Members of the House.
[25] Feb. 8, 1805. Foster Papers, II, 1864.

Occupation	72d	85th
Accounting		2
Advertising and public relations		5
Agriculture	12	20
Banking		5
Business and/or manufacturing	82	49
Civil service		2
Dentistry	2	1
Education	12	23
Engineering	5	1
Investments		3
Journalism, including radio	14	23
Labor		4
Law	274	233
Medicine and surgery	5	5
Pharmacist		1
Public official		23
Real estate and/or insurance		16
Secretary (congressional)		7
Social welfare		4
Miscellaneous	4	8
Not indicated	20	
Vacancies	5	
Total	435	435

Fragmentary data are available on the composition of the House of Representatives in earlier times. Of the 65 Members of the first House (1789–91), 24 were lawyers, 3 were physicians, and 22 were engaged in the ministry, farming, or business. Fifty-eight had previous legislative experience. Thirty-one had gone to college, 9 to high school, and 7 to grammar school. Their median age was 44.

Of 227 Members of the 29th House (1845–47), 163 were lawyers, 18 were farmers, and 8 were doctors. One hundred and fifty-seven of them had previous legislative experience. Ninety-four were college men, 43 had gone to high school, and 44 to grammar school. Their median age was 41.

Of the 357 Members of the 54th House (1895–97), 240 were lawyers, 76 were businessmen, and 9 were physicians. Eighty-two of them had previous legislative experience. Two hundred of them had gone to college, 64 to high school, and 74 to grammar school. Their median age was 48.

The first woman ever to become a Member of Congress was Miss Jeannette Rankin (Republican, Montana) who was elected to the 65th House in 1916. She served one term and was elected again in 1940 to the 77th Congress. Beginning with the 67th Congress there have always been one or more women in the National Legislature. Several of them succeeded their deceased husbands in the House. There were 10 women in the 79th House and 15 in the 85th, including such veterans as Frances P. Bolton, of Ohio, Edith Nourse Rogers, of Massachusetts, and Katharine St. George, of New York.

POLITICAL COMPLEXION

Five major political parties vied for control of the House of Representatives after 1789: the Federalists versus the Jeffersonian Republicans, 1789–1828; the Whigs versus the Democrats, 1829–55; the Republicans versus the Democrats, 1856–1960. The Federalists were in power in the first Chamber for 6 years (1789–93, 1799–1801) and later the Whigs for an equal span (1839–43, 1847–49). The number of Federalists in the House fluctuated from 53 in the 1st Congress to a low of 29 in the 9th Congress to a high of 85 in the 20th Congress after which they disappeared from the House scene. They were replaced in the 21st Congress (1829–31) by the Whigs who maintained a congressional party through the 33d Congress (1853–55) that ranged in size from 71 Members in the 21st Congress to 132 Members in the 26th and 27th Congresses.

Over the 170-year period since 1789 the Jeffersonian Republicans and the Democrats have controlled the House for 100 years and the Republicans for 58. After the decline of the Federalists the Jeffersonian Republicans and the Jacksonian Democrats held sway for 38 years (1801–39), but almost a century passed before they enjoyed another long period of supremacy during the New Deal era when they controlled the House for 14 years (1933–47). From 1801 down to the eve of the Civil War the Democrats kept control of the House of Representatives in all but four Congresses. Then, during the Civil War and Reconstruction period, the Republicans were in power for 16 years (1859–75). Thereafter the political pendulum swung back and forth between the two major parties, with the Republicans controlling the House for two long periods: from 1895 to 1911 and from 1919 to 1933. During the past century the dominant political complexion of the House has been Republican for 56 years and Democratic for 44 years.

More than 500 seats in the House have been held over the years by the representatives of minor parties and by a few Independents. During the 34th to 37th Congresses, inclusive, 108 seats were occupied by members of the American Party one of whom, Nathaniel P. Banks, of Massachusetts, was chosen Speaker in the 34th Congress. During the 46th to 49th Congresses members of the National Party held 27 seats in the House. Free Soilers held nine seats between 1851 and 1855. And the Populists elected 48 Members of the House during the decade of the 1890's. A few seats were held by Silverites and Laborites at the same time. Upward of 40 "Independents" have sat in the House of Representatives in the course of time, among them such memorable figures as George W. Norris, of Nebraska, and Fiorello La Guardia, of New York.

VARIOUS EVALUATIONS

Political cartoonists have lampooned Congress down through the years as a body composed of middle-aged windbags with open mouths, 10-gallon Texas hats, and flowing coattails. But the conventional picture underestimates the real character of our National Legislature. In plain fact—

remarks a close observer—

Congress is neither as doltish as the cartoonists portray it nor as noble as it portrays itself. While it has its quota of knaves and fools, it has its fair share of knights. And sandwiched between these upper and nether crusts is a broad and representative slice of upper-middle-class America.[26]

Of the thousands of Members who have sat in the Hall of the House since 1789, the overwhelming majority have been patriotic, conscientious, hard-working men and women. Many historic personages have marched across the congressional stage during its 170 crowded

26 Cabell Phillips, "A Profile of Congress," *New York Times Magazine*, Jan. 10, 1954, p. 16.

years and passed into the annals of history. Most of them have disappeared into the oblivion of the past, leaving only their biographies in the records of Congress. But a few mighty men of old writ large their names on the scroll of time and linger on in political memory.[27] Every decade in the history of the House has seen a little group of great debaters in that Chamber, arguing the changing issues of national concern and adorning the pages of the *Congressional Record* with their brilliant speeches.

As one studies the great debates of the past century—

remarked one authority—

the fact appears that speakers who have commanded the country's attention come in groups. Indeed, it may be said that the congressional firmament reveals constellations of genius as clearly as the heavens disclose brilliant stars cluster.[28]

Behind the bright stars in every session, however, have been the unsung heroes, the old professionals and committee specialists, the John McCormacks and Thor Tollefsons, who have carried on the unspectacular but essential work of lawmaking.

In concluding this chapter on the composition of Congress it is difficult to generalize regarding the quality of its membership down through the years. Any body as numerous as a national legislature has had its share of both mediocre and outstanding men. It seems safe to say that, in the long view, the caliber of Congress compares favorably with that of most other legislatures in the modern world.

When Alexis de Tocqueville first visited the American House of Representatives during the Jacksonian era, he was—

struck by the vulgar demeanor of that great assembly. Often—

he wrote—

there is not a distinguished man in the whole number. Its members are almost all obscure individuals * * * village lawyers, men in trade, or even persons belonging to the lower classes of society.[29]

Fifty years later James Bryce offered this evaluation: [30]

Watching the House at work, and talking to the members in the lobbies, an Englishman naturally asks himself how the intellectual quality of the body compares with that of the House of Commons. His American friends have prepared him to expect a marked inferiority. * * * A stranger who has taken literally all he hears is therefore surprised to find so much character, shrewdness, and keen though limited intelligence among the representatives. Their average business capacity did not seem to me below that of members of the House of Commons of 1880–85. True it is that great lights, such as usually adorn the British chamber, are absent; true also that there are fewer men who have received a high education which has developed their tastes and enlarged their horizons. The want of such men depresses the average. * * * In respect of width of view, of capacity for penetrating thought on political problems, representatives are scarcely above the class from which they came, that of second-rate lawyers or farmers, less often merchants or petty manufacturers. They do not pretend to be statesmen in the European sense of the word, for their careers, which have made them smart and active, have given them little opportunity for acquiring such capacities. As regards manners they are not polished, because they have not lived among polished people; yet neither are they rude, for to get on in American politics one must be civil and pleasant. The standard of parliamentary language, and of courtesy generally, has been steadily rising during the last few decades. * * * Scenes of violence and confusion such as occasionally convulse the French chamber, and were common in Washington before the War of Secession, are now unknown.

---

[27] *Cf.* George B. Galloway, *Congress at the Crossroads*, pp. 32–37.
[28] DeAlva S. Alexander, *op. cit.*, p. 299. For a description of these successive congressional galaxies, see pp. 299–312.
[29] Alexis de Tocqueville, *Democracy in America*, I, p. 204. Bradley edition (1945).
[30] James Bryce, *The American Commonwealth* (1888), I, pp. 143–144.

A statistical study of the composition of Congress indicates that the tendency since the Civil War has been for the age of first-term members to increase, for the length of service to increase, and for the average age of all the Members of the House of Representatives to rise. For example, in the 41st Congress, (1869–71), the median age of all members was 45, of first-term members was 42, and the average number of terms served was 1.04. In the 68th Congress (1923–25), the median age of all Representatives was 51, of first-term members was 47, and the average period of legislative service was 2½ terms.[31] When these figures are brought up to recent date, they show a continuation of these longrun trends. Thus, in the 79th Congress (1945–47), the median age of all Representatives was 52 years, of first-term members was 46, and the average number of terms served (including the 79th Congress) was 4½. Meanwhile, the median age of the potential voting population was 41. The increasing average age of Members of Congress compared with that of the electorate, and their longer average tenure of office, helps to explain perhaps why Congress is more conservative than the country.

[31] Stuart A. Rice, *Quantitative Methods in Politics* (1928), pp. 296–297.

CHAPTER 4

ORGANIZATION OF THE HOUSE

Under the Constitution as amended, Congress assembles at least once each year at noon on the 3d of January, unless they shall by law appoint a different day.[1] At the opening of the first regular session of each new Congress in the odd-numbered years, the House and Senate organize themselves anew. The manner in which the House organizes itself for business may be illustrated by the proceedings in that Chamber on January 3, 1957. Promptly at noon on that day Ralph Roberts, Clerk of the House during the 84th Congress, called it to order and, after the Chaplain's prayer, directed a clerk to call the roll by States of Members-elect whose credentials had been received. When the rollcall had been completed, the Clerk announced that 428 Members-elect had answered to their names and that a quorum was present. He also announced that credentials in regular form had been received showing the election of the Delegates from Alaska and Hawaii and of the Resident Commissioner from Puerto Rico.

The chairman of the Republican and Democratic Party conferences then nominated Mr. Joseph W. Martin, Jr., and Mr. Sam Rayburn, respectively, for the office of Speaker. The Clerk appointed tellers to canvass the vote on the election of the Speaker and Mr. Rayburn was elected, having received a majority of the whole number of votes cast. Thereupon the Clerk declared that Mr. Rayburn had been elected Speaker of the House of Representatives for the 85th Congress and appointed a committee to escort the Speaker to the Chair. The Speaker was escorted to the Chair by the committee and was introduced to the House by Mr. Martin. Mr. Rayburn then addressed the House, voicing his appreciation of his election and paying tribute to the principles and responsibilities of representative government. Mr. Vinson, of Georgia, next ranking Member of the House in point of continuous service, then administered the oath of office to Mr. Rayburn. The Members-elect and Delegates-elect then rose in their places and took the oath of office prescribed by law.

The respective conference chairmen then announced that the Honorable John W. McCormack, of Massachusetts, had been selected as majority leader of the House and that the Honorable Joseph W. Martin, Jr., of Massachusetts, had been chosen as minority leader.

Resolutions were then offered by the chairmen of the party conferences nominating their respective candidates for the offices of Clerk of the House, Sergeant at Arms, Doorkeeper, Postmaster, and Chaplain; and the candidates of the Democratic Party, which was in the majority, were elected. The officers then presented themselves at the bar of the House and took the oath of office.

Then, in quick succession, the House adopted resolutions notifying the Senate that it had assembled and chosen its Speaker and Clerk,

---

[1] Prior to the adoption of the 20th amendment in 1933, Congress met on the first Monday in December, in accordance with art. 1, sec. 4, of the original Constitution.

and authorizing the Speaker to appoint a committee of three members to join with a similar Senate committee to notify the President of the United States that Congress had assembled and was ready to receive any communication that he might be pleased to make.

Mr. Smith, of Virginia, who was to be the chairman of the Committee on Rules, then offered a resolution for the adoption of the rules of the 85th Congress, which was agreed to. Before the adoption of rules the House proceeds under general parliamentary law. The rules and orders of a previous Congress are not in effect until adopted by the sitting House.

Resolutions authorizing a joint session of Congress on January 7 to count the electoral vote and providing for the creation of a joint committee to make necessary arrangements for the inauguration of President-elect Eisenhower were then agreed to. Thus, in little less than 2 hours the House of Representatives had organized itself, elected its officers, and adopted its rules for the next 2 years.

ELECTION CONTESTS

In normal times the organization of the House has proceeded in the congenial manner described above. But during the first half of the 19th century the election of the Speaker gave rise to several minor contests, and on at least four occasions to sharp contests that ran on for days or weeks. From 1820 on, the slavery question underlay these disputes which grew more and more violent during the 1840's and 1850's. Before he left the House in 1861 to join the Confederacy, Representative John H. Reagan of Texas attributed the dissolution of the Union in large part to these passionate arguments.

Ordinarily a Speaker is chosen on the first ballot, if one political party in the House has a clear majority and if party lines are tightly held. But at least 10 contests for the Speakership took place during the decades before the Civil War. The first occurred in 1809 when the vote was divided among five candidates on the first ballot, with none receiving a majority. On the second ballot Nathaniel Macon of North Carolina, who had served as Speaker from 1801 to 1807, withdrew for reasons of health and Joseph B. Varnum of Massachusetts was elected.

The next contest took place in November 1820, after Henry Clay resigned the Speakership. On that occasion there were three candidates: John W. Taylor of New York, William Lowndes of South Carolina, and Samuel Smith of Maryland. The contest lasted 2 days and 22 ballots before Taylor, the antislavery candidate, was elected over Lowndes, the compromiser.

In 1821 Philip C. Barbour of Virginia was chosen on the second day and the 12th ballot over Taylor of New York by a majority of one. Taylor won in 1825 on the second ballot over two other candidates. In 1834, after Stevenson's resignation, John Bell of Tennessee was finally elected on the 10th ballot. In 1847 Robert C. Winthrop of Massachusetts was elected on the third ballot, and in 1861 Galusha Grow of Pennsylvania on the second vote.

The great prebellum fights for the speakership came in 1839, 1849, 1855, and 1859 and imposed a severe test upon our representative institutions. Those were exciting days in which the passions of sectional conflict and party strife inflamed the House and the qualifications and politics of candidates were closely inspected.

CONTEST OF 1839

The 1st session of the 26th Congress met on December 2, 1839, but did not succeed in electing a Speaker until December 16. The delay was caused by the fact that five of the six New Jersey seats were contested and by the refusal of the Clerk, who was presiding according to established usage, either to decide between the conflicting claimants or to put any question until a quorum of the House was formed. The effect of these two decisions was to prevent the transaction of any business as well as the organization of the House. Excluding the New Jersey delegation, there were 119 Democrats and 118 Whigs in the House. Control of the House depended upon which delegation from New Jersey was admitted.

After 4 days of debate and disorder, during which the Clerk persisted in his refusal to put any question until the House should be organized, John Quincy Adams arose and earnestly appealed to the House to organize itself by proceeding with the rollcall and ordering the Clerk to call the Members from New Jersey who held credentials from the Governor of the State. When someone asked who would put the question, Adams replied: "I will put the question myself." And when a resolution was offered that Adams be appointed chairman of the meeting, it was carried "by an almost universal shout in the affirmative." [2] Such was the confidence of that body in its leading statesman.

Under Adams' firm guidance the House finally agreed to vote on December 14. On the first day of voting an attempt was made to postpone election of a Speaker and to hear and decide the New Jersey contests first, but the House declined to let either delegation from that State take part in its organization. There were 6 candidates for Speaker on the 1st vote and 13 on the final 11th vote on December 16. Robert M. T. Hunter of Virginia was finally elected Speaker over John W. Jones of the same State who fell only five votes short of election on the first vote and who led the balloting on the first five rounds. As Adams concluded his eyewitness account of this furious struggle, Hunter "finally united all the Whig votes, and all the malcontents of the administration." [3]

CONTEST OF 1849

In 1849 a great battle for the speakership took place that lasted for 3 weeks and 63 ballots. No party had a majority in the Chamber when the 31st Congress met because several Free Soil Whigs and Democrats acted independently. The basic issue was whether or not the district and territorial committees were to have proslavery majorities, which would be determined by the identity of the Speaker who had the power to appoint the committees. The two leading candidates were Robert C. Winthrop of Massachusetts, the Whig candidate, who had been Speaker of the previous House; and Howell Cobb of Georgia, the Democratic candidate. At one stage in the proceedings it was proposed, in an effort to facilitate organization, that whoever was elected Speaker should be divested of power to construct the committees, but no action was taken on this motion. [4]

---

[2] *Memoirs of John Quincy Adams* (1876), vol. 10, p. 147.
[3] *Ibid.*, p. 165. See also I *Hinds' Precedents of the House of Representatives*, sec. 103.
[4] *House Journal*, 31st Cong., 1st sess., p. 91.

According to one Member, the committees had long been composed so as to pigeonhole all petitions for the abolition of the slave trade. On the first vote, on December 3, 1849, there were 11 candidates led by Howell Cobb who received 103 votes, 8 short of a majority. Viva voce voting for a Speaker continued daily until December 22. After the 13th vote a motion to elect a Speaker by a plurality of votes (made by Andrew Johnson), and a motion to select a Speaker from the top four or two candidates (made by Frederick P. Stanton), were made and tabled. After the 30th vote Mr. Lewis C. Levin proposed that the Speaker's chair be filled by lottery. Five names would be placed in a box, one by each of the five political parties or factions, and the first name drawn from the box by the Clerk would be Speaker. The five factions were the Whigs, Democrats, Native Americans, Free Soilers, and Taylor Democrats. This motion was also tabled. A similar proposal that the Speaker be chosen by lot, with only the names of Cobb and Winthrop in the box, was likewise tabled.

Other efforts to resolve the prolonged deadlock met a similar fate, including motions to elect a Speaker by ballot, or by plurality, or by less than a majority vote, or from the top three or two on the list, or to elect a Speaker pro tempore and other officers. After the 44th vote proposals were made but not adopted that Congressmen should receive no salary or mileage until a Speaker had been elected. On December 17 a proposal to appoint a committee to recommend some practicable and acceptable method of expediting the organization of the House was tabled by the margin of a single vote; and a motion to appoint certain named persons as officers of the House was also lost. Two days later Andrew Johnson suggested that ministers of the gospel be invited to attend and pray for a speedy and satisfactory organization, but even this appeal to the Deity was tabled, as was another motion to appoint a committee of one from each State delegation "to concert and report suitable measures for the speedy organization of this House." [5] Meanwhile, the Whig and Democratic Parties had appointed committees to confer and report some solution of the dilemma.

After a struggle of unprecedented duration and gravity, it was clear that a Speaker could not be elected by majority vote. Finally, on December 22, 1849, the House agreed by a vote of 113 to 106 to Stanton's motion to elect a Speaker by a plurality, provided it be a majority of a quorum. For the first time in its history the House surrendered the principle of majority rule. For 60 votes Cobb and Winthrop had been alternately in the lead. At long last, on the 63d vote, amid intense excitement, Howell Cobb received 102 votes out of 222, and Winthrop received 100, with 20 votes scattered among eight others. Cobb was chosen by a plurality of votes, being a majority of a quorum of the House, which then confirmed his election by majority vote.

Commenting on this contest in 1895, an eminent authority wrote: [6]

Southern suspense was now relieved. If the Whigs had elected their candidate in 1849 the Civil War might have been delayed, for the committees of this Congress affected the compromise of 1850. It is probable that Mr. Winthrop's prestige would have carried him into the Senate and eventually have affected

[5] Ibid., p. 130.
[6] Mary P. Follett, The Speaker of the House of Representatives (1896), p. 56.

the makeup of the Republican Party. The choice of a very pronounced pro-slavery and southern man at this crisis undoubtedly aggravated the struggles of the following decade.

CONTEST OF 1855

Another prolonged struggle over the election of a Speaker took place at the opening of the 34th Congress in December 1855. It continued for 2 months and took 133 ballots to decide. Here again the basic issue was whether the committees of the House would be organized in a manner hostile or friendly to slavery. The candidates were examined with respect to their political opinions, reflecting the political character of the contest and the power of the speakership position. Since 1849 the irrepressible conflict over slavery had gained momentum and the overriding question was whether Kansas should be on the side of freedom or slavery. The two leading political parties in the House were now the Republican Party, which emerged in the congressional elections of 1854 and replaced the Whigs, and the Democratic Party. The "Anti-Nebraska men" had a majority in the 34th Congress, but were unable to unite behind a single candidate.

On December 3, 1855, on the first vote for Speaker, votes were cast viva voce for 21 candidates, but none received a majority. William A. Richardson of Illinois led with 74 out of 225 votes. After the 23d vote Mr. Lewis D. Campbell of Ohio, one of the top two candidates in the voting, withdrew from the race. After the 59th vote a motion to drop the lowest candidates on the list progressively until two only should remain and that the higher of these two should then be the duly elected Speaker, was tabled. After 2 weeks of deadlock, a motion was offered that, after organizing, the House should do no business except pass the necessary appropriation bills and that then all the Members should resign their seats; but this, too, was tabled. As in 1839, it was suggested that the House solve the problem by appointing certain committees itself, but this proposal was not accepted. Weeks of maneuvering and negotiating passed, but neither the Democrats ñor the Free Soilers would yield in their determination to control the committees for or against slavery.

Meanwhile, on a long series of votes, Mr. Nathaniel P. Banks of Massachusetts fell only half a dozen votes short of the number necessary to a choice. After 2 months of tedious rollcalls the House finally decided to settle the contest, as it had in 1849, by a resort to plurality rule. And on February 2, 1856, on the 133d vote, Banks was declared Speaker of the House, having received 103 out of 214 votes cast. William Aiken of South Carolina was second with 100 votes.[7] Banks' election was subsequently confirmed by a resolution adopted by a majority vote. The House then proceeded to complete its organization by the election of a Clerk and other officers. According to Miss Follett—

Mr. Banks was elected above all because it was expected that he would constitute the committees in favor of the Free-Soilers. He justified this expectation by putting a majority of anti-slavery men on the Kansas Investigation committee, which act practically delayed the settlement of the Kansas episode until after 1857, and thus gave time for the anti-slavery forces to organize.[8]

---

[7] *House Journal*, 34th Cong., 1st sess., p. 444.
[8] Follett, *op. cit.*, p. 59. See also 5 *Hinds' Precedents*, sec. 6647, and Paul T. David et al., *The Politics of National Party Conventions* (1960), p. 24.

CONTEST OF 1859

The last great contest for the speakership in the 19th century occurred at the opening of the 36th Congress on the eve of the Civil War. The first session of this Congress met on December 5, 1859, but the House did not succeed in electing a Speaker until February 1, 1860, when William Pennington of New Jersey, a new Member, was chosen on the 44th ballot. No political party had a majority of the House which was then composed of 109 Republicans, 88 administration Democrats, 13 anti-Lecompton Democrats, and 27 Americans. The agitated state of public opinion on the slavery question was reflected in the desperate fight for the speakership that ensued.

After the first vote, on which 16 candidates received a total of 230 votes, the highest having 86 votes which was not a majority, Mr. John B. Clark of Missouri offered a resolution that no Member of the House who had endorsed and recommended a book hostile to slavery called "The Impending Crisis of the South: How to Meet It," written by one Hinton R. Helper, was fit to be Speaker.[9] The next day Mr. John A. Gilmer of North Carolina offered a second resolution calling on all good citizens to resist all attempts at renewing the slavery agitation in or out of Congress and resolving that no Member should be elected Speaker whose political opinions were not known to conform to such sentiments.[10] These resolutions were aimed at John Sherman, the Republican candidate, who had endorsed Helper's book. They set the stage for the bitter struggle that followed.

Voting for Speaker proceeded very slowly, amid scenes of uproar and confusion, as the clerk who was presiding declined to decide any questions of order. All such questions were submitted to the House and debated, so that it was impossible to expedite the proceedings. Sometimes only one vote would be taken during a day, the remainder of the time being consumed in passionate arguments. The galleries were packed with partisans of both sides whose applause and hisses goaded the gladiators on the floor. Members came armed with revolvers and bowie knives and it looked as if the Civil War might begin in the House itself. Filibustering by the southern Democrats was chiefly responsible for the long delay in the organization of the House.

On the second vote for Speaker, John Sherman of Ohio received 107 out of 231 votes, and on the third vote he had 110, only six short of the necessary majority. But by the end of January the Republicans realized that Sherman could not be elected because of the bitterness over the slavery issue, and so they swung their support to Mr. Pennington of New Jersey, a new Member and a political unknown. Finally, on February 1, 1860, almost 2 months after the beginning of the session, he was chosen Speaker of the House on the 44th vote, receiving 117 votes out of 233, the exact number necessary to a choice. Pennington's name first appeared on the 38th ballot on which he received one vote. On the 40th vote he jumped from 1 to 115, from the bottom to the top of the list, and remained in the lead until he was elected. In his speech of acceptance he said in part:[11]

After witnessing the almost insurmountable obstacles in the way of the organization of this House, I came to the conclusion that any gentleman, of any party, who could command a majority of the votes for Speaker, was bound, in deference

---

[9] *House Journal*, 36th Cong., 1st sess., p. 12.
[10] *Ibid.*, pp. 16, 17.
[11] *Ibid.*, p. 164. See also Follett, *op. cit.*, pp. 60–63.

to the public exigencies, to accept the responsibility as an act of patriotic duty * * *.

CONTEST OF 1923

No serious contest for the speakership took place on the floor of the House after the 36th Congress until the opening of the 68th Congress on December 3, 1923. At that time the political complexion of the House consisted of 225 Republicans, 205 Democrats, 1 Independent, 1 Farmer-Laborite, and 1 Socialist. But the balance of power in the chamber was held by about 20 Progressives who wore the Republican party label, but who presented a candidate of their own— Mr. Cooper of Wisconsin—as a "protest to the rules that have grown up in this body." [12] The regular Republicans nominated Mr. Frederick H. Gillett of Massachusetts for Speaker, the Democratic nominee was Mr. Finis J. Garrett of Tennessee, while Mr. Martin B. Madden of Illinois was also nominated by Mr. Reid of that State as a Republican candidate from the Middle West.

Four rollcalls were held on the first day and four more on the second day, all without result. On the first rollcall Gillett received 197 votes, Garrett 195, Cooper 17, and Madden 5. On the evening of the second day Mr. Longworth, the Republican floor leader, arrived at a gentlemen's agreement with the Progressives regarding a revision of the House rules, as a result of which Mr. Gillett was elected Speaker on the ninth rollcall on December 5, receiving 215 votes to 197 for Garrett and 2 for Madden.[13]

Since the 68th Congress there have been no unusual contests for the speakership, one party having always been in the majority and its candidate having always received a majority of the votes cast on the first ballot.

SEATING ARRANGEMENTS

During the 19th century it was customary, following the organization of the House and the adoption of the usual resolutions, for the members to draw lots for their seats in the Hall. Up to the 29th Congress, when the drawing began, seats were taken on a first-come, first-choice basis. Members living near Washington who arrived early for a session secured the best seats and kept them for the duration of the session. Before the drawing began, ex-Speakers and one or two Members of long service in the House were allowed to select their seats.

On February 13, 1847, while the House was in Committee of the Whole House on the State of the Union, John Quincy Adams entered the Hall for the first time since his attack of paralysis. At once the Committee rose in a body to receive him and Mr. Andrew Johnson said:

In compliance with the understanding with which I selected a seat at the commencement of the present session, I now tender to the venerable member from Massachusetts the seat which I then selected for him, and will furthermore congratulate him on being spared to return to this House.[14]

---

[12] *Congressional Record*, 68th Cong., 1st sess., p. 8.
[13] Chang-Wei Chiu, *The Speaker of the House of Representatives Since 1896* (1928), pp. 32–33.
[14] I *Hinds' Precedents of the House of Representatives*, sec. 81.

In 1857, when the House moved into its present Chamber, Representatives had individual carved oak desks and chairs. These were replaced in 1859 by circular benches with the parties arranged opposite each other, but the desks were restored in 1860. As the membership grew, smaller desks were installed in 1873 and again in 1902. The places at the extreme right and left of the rostrum were the least desirable. Members usually tried to secure seats near their friends or colleagues from the same State. The Republicans sat, as now, on the left of the Speaker and the Democrats on his right. But when one of these parties was in a small minority, the surplus of the majority party sat to the extreme left or right of the Hall.

Commenting on these arrangements in 1888, James Bryce said:

It is admitted that the desks are a mistake, as encouraging inattention by enabling men to write their letters; but though nearly everybody agrees that they would be better away, nobody supposes that a proposition to remove them would succeed.[15]

But by 1914, when the membership had grown to 435, the House was forced to remove the desks and replace them with chairs arranged in long benches. Today there are 448 medium-tan leather-covered chairs with walnut frames, bronze feet, and leather-padded arm rests. This change put an end to the drawing of seats by lot and Members now occupy any vacant chair on their side of the aisle.

[15] James Bryce, *The American Commonwealth* (1888), vol. I, p. 140.

CHAPTER 5

EVOLUTION OF THE HOUSE RULES

Under the Constitution each House may determine the rules of its proceedings. And in practice each House of Representatives has done so from the beginning of congressional history either by explicitly adopting rules or by acquiescing in those of a preceding House. As we saw earlier, the House of Representatives adopted a short code of four rules on April 7, 1789, and agreed to six additional rules a few days later. From then until 1860 the House rule book gradually expanded by a process of accretion, as the rules were enlarged by amendments offered mainly by individual members. Each new House customarily adopted the rules of its predecessor, sometimes with changes or additions, thus erecting a code that became continuous in character and substantially constant in content.

After 70 years of gradual expansion the rules of the House had grown to more than 150 in number, consuming some 20 pages of the journals, when a select committee of five was appointed, at the close of the first session of the 35th Congress on June 14, 1858, "to digest and revise the rules * * * and to suggest alterations and amendments" therein.[1] From time to time over the years they had been criticized as cumbersome and useless. Warren Winslow, ex-speaker of the North Carolina Senate, was the author of this resolution which provided that the Speaker, James L. Orr of South Carolina, should be a member of the select committee. This was the first time in the history of the House that its presiding officer had served on one of its committees. On December 20, 1858, the select committee reported some 31 amendments of the rules, a dozen of which were to strike out existing rules.[2] Its report was recommitted without further action in that Congress.

Continued criticism of the rules and parliamentary practice of the House led to the reappointment of the select committee on February 1, 1860, under the chairmanship of Israel Washburn, Jr., of Maine, a distinguished parliamentarian. Six weeks later the Washburn committee submitted its famous report which embraced some 38 amendments of the rules, consisting mainly of the changes that had been recommended in December 1858.

They need to be amended—

Washburn declared.

But their observance is most needed. The good nature of members in granting unanimous consent breeds ignorance, and when applied they provoke criticism because a different practice obtains.[3]

After extensive debate the House agreed to numerous amendments on March 16 and 19, 1860.[4] Just as the Union was breaking up on

---

[1] *Congressional Globe*, June 14, 1858, p. 3048.
[2] H. Rept. No. 1, 35th Cong., 2d sess.
[3] *Congressional Globe*, 36th Cong., 1st sess., pp. 1178, 1209.
[4] *House Journal*, 36th Cong., 1st sess., pp. 526–533, 545–551.

46

the eve of the Civil War, the House of Representatives adopted the first sweeping revision of its rules since 1789.

Many of the changes in the revision of 1860 were technical in character, correcting inconsistencies, combining related rules, and adjusting others to the existing practice. But several drastic modifications were made.

One destroyed the trick of striking out the enacting clause in Committee of the Whole and then disagreeing to the report in the House. Another provided that the previous question, when negatived, should leave the pending business undisturbed, and when ordered on a motion to postpone, should act only on such motion; or, if on an amendment or an amendment thereto, that it should not preclude debate on the bill. This gave the House the facility for amendment enjoyed in Committee of the Whole. To avoid a repetition of the riotous scenes preceding the election of Speaker Pennington, the rules of one House were made binding upon its successors, unless otherwise ordered. Although parliamentarians generally held this rule invalid whenever seriously questioned, it survived for thirty years.[5]

With the postwar increase in the size and business of the House, dissatisfaction with the strictness of its rules recurred, the burden of complaint being that the liberty of the individual Member suffered under them. On May 24, 1872, the House agreed to the Banks resolution providing for the appointment of a commission to revise the rules and report—

such changes as will facilitate the presentation of reports of committees, enlarge the means of an intelligent transaction of general business, and secure to every member a proper opportunity to examine all legislative measures before they are submitted for consideration and action by the House.[6]

This commission does not appear to have reported, but meanwhile more than two-score rules were added to the House Manual and many new precedents were established.

In response to continued criticism, the House in 1879 instructed a committee of able parliamentarians to sit during the recess in order to revise, codify, and simplify the clumsy accretion of 169 rules that had accumulated since the revision of 1860. Samuel J. Randall, Joseph C. S. Blackburn, Alexander H. Stephens, James A. Garfield, and William P. Frye composed the committee. Their unanimous report rearranged and grouped the orders by subject into 44 main rules with the avowed object to "secure accuracy in business, economy of time, order, uniformity, and impartiality." Thirty-two rules were dropped as obsolete or unnecessary, 12 were retained intact, and 125 were condensed into 32, making a total of 44, each subdivided into clauses. The House debated the new code at intervals for 2 months and finally adopted it as the general revision of 1880.[7]

Hailed as a brilliant achievement, the new code had far-reaching effects on committee access to the floor, the distribution of the appropriation bills, the privilege of reporting at any time, on suspension of the rules, special orders, and the Committee on Rules which became a standing committee at this time. Alexander has summarized the historic revision of 1880 as follows:

It stopped voting after the second call of the roll; it dropped the penalty system of absenteeism without leave; and it authorized the clerk to announce "pairs" instead of members. It abolished the practice of changing a few words in a

5 DeAlva S. Alexander, *History and Procedure of the House of Representatives* (1916), pp. 192–193.
6 *Congressional Globe*, 42d Cong., 2d sess., p. 3819.
7 For report and debate see *Congressional Record*, 46th Cong., 2d sess., pp. 108–208, 478–491, 551–558, 575–579, 603–614, 658–665, 708–713, 727–735, 954–959, 1195–1208, 1255–1267.

pending bill to make it germane as an amendment; it caused a motion to reconsider, made during the last six days of a session, to be disposed of at the time; it sent a bill, to which objection was made to its present consideration, to the Committee of the Whole or to the House calendar; it gave preference to revenue and appropriation bills in Committee of the Whole; it required bills on the private calendar to be taken up and disposed of in order; and it provided that the previous question should bring the House to a direct vote upon a single motion, a series of allowable motions, or upon an amendment or amendments, the effect being to carry the bill to its engrossment and third reading, and then, on a renewal of the motion, to its passage or rejection. To afford "the amplest opportunity to test the sense of the House as to whether or not the bill is in the exact form it desires," it authorized a motion, pending the passage of a bill, to recommit it with or without instructions. Other changes of less note modified the duties of minor officers, extended former members' admission to the floor, safeguarded the filing, disposition, and withdrawal of papers, made the Committee on Rules a standing committee of five members, gave a conference report precedence over all other business, created the House calendar, to which were referred all public bills not carrying an appropriation, and added an hour to the time of the member closing a debate whenever it extended over a day.[8]

But the revisers of 1880 left untouched such "disreputable practices" as "riders" on appropriation bills and the "disappearing quorum."

Except for the exciting contests that marked the general revisions of 1860 and 1880, the customary practice in *post bellum* days, when a new House met, was to proceed under general parliamentary law, often for several days, with unlimited debate, until a satisfactory revision of former rules had been effected. Proposed changes in the old rules were discussed on these occasions in a leisurely, good-natured way and the meaning of the complex code of the House was explained to the new Members. In describing these biennial field-days McConachie wrote:[9]

Discussion of the rules does not mean cold argument over phraseology, clear reasoning upon scientific legislative methods. It is the impassioned utterance of men newly gathered together, and as yet unacquainted with each other, but fresh from constituencies whose districts completely cover the broad surface of the United States. It is the airing-ground where the people through their representatives pass judgment upon the Congress which has gone before, and express their desires concerning great living political issues as an enlightenment preliminary to the formulating of laws by the committee workers. Usually one, two, or three changes in the former code, involving, it may be, the power of some committee whose business has become suddenly of first importance, or relating to the adjustment of majority and minority rights, have constituted the central themes. In these discussions upon the broad subject of the State of the Union, a large part, often the largest part, of the talking is made up of random speeches by the newer members. The older fellows sit back, say nothing, listen. The new man may break some ice as to the meaning of the complex code which governs proceedings, but the old man gathers large ideas as to the character of the complex mass of membership which will soon come under his directing and governing hand. * * *

After the revision of 1880 general debate upon the adoption of the rules often continued for several days at the opening of a new Congress. Two days were so consumed at the beginning of the 48th Congress (1883), 4 days at the 49th (1885), 6 days at the 51st (1889), 9 days at the 52d (1891), and 6 days at the opening of the 53d Congress (1893). On three of these occasions 2 months or more elapsed before the amended code was finally adopted, in striking contrast to the celerity with which the old rules have been rushed through in recent times.[10]

---

[8] Alexander, *op. cit.*, pp. 194–195.
[9] L. G. McConachie, *Congressional Committees* (1898), pp. 111–112.
[10] See ch. 9 for a detailed description of the uses of the House rules during this period and the struggle for their reform.

REED RULES OF 1890

The next major development in the evolution of the House rules came in 1890 with the adoption of the famous "Reed Rules." Thomas Brackett Reed had entered Congress from Maine in March 1877; during the intervening years he had often seen how the business of the House could be paralyzed and the will of the majority frustrated by minority groups. The tactics of obstruction then employed included such devices as the "disappearing quorum," repeated rollcalls, and various dilatory motions.

Reed was a bold and courageous man with a powerful personality and an acid tongue. He had been a leading figure in the Maine legislature and he was destined to become a masterful Speaker of the House of Representatives. In his view the business of an organism was to function and the duty of a legislature was to legislate. During the 1880's Mr. Reed became an expert in parliamentary strategy and tactics, biding his time until he should be in a position to overcome the techniques of minority rule. The need of reform in House procedure impressed him deeply and he was convinced that the traditional practice must be changed. Minority rights, he felt, should not be allowed to override the rights of the majority.

Reed's opportunity to carry out his ideas came with his elevation to the Speakership in the 51st Congress. When the House met in December 1889, it declined to adopt rules at its organization, thus bringing general parliamentary law into operation. On January 29, 1890, the contested election case of Smith vs. Jackson was called up for consideration. When Mr. Crisp of Georgia raised the question of consideration, the vote stood: yeas 161, nays 2, not voting 165, three less than a quorum. But when the objection of "no quorum" was raised, the Speaker directed the Clerk to record the names of those present and refusing to vote: a long-standing minority maneuver, and then he declared a quorum present and consideration of the election case in order.

Immediately the House was in an uproar. Members poured into the aisles and denounced the Speaker as a "tyrant" and a "czar." The commotion continued for several hours amid scenes of unprecedented disorder. In support of his ruling Mr. Reed cited the practice of the English House of Commons, the rules and precedents of the House of Representatives, and the Federal Constitution. A Democratic Member appealed from the decision of the Chair, but the appeal was tabled by a majority of a quorum.

The next day the Speaker again counted those present but not voting in order to make a quorum for the approval of the Journal, and refused to entertain any appeal from his decision, stating that the House had already decided the question of a quorum. Despite violent abuse, Mr. Reed maintained his position with calmness and dignity until at last the crisis passed. And he declared his intention thenceforth to disregard all motions and appeals, however, parliamentary in themselves, which were made merely for the sake of delay.

These two historic decisions of the Chair: that a vote is valid if a quorum be actually present, though not voting, and that obviously dilatory motions designed to obstruct business need not be entertained, were both incorporated among the 45 rules that the House adopted after long debate on February 14, 1890. Thus, after a century of warfare over minority obstruction, the adoption of the "Reed Rules" in 1890 finally doomed the dilatory tactics of a minority in the House to defeat.[11]

In addition to these major reforms, the Reed Rules as adopted in 1890 also provided for a readjustment in the order of business, reduction of the quorum in Committee of the Whole to 100, the relief of the morning hour by filing bills and reports with the Clerk, and the adoption of special orders by a majority vote—a major change. Under the new system, the Speaker referred all public bills to their respective committees and was authorized to dispose of business "on the Speaker's table" without action by the House, except on House bills with Senate amendments which usually go to conference without debate. Likewise he minimized "unfinished business" by limiting its jurisdiction to business transacted by the House in its general legislative time as distinguished from business transacted in special periods. Under the revised "order of business," adopted in 1890, the House has since been able to move freely from one calendar to another and from the House to the Committee of the Whole.

In defense of these new arrangements the Committee on Rules reported to the House that:

The abuse [of obstruction] has grown to such proportions that the parliamentary law which governs American assemblies has found it necessary to keep pace with the evil, and to enable the majority by the intervention of the presiding officer to meet by extraordinary means the extraordinary abuse of power on the part sometimes of a very few members.[12]

By empowering the Speaker to prevent obstruction, the reforms of 1890 went far to regularize House procedure, to expedite the conduct of its business, to enhance its dignity, and to fix legislative responsibility upon the majority. The Reed Rules won lasting fame for their author in the annals of Congress and have proved generally satisfactory in practice.[13]

REVOLUTION OF 1910

Under the operation of the Reed system the Speaker of the House developed far-reaching powers. They included his power to appoint the standing committees of the House, to designate their chairmen, and thus determine the legislative opportunities of the individual members. As chairman of the Committee on Rules he was able to determine what business the House should consider. And through his unlimited power of recognition he could decide what matters would come before the House and discipline Members who failed to comply with his wishes. After a long process of evolution the Speaker of the House had become an officer second only to the President of the United States in influence and power.

It was not long, however, before a reaction set in. Under Speaker Cannon, first elected to that office in 1903, there developed growing discontent both in Congress and throughout the country with the manner in which and the purposes for which the powers of the Speaker were being exercised. This discontent finally broke out in open rebellion on the floor of the House on March 16, 1910, when a coalition of insurgent Republicans and Democrats, led by George Norris of Nebraska, succeeded in effecting a radical revision of the House rules.

---

[11] *House Journal*, 51st Cong., 1st sess., pp. 209, 214, 216, 219–221, 224–227, 227–233.
[12] *Congressional Record*, 51st Cong., 1st sess., pp. 1131–1132.
[13] *Cf.* Alexander, *op. cit.*, pp. 165–168, 206, 220–221.

They removed the Speaker from the Rules Committee of which he had formerly been chairman. They stripped him of the power to appoint the standing committees of the House and their chairmen which he had previously possessed and exercised as a powerful weapon of party discipline. And they restricted his former right to recognize or refuse to recognize Members seeking to address the House. It was also provided that the Committee on Rules, which had been composed of 5 members appointed by the Speaker, should henceforth be elected by the House and be composed of 10 members, 6 from the majority party and 4 from the minority. The Speaker was excluded from membership on this committee which was to elect its chairman from its own members.

The Norris resolution was adopted by a vote of 191 to 156, on March 19, after a great debate and continuous session lasting 29 hours. In a vivid description of this successful *coup d'etat*, which he had witnessed from the press gallery, George Rothwell Brown wrote that—

As Mr. Cannon's gavel fell an epoch in the long and brilliant history of the American House of Representatives came to an end. A new era had begun.[14]

The revolution of 1910 was not only political in character; it was also social in the sense that it reflected an aroused public opinion which felt that legislative power, under "Czar" Cannon's leadership, had grown so great as to upset the balance of power in the American constitutional system. The insurgents who thus succeeded in destroying the strong system of party government, party discipline, and majority rule in the House of Representatives, which their party had erected under the masterful leadership of Mr. Reed and Mr. Cannon, sought to liberalize the rules of the House as a prelude to the introduction and passage of measures liberalizing the laws. Their grievances were voiced by Mr. Nelson of Wisconsin who said:

Have we not been punished by every means at the disposal of the powerful House organization? Members long chairmen of important committees, others holding high rank—all with records of faithful and efficient party service to their credit—have been ruthlessly removed, deposed, and humiliated before their constituents and the country because, forsooth, they would not cringe or crawl before the arbitrary power of the Speaker and his House machine * * *. We are fighting for the right of free, fair, and full representation in this body for our respective constituencies * * *. We are fighting with our Democratic brethren for the common right of equal representation in this House, and for the right-of-way of progressive legislation in Congress.[15]

The Republican system of party government in Congress, based upon the party caucus and strict party discipline, also had its eloquent defenders in the debate. Among them was Mr. James R. Mann of Illinois, one of Speaker Cannon's lieutenants, who said:

On the whole, the rules of the House are probably the best considered, most scientifically constructed and finely adjusted rules governing any parliamentary body on earth. * * * It is not true that Speaker Cannon or any other Speaker is an autocrat in the House. It is true that the present Speaker is the leader and strongest influence in the House, and that he has been so for ten years, dating back to the time before he was Speaker and from the time that Speaker Reed left the House. We may some of us revile him temporarily. Great men have been abused at all times—such is the history of mankind—but when the book of history of this generation shall have been written, together with the legislation that has been enacted, the years of the Speakership of Mr. Cannon will stand out among the most brilliant in the history of our country.[16]

14 George Rothwell Brown, *The Leadership of Congress* (1922), p. 152. See also 8 *Cannon's Precedents* 3376.
15 Ibid., pp. 158–159.
16 Ibid., p. 163.

Mr. Champ Clark of Missouri, who was soon to become Speaker himself, expressed the attitude of the Democrats in the House toward the impending changes as follows:

* * * this is a fight against a system. We think it is a bad system, as far as this Committee on Rules has been concerned. It does not make any difference to me that it is sanctified by time. There never has been any progress in this world except to overthrow precedents and take new positions. There never will be. Reformers and progressives are necessarily and inevitably iconoclasts. * * * I have believed ever since I was in the House long enough to understand the work of the Committee on Rules that the fact that the Speaker of the House was chairman of that committee, and practically the Committee on Rules, gives the Speaker of this House more power than any one man ought to have over the destinies of this republic. * * * We had made up our minds months ago to try to work the particular revolution that we are working here today, because, not to mince words, it is a revolution. * * * I am not giving my adhesion to any proposition concerning this rules business that does not remove the Speaker now, and, so far as we can control it, for all time to come, from the Committee on Rules. That is my position, and in that I speak for the Democrats of the House and the insurgent Republicans. We are fighting to rehabilitate the House of Representatives and to restore it to its ancient place of honor and prestige in our system of government.[17]

When the House adopted the Norris resolution amending its rules on March 19, 1910, Speaker Cannon signified his recognition of its importance by announcing that he would entertain a motion that the Chair be vacated so that the House could elect a new Speaker. Such a motion was made, but defeated. The Republican insurgents were willing to form a coalition with the Democrats to revise the rules, but not to elect a Democratic Speaker. The Democrats captured control of the House, however, in the following November, and when the 62d Congress convened in special session on April 4, 1911, Champ Clark was chosen Speaker.

Back in power after 16 years, the Democrats proceeded to adopt a radically revised code of rules based upon the Crisp rules of the 53d Congress and incorporating substantially all the changes effected by the Norris resolution. The rules of the 62d House dealt the final *coup de grace* to the traditional powers of the speakership by depriving him of the right to appoint the standing committees of the House, providing instead that they should be "elected by the House, at the commencement of each Congress." They provided further that committee chairmen should be elected by the House and not be appointed by the Speaker. They retained and strengthened the Calendar Wednesday rule, first adopted in 1909, under which every standing committee had a chance to call up its reported bills without getting a "green light" from the Rules Committee. And they also preserved the unanimous-consent calendar, another 1909 procedural innovation of progressive origin, whereby 2 days a month were expressly reserved for the consideration of minor bills, important to individual Members, without requiring the recognition of the Chair.

On the surface the 1911 rules had apparently succeeded in transferring control of the legislative process in the House of Representatives from the Speaker to the House itself. To many students of these tremendous events it appeared, not that the House had rejected the principle of leadership, but rather that the House had rebelled against the dictatorial manner in which Speaker Cannon exercised his powers, and had determined to shift the leadership of the House from the Chair to the floor, leaving the Speaker on the rostrum as merely a moderator of the legislative machine.[18] This interpretation

17 Ibid., pp. 165–67.
18 Cf. W. F. Willoughby, *Principles of Legislative Organization and Administration* (1934), pp. 544–545.

of these events seemed to be confirmed by the role assumed in the 62d Congress by Mr. Oscar W. Underwood who was, at once, both the majority floor leader and the chairman of the Ways and Means Committee to which the Democratic caucus assigned the function of naming the committees of the House, including the Committee on Rules.

In the perspective of half a century, however, the changes made in 1911 have proved to be less drastic than they appeared at that time. Although the Speaker is no longer a member of the Rules Committee, he still influences it. Although he lost his power of appointing the standing committees of the House, he still appoints the select committees, the House Members of conference committees, and the chairman of the Committee of the Whole. Through these and other prerogatives and channels of influence, the Speakership continues to be an exceedingly powerful office.

DEVELOPMENTS SINCE 1912

Since the revision of 1911 at least four noteworthy developments have taken place in the rules of the House. The first of these concerned jurisdiction over appropriations for the support of the Government. The Committee on Appropriations was first established in 1865 and for 20 years it reported all the general appropriation bills. But in 1885 authority to report the supply bills was divided among nine committees of the House and this allocation continued until July 1, 1920, when by an amendment of the rules the House again concentrated in the Committee on Appropriations the power to report all the general appropriation bills and readopted the rule in the form provided by the revision of 1880. Meanwhile, Congress enacted the Budget and Accounting Act of 1921 and the change in the general supply bills to conform to the new budget law was made in the 2d session of the 67th Congress.[19] Thus, since 1920, the Committee on Appropriations has had exclusive jurisdiction over all the general appropriation bills.

The second significant development took place on December 5, 1927, when some 11 separate committees on expenditures in the executive departments were consolidated into a single such committee. The first of these expenditure committees had been created in 1816, and others were added as new departments were established. In reporting a resolution from the Committee on Rules to abolish these "deadwood committees," Chairman Snell of the Rules Committee remarked:

I think there is no one on either side but that will agree that it is foolish and ridiculous for us to carry from year to year 16 committees [of which 11 were expenditures committees] that have practically no work to do in connection with the work of the House and are only deadwood, used simply to furnish assignments to Members. The majority of the committees that we are abolishing have not met in several years and there is no probability that there will be any work for them in the immediate future.

The resolution was passed on the same day it was reported and the 11 expenditures committees, which Mr. Alvin Fuller of Massachusetts described as "ornamental barnacles on the ship of state," were abolished.[20] On July 3, 1952, the name of this committee was changed

19 7 *Cannon's Precedents* 1741.
20 Lucius Wilmerding, Jr. *The Spending Power* (1943), pp. 292–293. See also 7 *Cannon's Precedents* 2041.

from "Expenditures in the Executive Departments" to "Government Operations.'

REFORMS OF 1946

The outstanding development in the organization and operation of Congress during the past 50 years was the Legislative Reorganization Act of 1946. Hailed at its passage as a legislative miracle, this act was the culmination of a long and sustained campaign in Congress and the country to "modernize" the National Legislature. The alleged decline of Congress in relation to the executive was a widely observed phenomenon. For several years Members of both Houses and both political parties had been offering various proposals for specific reforms or wider action which had been the subject of lively discussion on the floor of the House and Senate. These members recognized that the problem of making Congress a more efficient democratic machine was becoming increasingly acute, that it was not a party problem, and that it required solution regardless of the party situation in Congress. Meanwhile, articles urging legislative rehabilitation were appearing in the lay and learned magazines, while the press, ever alert to significant public questions, was arousing and informing public opinion on the need of "congressional reform." The radio networks broadcast debates on the machinery and methods of Congress as part of their educational programs and various civic and professional groups put their weight behind the movement.

Congress responded to this campaign by setting up a joint select committee of its own Members which held extensive hearings and produced an act "to provide for increased efficiency in the legislative branch of the Government" which was approved by President Truman on August 2, 1946. The Legislative Reorganization Act had 10 objectives:

1. To streamline and simplify the committee structure;
2. To eliminate the use of special or select committees;
3. To clarify committee duties and reduce jurisdictional disputes;
4. To regularize and publicize committee procedures;
5. To reduce the workload on Congress;
6. To strengthen legislative oversight of administration;
7. To reinforce the power of the purse;
8. To improve congressional staff aids;
9. To regulate lobbying; and
10. To increase the compensation of Members of Congress and provide them retirement pay.

Of these objectives the first seven found expression in extensive changes in the rules of the House and Senate and were set forth in the first title of the 1946 act. This was divided into three parts of which the first amended the standing rules of the Senate by streamlining its committee system, part 2 amended the rules of the House of Representatives in the same way, and part 3 contained 12 sections applicable to both Houses.

Modernization of the standing committee system was the first aim of the act and the keystone in the arch of congressional "reform." By dropping minor, inactive committees and by merging those with related functions, the act reduced the total number of standing committees from 48 to 19 in the House of Representatives and from 33 to

15 in the Senate. These changes in committee structure have survived except that so-called "select" Committees on Small Business have been set up in each House and have become standing committees in everything but name. The House established a standing Committee on Science and Astronautics on July 21, 1958, and the Senate created a standing Committee on Aeronautical and Space Sciences on July 24, 1958.

In the form in which it passed the Senate, the act prohibited special committees. Although this provision was stricken in the House, the spirit of the act clearly frowns on the creation of special committees. Its authors had recommended that the practice of creating special investigating committees be abandoned on the ground that they lack legislative authority and that the jurisdiction of the new standing committees would be so comprehensively defined, in the reformed rules, as to cover every conceivable subject of legislation. In practice, special committees have not been abandoned, but their number has diminished.

The act also amended rule XI of the House rules by clarifying the duties of the reorganized standing committees which were defined in terms of their jurisdiction over specific subject-matter fields and administrative agencies. Although House bills are occasionally re-referred by unanimous consent, open conflicts between committees in the first chamber have almost disappeared. But it must be admitted that jurisdiction over the various aspects of several subject-matter fields is still split among many standing committees in both Houses of Congress. National defense policies and expenditures are reviewed in piecemeal fashion by several committees in both Houses; jurisdiction over various phases of our foreign relations is widely scattered; and the fiscal machinery of Congress is also splintered and fragmented.[21]

Under section 133 of the 1946 act, committee procedure has been regularized in regard to periodic meeting days, the keeping of committee records, the reporting of approved measures, the presence of a majority of committeemen as a condition of committee action, and the conduct of hearings. Under the rule, proxy voting is permissible in committee only after a majority is actually present. Each committee may fix the number of its members to constitute a quorum for taking testimony and receiving evidence, which shall be not less than two. The requirement that witnesses file written statements of their testimony in advance of hearings is observed by some committees and ignored by others; hearings are sometimes called on too short notice for this action to be possible. Most committees hold open hearings, except the House Committee on Appropriations which has availed itself of the allowed option of holding its hearings in camera.[22] Committee offices, staff personnel, and records are now kept separate and distinct from those of committee chairmen: another requirement of the 1946 act. In practice, to be sure, these committee regulations are not always complied with.

Section 131 of the act sought to reduce the workload on Congress by banning the introduction of four categories of private bills, e.g., pension bills, tort claims bills, bridge bills, and bills for the correction

---

[21] Cf. The Organization of Congress: Some Problems of Committee Jurisdiction. S. Doc. No. 51, 82d Cong., 1st sess. July 1951.
[22] Congressional Quarterly News Features reports that in recent years about one-third of all congressional committee hearings have been closed to the public.

of military or naval records. But this gain has been offset by the postwar flood of private immigration bills that has engulfed the judiciary committees: 2,181 were introduced in the House in 1955.

Another main objective of the 1946 act was to strengthen legislative "oversight" of administration. To this end section 136 provided that—

each standing committee of the Senate and the House of Representatives shall exercise continuous watchfulness of the execution by the administrative agencies concerned of any laws, the subject matter of which is within the jurisdiction of such committee * * *.

This provision, coupled with the professional staffing of congressional committees, has contributed mightily to the extraordinary increase in the exercise of the investigative function of Congress after World War II. In practice, the armory of legislative surveillance of the executive has included such weapons as committee investigations, question periods at the committee stage, the statutory requirement of prior committee clearance of contemplated administrative action, the requirement of periodic reports to Congress, the control of administrative action by congressional resolutions, and demands for the production of executive documents and testimony: all of which have been increasingly used in recent years to strengthen the "watchdog" function of Congress.[23]

A final major aim of the 1946 act was to strengthen the congressional power of the purse. There was a growing feeling in Congress and the country that Congress was losing control of the purse strings. This aim found expression in several sections of the act of which the most ambitious was that (sec. 138) for the creation of a Joint Committee on the Budget which was to formulate a "legislative budget" and fix a ceiling on expenditures. Attempts to carry out the legislative budget provisions during 1947–49 proved abortive and the Joint Budget Committee has failed to function since 1949. The McClellan bill to recreate a Joint Committee on the Budget has passed the Senate five times in the last decade, only to be lost on the House side. The House is jealous of its fiscal prerogatives and perhaps feels that the proposed Joint Budget Committee would trespass upon the jurisdiction of its Committee on Appropriations.[24]

For the most part, the reforms of 1946 were enacted by Congress as an exercise of the rulemaking power of the respective Houses and were incorporated in their standing rules. In retrospect, we see that the standing committee structure, streamlined in 1946, continues virtually intact, and that there has been a gradual increase in the use of joint committees and a rapid growth of subcommittees. As if to compensate for the decline in the policy-making role of Congress, with the shift of the initiative in policy making in recent decades from Congress to the Executive, there has been an extraordinary rise in the exercise of the investigative function of Congress since the Second World War and initial steps have been taken to correct its alleged abuses. Supervision of the executive branch continues to be a major preoccupation of the National Legislature, and some new techniques for the purpose have been developed, including prior committee clearance and the use of congressional resolutions to control administrative action. Not

[23] See George B. Galloway, *Congressional Reorganization Revisited*, Bureau of Governmental Research, University of Maryland, 1956, pp. 9–14. See also J. Malcolm Smith and Cornelius P. Cotter, *Administrative Accountability: 1 Reporting to Congress*, Stanford University Political Science Series, No. 60, 1957.
[24] For a recent study of this subject see Robert A. Wallace, *Congressional Control of Federal Spending* (1960).

legislation but control of administration is becoming the primary function of the modern Congress. Although the fiscal control features of the 1946 act failed to work in practice, numerous proposals for strengthening congressional control of public expenditure were offered by Members of Congress, the Hoover Commissions, and interested private research organizations. The Legislative Reorganization Act of 1946 was largely the result of an internally felt need. The Members of the House who assisted in formulating the act and who were instrumental in its passage in that chamber were Mike Monroney, of Oklahoma; Everett M. Dirksen, of Illinois; E. E. Cox, of Georgia; Thomas J. Lane, of Massachusetts; Earl C. Michener, of Michigan; and Charles A. Plumley, of Vermont.

STRUGGLE OVER THE 21-DAY RULE

The most recent episode in the evolution of the House rules involved the struggle over the so-called 21-day rule in 1949–51. In 1937 the New Deal lost control of the House Rules Committee when three of its Democratic members joined with the four Republican members to block floor consideration of controversial administration bills. The coalition succeeded in preventing a score or more of New Deal-Fair Deal measures from reaching the House floor, except by the laborious discharge route which required 218 signatures on a discharge petition to take a bill away from a committee. After the Second World War a rising demand developed for reform of the powers of the Committee on Rules. Rebellion against the committee found expression in a letter which Representative Eberharter wrote his House colleagues in December 1948.

In theory—

he said—

the Rules Committee is a traffic director on the legislative highway, determining the order of business on the floor of the House. In practice this committee has become an obstruction to orderly traffic. The committee often allows bills to come before the House only on its own terms. It frequently usurps the functions of the regular legislative committees of the House by holding hearings and reviewing the merits of bills that have already been carefully studied by the proper legislative committees. A reform of this undemocratic system is long overdue. Congress is constantly engaged in a struggle for the respect of the people. The people never have and never will be able to understand how the will of a majority of the House of Representatives can be set aside by the judgment of a few men on a powerful committee.

The fight against the "obstructive tactics" of the Rules Committee finally came to a head on January 3, 1949, when the House adopted the so-called "21-day rule" by a vote of 275 to 142. Under this rule, the chairman of a legislative committee which had favorably reported a bill could call it up for House consideration if the Rules Committee reported adversely on it or failed to give it a "green light" to the House floor within 21 days. The 21-day rule remained in effect throughout the 81st Congress (1949–50), despite a determined effort to repeal it early in the 2d session. A coalition led by Congressman Cox of Georgia was defeated on January 20, 1950, by a vote of 236 to 183; 85 southern Democrats voted for the Cox repeal resolution, while 64 Republicans sided with the administration against their own leadership.

During the 1st session of the 81st Congress, the 21-day rule brought the anti-poll-tax bill to the House floor for a successful vote and forced action on the housing and minimum wage bills. During the second session it enabled the House to vote for the National Science Foundation, Alaska and Hawaii statehood legislation, and other important measures. Altogether during the 81st Congress, eight measures were brought to the floor of the House and passed by resort to the 21-day rule, and its existence caused the Rules Committee to act in other cases.

On January 3, 1951, a hostile coalition regained control of the situation and obtained repeal of the 21-day rule by a vote of 247 to 179 after a bitter fight. As a result, the power of the Rules Committee to blockade bills was restored and has since remained in effect.

Two opposing principles were involved in the struggle over the powers of the House Committee on Rules: whether legislative action should be controlled by a majority of the entire House or whether the majority party should control through its nominal agent. Those who believed in the principle of majority rule by the whole House favored reducing the Rules Committee to a traffic director on the legislative highway and a more liberal discharge rule. Their fundamental objection to the existing setup was that it vests power in a small group of Rules Committee men to prevent the House from considering and taking action upon measures not favored by the committee. Under the present system, they say, many cases arise where a bill or resolution that would receive favorable action by the House, if it had a chance to consider it, is killed in committee. Such a system, it is argued, denies the House its constitutional right to legislate and violates the principle of representative government.

On the other hand, those who believed that the party in power should control legislative action, as a means of fulfilling its responsibility to the electorate, favored strengthening party government in the House through a strong Rules Committee and a strict discharge rule. To curtail the authority of the committee, they asserted, would (1) go far to destroy the effective working of party government and responsibility, and (2) tend to facilitate the attempt of self-seeking special interests and minority groups to secure the passage of legislation detrimental to the general welfare.

While conceding the force of these objections, advocates of a change maintained that, under existing political conditions in the Rules Committee, it is possible for the will of the majority party, as expressed at the polls, to be frustrated by a hostile coalition within the committee. Under these circumstances, ran their argument, only a reform of the powers of the committee would, in crucial cases, enable the true majority will to prevail.

CHAPTER 6

DEVELOPMENT OF COMMITTEE SYSTEM

From the beginning our National Legislature has conducted its work in large part through committees of its members. The use of select and standing committees, as well as the Committee of the Whole, was derived by Congress from the practice of the English House of Commons via the colonial assemblies, especially those in Pennsylvania and Virginia.[1] In the early days the House of Representatives referred its business to a host of select committees. For every bill and petty claim a special committee was "raised." Select committees are special or temporary groups created for a particular purpose, whereas standing committees are permanent groups that continue from Congress to Congress.

Although select committees and the Committee of the Whole were largely relied upon by the House during its first quarter century, the standing committee system had its inception in the earliest days. The Committee on Elections created in 1789 (since 1946 a standing subcommittee of the Committee on House Administration) has the honor of being the oldest standing committee of the House. Claims, established in 1794, was the second to join this category. It was followed in 1795 by Interstate and Foreign Commerce and Revisal and Unfinished Business. As the 19th century advanced, the select committees were converted into standing committees which gradually grew in number. Six of them were set up in the first decade of that century and 11 in the second decade. By midcentury the House had 34 standing committees and by 1900 it had 58. Nine more were added during the 20th century up to 1930 when the process of fission stopped, save for the creation of the Committee on Un-American Activities in 1945 and in 1958 of the Committee on Science and Astronautics. With the consolidation in 1920 of jurisdiction over appropriations in a single Committee on Appropriations (previously divided among 9 committees), and with the merger in 1927 of 11 expenditures committees into a single Committee on Expenditures in the Executive Departments, a net reduction of 18 in the number of standing committees in the House was effected. In 1946 the committee structure in the first chamber was streamlined when 48 standing groups were reduced to 19.

CHRONOLOGICAL DEVELOPMENT

The following tables reflect the chronological development of the standing committee system of the House of Representatives.

---

[1] On the evolution of the committee system see J. F. Jameson, "The Origin of the Standing Committee System in American Legislative Bodies," *Annual Report of the American Historical Association*, 1893.

Growth of standing committees by decades

1789–1800	4	1881–90	3
1801–10	6	1891–1900	9
1811–20	11	1901–10	3
1821–30	6	1911–20	3
1831–40	6	1921–30	2
1841–50	1	1931–40	0
1851–60	1	1941–50	1
1861–70	7	1951–60	1
1871–80	4		

Growth of standing committees by periods

Congress:	Number	Congress—Continued	Number
14th	20	56th	58
28th	36	70th	45
42d	42	86th	20

Chronology of House standing committees

Committee	Created
Elections No. 1	1789
Claims	1794
Interstate and Foreign Commerce	1795
Revisal and Unfinished Business	1795
Ways and Means	1802
Accounts	1805
Public Lands	1805
District of Columbia	1808
Post Office and Post Roads	1808
Library	1809
Judiciary	1813
Revolutionary Claims	1813
Public Expenditures	1814
Private Land Claims	1816
Expenditures in Executive Departments (5)	1816
Manufactures	1819
Agriculture	1820
Indian Affairs	1821
Military Affairs	1822
Naval Affairs	1822
Foreign Affairs	1822
Military Pensions	1825
Territories	1825
Invalid Pensions	1831
Railways and Canals	1831
Militia	1835
Patents	1837
Public Buildings and Grounds	1837
Mileage	1837
Engraving	1844
Expenditures in Interior Department	1860
Coinage, Weights, and Measures	1864
Appropriations	1865
Banking and Currency	1865
Mines and Mining	1865
Pacific Railroads	1865
Education and Labor (separated in 1883)	1867
Revision of the Laws	1868
War Claims	1873
Expenditures in Department of Justice	1874
Levees and Improvements of Mississippi River	1875
Rules	1880
Rivers and Harbors	1883
Merchant Marine and Fisheries	1887
Expenditures in Department of Agriculture	1889
Election of President, Vice President, and Representatives	1893
Immigration and Naturalization	1893

Chronology of House standing committees—Continued

Committee	Created
Irrigation and Reclamation	1893
Civil Service	1893
Alcoholic Liquor Traffic	1893
Ventilation and Acoustics	1895
Elections No. 2	1895
Elections No. 3	1895
Insular Affairs	1899
Census	1901
Industrial Arts and Expositions	1901
Expenditures in Department of Commerce and Labor	1905
Roads	1913
Flood Control	1916
Woman Suffrage	1917
World War Veterans' Legislation	1924
Memorials	1929
Un-American Activities	1945
Science and Astronautics	1958

A mere listing of the names of these 68 standing committees set up by the House of Representatives over a century and a half reflects the growing diversity of interests in the expanding Nation and, concomitantly, the rising business of the House. With a little imagination the committee list may be viewed as an outline of American history, for the creation of each major committee was associated with some important historical event or emerging public problem. Thus, the increasing domestic and foreign trade of the new Republic was soon followed by the creation of the Committee on Interstate and Foreign Commerce in 1795. The Louisiana Purchase in 1803 gave rise to the Committee on Public Lands in 1805. The location of the seat of the National Government on the shores of the Potomac in 1800 led to the District of Columbia Committee in 1808. The Committee on Public Expenditures was created in 1814 in order to relieve Ways and Means of some of its duties and to inquire into the economical management of the departments and the accountability of officers. The expanding relations of the United States with foreign nations produced the Committee on Foreign Affairs in 1822. It had been in continuous existence as a select committee since 1808. The Appropriations Committee dates from 1865 when it was created to relieve Ways and Means, then overburdened by the weight of war legislation. Long opposed by southern Members, the establishment of the Committee on Education and Labor in 1867 marked the emancipation of the slaves. And so on down the long list to the creation of the Un-American Activities Committee in 1945, reflecting postwar fears of internal subversion, and the Committee on Science and Astronautics in 1958, marking the advent of the space age.

APPOINTMENT OF COMMITTEES

From 1790 until 1911 the Speaker generally appointed the members and the chairmen of the standing and select committees of the House of Representatives, although the annals reveal several instances in which committees chose their own chairmen.[2] From 1857 he made these appointments, with few exceptions, at the commencement of each Congress. But this power was taken away from the Speaker in 1911, as we have seen, and since that time the committees and their

_____
[2] 4 Hinds' Precedents 4524, 4525, 4526, 4527, 4528, 4529.

chairmen have been elected by the House as soon as the two political parties in the Chamber have had time to perfect their lists and present resolutions for their ratification.[3] In the earlier usage the Member moving a select committee was named as its chairman. Prior to 1880 when the rule relating to the appointment of select committees was adopted, the House occasionally deprived the Speaker of the appointment of a select committee; but the practice of leaving the appointment of House Members of conference committees and the Chairman of the Committee of the Whole to the Speaker dates from the earlier years.

During early Congresses an attempt was made to give each State representation on important committees. As the number of States in the Union gradually grew, this practice was discontinued but geographical representation remains a significant factor in committee assignments. Formerly Members sometimes complained about undue delay on the part of the Speaker in assigning committee posts. In the 42d Congress (1871) the Speaker waited 275 days (March 4 to December 4) before submitting committee lists.

In the modern practice the lists of committee assignments are prepared by the "committees on committees" of the major parties. The Republican conference selects its "committee on committees" and the Democratic members of the Ways and Means Committee act as their "committee on committees." The lists drawn up by these groups are approved in party conference and then ratified by the House. Party representation on the standing committees of the House is determined by the selection committee of the majority party and reflects the party ratio in the Chamber. Freedom of choice in making committee assignments is limited both by the number and size of the committees, which are fixed by the standing rules, and by the number of vacancies resulting from the death, defeat, or resignation of committeemen.

In filling vacancies in committee chairmanships the unwritten rule of seniority has usually, but not invariably, been followed. Seniority is the custom by which the chairmanships of the standing committees automatically go to the majority party members who have the longest continuous service on the committees. On rare occasions this custom has not been followed. For example, in 1903 Representative Jesse Overstreet, of Indiana, was appointed chairman of the Committee on Post Offices and Post Roads, giving him precedence over two members who had served 16 and 32 years, respectively. In 1905 Representative James A. Tawney, of Minnesota, was made chairman of Appropriations although two other members outranked him. Both of these departures were made by Speaker Cannon in order to promote his policies. In 1909 Representative James R. Mann, of Illinois, was advanced to the chairmanship of Interstate and Foreign Commerce out of his turn. In 1915 Representative Claude Kitchin, of North Carolina, was promoted to the chairmanship of Ways and Means over Representative Shackleford, of Missouri, who stood next in line because the incumbent of this post at that time was also the Democratic floor leader, a position for which Mr. Kitchin was preferred. And in 1921 Representative Martin B. Madden, of Illinois, was elevated to the chairmanship of Appropriations, of which he had only recently become a member, because the committeeman next in line

³ 4 *Hinds' Precedents* 4513; 8 *Cannon's Precedents* 2201–2202.

was considered too old to assume the heavy duties of launching the new budget system.[4]

ROLE OF COMMITTEE CHAIRMAN

The powers and duties of the chairmen of the standing committees of Congress gradually evolved over the years and have not been codified, but are scattered through the rules and statutes. Statements on the subject are found in House rule XI, in the standing orders adopted by some committees, in certain sections of title 2 of the United States Code, in the Legislative Reorganization Act of 1946, and in Hinds' and Cannon's *Precedents of the House of Representatives*.

The earliest light on the role of committee chairmen is shed by Jefferson's famous manual of parliamentary procedure. Although this manual was prepared by Thomas Jefferson for his own guidance as President of the Senate from 1797 to 1801, it reflects both the theory and practice of the House of Representatives in the last decade of the 18th century, so far as the functioning of committees and their chairmen is concerned. In the early Congresses most important matters were first considered in a Committee of the Whole for the purpose of rational discussion and the definition of guiding principles, before bills were allowed to be introduced and before reference to smaller committees which were appointed to establish facts and arrange details. When standing committees were appointed, *Jefferson's Manual* states in section XI that:

> The person first named is generally permitted to act as chairman. But this is a matter of courtesy; every committee having a right to elect their own chairman, who presides over them, puts questions, and reports their proceedings to the House.

If a bill or resolution were committed to a select committee, the member who moved its appointment was usually named as chairman. The Jeffersonians believed that these committees and their chairmen should be sympathetic to the purpose of the matters committed to them. Thus, Jefferson notes in section XXVI of his manual that:

> Those who take exceptions to some particulars in the bill are to be of the committee, but none who speak directly against the body of the bill; for he that would totally destroy will not amend it; or as is said, the child is not to be put to a nurse that cares not for it. It is therefore a constant rule "that no man is to be employed in any matter who has declared himself against it." And when any member who is against the bill hears himself named of its committee he ought to ask to be excused.

The *Annals* of the early Congresses indicate that special knowledge or experience of a particular subject was sometimes considered a qualification for committee appointment, but that the principle of seniority had not yet become customary in selecting committee chairmen. Joseph Cooper reports that the standing Committee on Elections in the Third Congress and the standing Committees on Claims and on Commerce and Manufacturing in the Fourth Congress had different chairmen in one session than in another. The successive chairmen were not the ranking members, members were not listed by party on the committee lists, and the composition of the standing committees underwent substantial changes from session to session.[5]

---

[4] Paul DeWitt Hasbrouck, *Party Government in the House of Representatives* (1927), p. 48.
[5] In his unpublished doctoral dissertation, Harvard, 1960, on committee theory and practice in Congress. This excellent work analyzes committee theory and practice in the House of Representatives in three periods: The Jeffersonian, 1789-1829, the Progressive 1909-34, and the Modern Reform, 1944-59.

As regards committee reports Jefferson went on to say in the same section of his manual that:

A committee meet when and where they please, if the House has not ordered time and place for them; but they can only act when together, and not by separate consultation and consent—nothing being the report of the committee but what has been agreed to in committee actually assembled.   A majority of the committee constitutes a quorum for business.

During the first 20 years (1789–1809), when the House largely relied on select committees to perfect the details of bills after their general principles had been formulated in Committee of the Whole, committee reports were made by the chairman standing in his place on the House floor.   He would read the committee amendments and explain the reasons for them and then deliver the bill at the Clerk's table.   The Clerk would read the reported amendments and the papers would lie on the table until the House, at its convenience, took up the report.   The report being made, the committee was dissolved (*Jefferson's Manual*, sec. XXVII).   This procedure has long been obsolete.   In the modern practice, most of the reports of committees are made by filing them with the Clerk without reading, and only the reports of committees having leave to report at any time are made by the chairman or other member of the committee from the floor. While privileged reports are frequently acted on when presented, yet the general rule is that reports shall be placed on the calendars of the House, there to await action under the rules for the order of business. Since 1946 it has been the duty of the chairman of each committee to report, or cause to be reported promptly to the House, any measure approved by his committee and to take or cause to be taken necessary steps to bring the matter to a vote (rule XI, par. 26(d)).

As time went on disparities developed between theory and practice regarding the role and prerogatives of committee chairmen.   Originally conceived as merely the moderator or agent of the committee, the chairman began to play a more active part both in advancing and retarding committee reports.   Evidence of this is reflected in two resolutions introduced in the House at the end of the first session of the ninth Congress (1805–06) by Representative James Sloan of New Jersey.   One resolution required all committees to make weekly reports unless excused from so doing by unanimous consent.   The other required that all standing committees be elected by ballot and choose their own chairmen.   These resolutions were aimed at John Randolph, chairman of Ways and Means, in order, said Sloan—

to prevent in future the most important business of the nation from being retarded by a Chairman of the Committee of Ways and Means, or any other committee, by going to Baltimore or elsewhere, without leave of absence * * * to prevent in future the Chairman of the Committee of Ways and Means from keeping for months the estimates for the appropriations necessary for the ensuing year in his pocket, or locked up in his desk * * * and, finally, to prevent hereafter bills of importance being brought forward, and forced through the House, near the close of a session, when many members are gone home. * * * [6]

In the 1st session of the 10th Congress (1807–8) John Randolph was removed from Ways and Means when the committee was completely reformed.   Meanwhile, the House adopted a rule in the second session of the 8th Congress (1804–05), and renewed it in the 9th and 10th Congresses, allowing committees to choose their own chairmen if they wished.   As the 19th century advanced, however, previous service

[6] *Annals*, 9th Congress, 1st sess., pp. 1114–1115.   Quoted by Cooper, *op. cit.*, pp. 35–36.

on a committee increased in importance and the tendency grew to appoint the senior Members of the House to the committee chairmanships.

The precedents of the House of Representatives, as compiled by Asher Hinds and Clarence Cannon, shed further light on the evolution of the role of committee chairmen during the 19th century. The rule providing for the appointment of clerks of committees dates from December 14, 1838, when Representative Samuel Cushman of New Hampshire proposed that no committee should be permitted to employ a clerk at public expense without first obtaining leave of the House for that purpose. This suggestion was adopted and became old rule No. 73. In the rules revision of 1880 it became section 4 of rule X. (*Hinds' Precedents*, vol. 4, sec. 4533). In 1911 an amendment was added to this rule including other committee employees, making the rule read as follows:

> The chairman shall appoint the clerk or clerks or other employees of his committee, subject to its approval, who shall be paid at the public expense, the House having first provided therefor (*Cannon's Precedents*, vol. 8, sec. 2206).

Under the Legislative Reorganization Act of 1946, as amended, each standing committee of the House is authorized to appoint professional and clerical staffs, by majority vote of the committee, who shall be assigned to the chairman and ranking minority member, as the committee may deem advisable, and whose compensation shall be fixed by the chairman.

As regards their meetings, committees of the House originally met when and where they pleased, as noted above, the time and place being largely determined by the chairman. The failure of chairmen to take action responsive to the wishes of committees occasioned discussion in later Congresses, and on December 8, 1931, the first rule on this subject was adopted by the House (*Cannon's Precedents*, vol. 8, sec. 2208). The present rule, which combines the 1931 rule and section 133(a) of the Legislative Reorganization Act of 1946, provides that:

> Each standing committee of the House (other than the Committee on Appropriations) shall fix regular weekly, biweekly, or monthly meeting days for the transaction of business before the committee, and additional meetings may be called by the chairman as he may deem necessary and each such committee shall meet to consider any bill or resolution pending before it (a) on all regular meeting days selected by the committee; (b) upon the call of the chairman of the committee; (c) if the chairman of the committee, after three days' consideration refuses or fails, upon the request of at least three members of the committee, to call a special meeting of the committee within seven calendar days from the date of said request, then upon the filing with the clerk of the committee of the written and signed request of a majority of the committee for a called special meeting of the committee, the committee shall meet on the day and hour specified in said written request. It shall be the duty of the clerk of the committee to notify all members of the committee in the usual way of such called special meeting (rule XI, par. 24).

As regards committee procedure, the House amended its rules on March 23, 1955, by adopting a set of standards for the conduct of investigative hearings which imposed certain duties on the chairman at such hearings, including the making of an opening statement, the punishment of breaches of order and decorum, and the disposition of requests to subpena witnesses (rule XI, par. 26).

It often happens in human affairs that law or theory and actual practice do not precisely correspond. An account of the powers of committee chairmen would be incomplete, therefore, which did not include some description of the actual operation of the rules as seen by close students of congressional government down through the years. Writing in 1885, Woodrow Wilson said:[7]

It is now, though a wide departure from the form of things, no great departure from the fact to describe ours as a government by the Standing Committees of Congress * * *. The leaders of the House are the chairmen of the principal Standing Committees. Indeed, to be exactly accurate, the House has as many leaders as there are subjects of legislation; for there are as many Standing Committees as there are leading classes of legislation, and in the consideration of every topic of business the House is guided by a special leader in the person of the chairman of the Standing Committee, charged with the superintendence of measures of the particular class to which that topic belongs * * *. I know not how better to describe our form of government in a single phrase than by calling it a government by the chairmen of the Standing Committees of Congress. * * *

Writing in 1898, L. G. McConachie, historian of the development of congressional committees during the 19th century, said:[8]

The committee chairman, partly lifted by the Speaker in his rise, partly made important by the same conditions which have elevated the Speaker, has taken on function after function. His position was honorary to begin with; almost a mere matter of being named first * * *. While, from a present view, the chairman has enlarging powers within his increasingly crowded committee, upon whose room, with its conveniences, he has the lion's share of claim and control, whose clerk he appoints, and uses as a private secretary when committee business is dull, and to whose subcommittees he distributes the favors of legislation; yet the place to behold him in his largest influence is in the arena of striving interests, with its competition growing sharper and sharper—in the daily assembly of all the Representatives. There the Speaker sits as umpire, while his party leaders contend each for the cause of his own committee * * *. The chairman's steering qualities do not cease to be necessary when he has vanquished the chiefs of other committees by securing attention to his bills in preference to theirs. It has come about that the kind and length of consideration given to committee measures before the final vote are placed almost solely on his responsibility, and vary with his judgment of the sentiments of the majority. To him, by way of defining his previously existing right to open and close a debate, has been given, since 1880, one or two golden hours of time which he may dole out in quarter hours or ten-minute pieces to whomsoever he pleases. If he thinks it safe or wise, he insists upon the previous question without permitting talk or amendment.

Writing in 1943, Roland Young remarked:[9]

The chairmanship of an important congressional committee is coveted because of the political power which it gives the chairman. The power of a committee chairman varies from committee to committee and from chairman to chairman, but ordinarily a strong chairman, no matter what his views, is very influential even though it may not be possible for him to prevent the reporting of all legislation of which he disapproves or to get reported all legislation of which he approves. The chairman is powerful because he can call committee meetings whenever he wishes, because he has a large amount of freedom in preparing the legislative agenda for the committee, and because he is officially consulted on questions relating to his committee. A chairmanship also offers certain prerogatives in the form of additional secretarial assistance, but, more than that, it gives the member a status with Congress, with the bureaucracy, and with the general public.

In its 1945 report on the reorganization of Congress, a committee of the American Political Science Association said in part:[10]

The real work of Congress is done, not on the floor, but in the committee rooms. There the effective decisions are made in vital matters and are usually approved by the House. In this business the committee chairmen exercise great power. They arrange the schedules of work and the agenda of committee meetings.

[7] Woodrow Wilson, *Congressional Government*, pp. 56, 60–61, 102.
[8] L. G. McConachie, *Congressional Committees*, pp. 155, 157–159.
[9] Roland Young, *This Is Congress*, p. 108.
[10] Committee on Congress of the American Political Science Association, *The Reorganization of Congress*, p. 45.

They parcel out the personnel of subcommittees and determine the scope of their work. They or their subordinate chairmen of the subcommittees report to Congress on decisions for legislation and manage the floor debates in defense of such decisions. In these debates the committee chairman's work carries great weight because the subject is his peculiar province. In effect, the committee chairmen are able in large measure to dictate what proposals for legislation may be considered by Congress. The ordinary member proposes, but the chairman disposes. It is contrary to human nature to expect that the committee chairmen who are the leaders of Congress, will voluntarily surrender such great powers.

Writing in 1953, George B. Galloway summed up current practice by saying: [11]

Just as the standing committees control legislative action, so the chairmen are masters of their committees. Selected on the basis of seniority, locally elected and locally responsible, these "lord-proprietors" hold key positions in the power structure of Congress. They arrange the agenda of the committees, appoint the subcommittees, and refer bills to them. They decide what pending measures shall be considered and when, call committee meetings, and decide whether or not to hold hearings and when. They approve lists of scheduled witnesses, select their staffs and authorize staff studies and preside at committee hearings. They handle reported bills on the floor and participate as principal managers in conference committees. They are in a position to expedite measures they favor and to retard or pigeonhole those they dislike. Strong chairmen can often induce in executive sessions the kind of committee actions that they desire. In the House of Representatives, where debate is limited, the chairman in charge of a bill allots time to whomever he pleases during debate on the floor; he also has the right to open and close the debate on bills reported by his committee; and he may move the previous question whenever he thinks best. In short, committee chairmen exercise crucial powers over the legislative process. In his little classic on *Congressional Government*, written sixty-eight years ago, Woodrow Wilson described our form of government in a single phrase by calling it "a government by the chairmen of the standing committees of Congress." So far as Congress is concerned, this description is, in a large sense, still true.

REGIONAL DISTRIBUTION OF CHAIRMANSHIPS

In view of the potent place of committee chairmen in the power structure of Congress, it is interesting to note the regional distribution of these influential posts. When the Republicans controlled the House in the 83d Congress, the Central States had 14 of the 19 standing committee chairmanships, the Middle Atlantic States had 4, and New England had 1. Illinois alone had five chairmanships, including Foreign Affairs, Judiciary, and Rules. Michigan had three: Banking and Currency, Government Operations, and Public Works. In the second session of the 85th Congress, when the Democrats were in power, the South had 12 of the 19 chairmanships in the House, the Middle Atlantic States had 4, the Central States had 2 and the Pacific coast 1. This pattern of committee power has existed for many years, with the Middle West in the seats of the mighty when the Republicans dominate the House and the South controlling the committee strongholds when the Democrats are in the ascendancy. The long-run trends in the geographical distribution of committee chairmanships in the House since 1820 are reflected in the accompanying table.

[11] George B. Galloway, *The Legislative Process in Congress*, p. 289.

Regional distribution of committee chairmanships in the House of Representatives, 1820–1960

Region	Democrats, 1820	Republicans,[1] 1860	Republicans, 1900	Democrats, 1940	Democrats, 1960
New England	4	7	8	0	0
Middle Atlantic	11	13	12	8	4
North Central	2	9	33	10	2
South Atlantic	8	2	1	10	6
South Central	5	3	0	13	7
Mountain	0	0	0	2	1
Pacific	0	0	3	4	0
Total	[2] 30	34	57	47	20

[1] In 1860 the Republicans had a plurality, not an absolute majority, of House seats.
[2] Includes several committees that were standing in fact though not in name.

Source: *Congressional Directories*, 16th Cong., 2d sess.; 36th Cong., 1st sess.; 56th Cong., 2d sess.; 76th Cong., 3d sess.; 86th Cong., 2d sess.

JURISDICTION AND DUTIES

From the earliest days the rules of the House have given its standing committees jurisdiction over the various subjects of legislation. The entire legislative domain has been divided into distinct categories defined by the rules, and jurisdiction over each category has been allocated to a separate standing committee. The Legislative Reorganization Act of 1946 not only streamlined the committee structure of the House, but also redefined and clarified the jurisdiction of the 19 streamlined committees. Every subject of legislation then conceivable was listed under the appropriate standing committee, no one then foreseeing that the amazing advance of science and the exploration of outer space by man-made moons and satellites would create new fields of legislative interest and inquiry. The same act sought to reduce the scope of lawmaking by prohibiting the reception or consideration of certain private bills relating to claims, pensions, construction of bridges, and the correction of military or naval records. Upon their introduction all bills are referred to the appropriate standing committees which must consider and report them before they can be taken up on the floor.

The rules of the House are the rules of its committees, so far as applicable, and committees may adopt additional rules not inconsistent therewith. Several House committees have adopted their own standing orders and customarily print them in their committee calendars together with the appropriate provisions regarding committee powers and procedures from sections 133 and 134 of the Legislative Reorganization Act of 1946.

EVOLUTION OF COMMITTEE POWERS

During the Federalist and Jeffersonian periods it was the general practice of the House of Representatives to refer legislative subjects to a Committee of the Whole in order to develop the main principles of legislation, and then to commit such matters to select committees to draft specific bills. In those early years, before the rise of the standing committee system, the committees were regarded as agents of the House which kept control over them by giving them specific instructions as to their authority and duties. Jefferson's Manual, in section XXVI, provided:

The committee have full power over the bill or other paper committed to them, except that they can not change the title or subject.

The committee may not erase, interline, or blot the bill itself; but must, in a paper by itself, set down the amendments, stating the words which are to be inserted or omitted, and where, by reference to page, line, and word of the bill.

And in section XXVIII:

If a report be recommitted before agreed to in the House, what has passed in committee is of no validity; the whole question is again before the committee, and a new resolution must again be moved, as if nothing had passed.

The guiding principles of legislation were settled in the House before a matter was referred to a committee, and a committee in reporting a bill back to the House was obliged to conform to the terms of the resolution of reference. The decisions reached in the House were binding upon its committees.

The House retained control of its committees in early days, first, by assigning specific tasks to *ad hoc* groups; second, by requiring them to report back favorably or unfavorably; third, by dissolving a select committee when it had completed its work; and, fourth, by passing judgment upon the committee reports. Scores of special committees were raised by the Federalists and the Jeffersonian Republicans to consider specific matters or draft bills and were dismissed upon the submission of their reports. There was no discharge problem in those days because committees were expected to report back, one way or another; should a committee fail to report, a discharge motion could easily be made and carried by a simple majority vote.

Moreover, at the outset, the introduction and reference of bills was strictly controlled by the House. The power of a committee to report by bill was not allowed until principles had first been settled by the House, usually in Committee of the Whole. And the right of an individual member to introduce a bill depended upon a grant of leave so to do by the House, in striking contrast to the modern practice under which Congressmen enjoy complete freedom in this respect. This rule was adopted by the House in the first Congress:

Every bill shall be introduced by motion for leave or by an order of the House on the report of the committee; and in either case a committee to prepare the same shall be appointed. In cases of a general nature, one day's notice at least shall be given of the motion to bring in a bill; and every such motion may be committed.

In the early decades bills were customarily introduced on the report of a committee by order of the House, but as time went on the practice developed of permitting committees to report by bill at their own discretion; and finally in 1822 a rule was adopted which recognized this practice and provided that "the several standing committees of the House shall have leave to report by bill or otherwise." [12] Meanwhile, the introduction of bills on leave by individual members revived after 1835 and has been unchecked since 1880.

As regards the reference of bills, the original practice, as we have seen, was to refer important matters to a Committee of the Whole for a decision on principles and this continued to be prevailing practice down to the end of Jefferson's first administration. But with the

---

[12] For a description of the gradual evolution of the present system for the introduction of bills, see *Hinds' Precedents*, vol. 4, sec. 3365. For a lucid discussion of this subject see also Cooper, *op cit., passim.*

growth of the standing committee system in 1816 and thereafter, the Committee of the Whole declined and their roles were reversed. With increasing frequency legislative subjects came to be referred initially to the smaller standing committees which grew in power and prestige. "Thus, by 1825, if not earlier," writes Joseph Cooper, "we may conclude that both in theory and in fact the standing committee had become predominant with regard to the first reference of legislative subjects." [13]

As regards committee meetings, the original rule provided that—

A committee meet when and where they please, if the House has not ordered time and place for them; but they can only act when together, and not by separate consultation and consent—nothing being the report of the committee but what has been agreed to in committee actually assembled (*Jefferson's Manual*, sec. XXVI).

A rule that dates back to 1794 provides that no committee of the House shall sit, without special leave, while the House is in session. Exceptions were inserted for the Committee on Rules in 1893 and for the Committees on Government Operations and Un-American Activities in 1953. In the absence of direction by the House, standing committees fix regular meeting days and also meet on call of the chairman, or conditionally on the signed request of a majority of the committee. On February 25, 1952, Speaker Rayburn ruled that committees may not televise or otherwise broadcast their proceedings, either in Washington or elsewhere.[14]

From earliest days the House has delegated the conduct of investigations to its select and standing committees and has authorized them to send for persons and papers. This power, whose origin has been traced back to the ancient practice of the English House of Commons in the 16th century, was first conferred by the House on a select committee that investigated the defeat of General St. Clair by the Indians in 1792 and compelled witnesses to attend and testify under oath.[15] Since then the House has frequently granted the power to compel testimony, even to subcommittees, and it has been used in scores of cases down through the years in investigations of the conduct of public officials, Members of Congress, election contests, and economic and social problems. The power to send for persons and papers has been upheld by the courts, within certain limits, and many contumacious and recalcitrant witnesses have been cited for contempt of the House for their refusal to answer questions or produce papers. During the 19th century the House of Representatives was the chief inquisitor and much American history can be gleaned from the reports of its investigating committees. In recent years the pace of the investigative process has increased, partly as a result of the authority granted each standing committee of the House and Senate in 1946 to "exercise continuous watchfulness" of the execution of the laws within its jurisdiction. Some committees have recently adopted rules of procedure for the conduct of their inquiries and on March 23, 1955, the House adopted a set of rules for the guidance of all its investigating committees (rule XI, pars. h–q).

[13] *Ibid.*, p. 53.
[14] *Congressional Record*, 82d Cong., 2d sess., p. 1334.
[15] See article on "Governmental Investigations", by George B. Galloway in the *Encyclopedia of the Social Sciences*. For the House precedents see *Hinds' Precedents*, vol. 3, ch. 54–56; "Congressional Power of Investigation," S. Doc. No. 99, 83d Cong., 2d sess., pp. 36–39; Marshall E. Dimock, *Congressional Investigating Committees* (1929); Ernest J. Eberling, *Congressional Investigations* (1928); George B. Galloway, "The Investigative Function of Congress," *American Political Science Review*, February 1927; and M. Nelson McGeary, *The Developments of Congressional Investigative Power* (1940).

The role of the House as the "inquest of the Nation" and the proper scope of committee inquiries into the conduct of administration was a subject of frequent debate during the early Congresses. Federalists and Jeffersonians argued at length over the appropriate limits of legislative oversight of the executive. Joseph Cooper identifies three areas in which this debate raged: [16]

(1) Investigations of offenses committed by executive officers to ascertain whether they were serious enough to sustain an impeachment proceeding;
(2) Investigations aimed at informing the nation as to possible abuses in the administration of the law or aimed at supplying the House with sufficient information to enable it to control administration legislatively; and
(3) Investigations into the use of public money to secure the information necessary to enable the House to appropriate wisely.

The Jeffersonians believed that these were proper fields for congressional inquiry of administration, but that Congress should not interfere with the administration of the law. Discrepancies developed, however, between their theory and practice and after 1809 the practice of the House was marked by a noteworthy expansion of special investigations into administrative conduct of the government and of the exercise of the oversight function by House committees. In a searching and original analysis of the "postnatal role" of the House and its committees during the period, 1789–1829, Joseph Cooper concludes that after 1809 there was [17]—

* * * a turning away from oversight or superintendence toward supervision, a turning away from the notion that the President is primarily responsible for administration toward the notion that all rests with Congress * * * it is clear that a different sense of responsibility for administration activated the generations of Republicans who served in Congress after 1809 and that the thrust of that new sense of responsibility was toward Congressional supremacy in administration as well as in legislation.

Beginning with the Committee on Enrolled Bills in 1812, several House committees at intervals over the years were granted leave to report at any time on stated matters, as a method of expediting the most important matters of business. The privilege carried with it the right of immediate consideration by the House. Privileged reports are made from the floor. In the revision of the rules in 1880 these various privileges were consolidated in one rule. The rule was amended in 1946 to provide that no general appropriation bill shall be considered in the House until printed committee hearings and a committee report thereon have been available for the Members of the House for at least 3 calendar days. The privilege of reporting at any time is now enjoyed by the following committees: Appropriations, House Administration, Interior and Insular Affairs, Public Works, Rules, Veterans' Affairs, and Ways and Means, on the matters specified in paragraph 21 of rule XI.[18]

From this review of the development of committee powers, it will be seen that the committees were regarded in early years as creatures of the House and were subject to its direction, that they received most of their major rights and powers during the first quarter century of congressional history, and that by 1825 at the latest the pattern of committee powers had assumed its modern form. No basic change in this pattern took place thereafter. Meanwhile, as the 19th century advanced, the standing committee system expanded, their prestige

---

[16] Joseph Cooper, *op. cit.*, pp. 42–47.
[17] *Ibid.*, p. 60.
[18] For the history of this rule, see *Hinds' Precedents*, vol. 4, sec. 4621.

and influence were steadily enhanced, and they became increasingly autonomous in their operations. By 1885 as acute an observer of the system as Woodrow Wilson correctly described congressional government as government by the standing committees of Congress. And at the end of the century Miss Follett truthfully remarked that "Congress no longer exercises its lawful function of lawmaking; that has gone to the committees as completely as in England it has passed to the cabinet." [19]

Summarizing this section, the standing committees of the House have acquired power over the years to receive legislative proposals, messages, petitions, and memorials on matters within their defined jurisdiction; to sit and act when and where they deem it advisable during sessions (by special leave), recesses, and adjourned periods; to send for persons and papers; to take testimony and make expenditures; to conduct authorized investigations and to report by bill or otherwise upon any matter within their jurisdiction; to oversee the execution of the laws; to certify contumacious witnesses for contempt; to adopt rules and appoint subcommittees; to report in certain cases at any time or not to report. Measures that the whole House might approve are sometimes "killed in committee" by a few Members. Congressional committees usually report only those bills that a majority of their members favor, unlike some State legislatures and the English House of Commons where all referred bills are reported back one way or another.

Subject to some limitations, the committees of Congress have thus come to play a leading role in lawmaking. Each composed of comparatively few members, each normally acting independently of the others, they have long determined the agenda of the House which has largely delegated to its standing committees the power to decide what matters shall be considered on the floor and to control the proceedings there, subject to the terms of the Rules Committee. They can amend or rewrite bills to suit themselves. They can report bills or pigeonhole them. They can initiate measures they desire and bury or emasculate those they dislike. They can proceed with dispatch or deliberate at length. Thus, the real focus of the legislative power is not in the House or Senate; it is in their standing committees. The tendency is for the standing committees to frame policy that the whole legislature usually follows.

TYPES OF COMMITTEES

There are four types of congressional committees: (1) standing or permanent committees that continue from Congress to Congress; (2) special or temporary committees created for a particular purpose; (3) joint committees (including conference committees) composed of Members from both Houses; and (4) subcommittees (both standing and special) created to divide the labor of the standing committees.

In the House of Representatives there are also two Com-ittees of the Whole, in effect standing committees: the Committee of the Whole House, which considers business on the Private Calendar, and the Committee of the Whole House on the State of the Union, which considers business on the Union Calendar.

The committees of Congress may also be classified by function as: (1) legislative committees having jurisdiction defined in the rules over

---

[19] Mary P. Follett, *The Speaker of the House of Representatives* (1896), p. 246.

the several fields of legislation; (2) supervisory co amittees concerned with supervising the administration of the laws; (3) fiscal committees, which handle the revenue and appropriation bills; (4) investigating committees, which make inquiries of various kinds; (5) housekeeping committees, which oversee the internal housekeeping functions of Congress; and (6) political committees, which perform various functions for the political parties.

The size of the standing committees is fixed by the rules of the House; of special committees by the resolutions creating them; and of joint committees by the statutes or resolutions establishing them. In 1958 the standing committees of the House of Representatives ranged in size from 9 to 50 Members, but typically they had 25 or 27 or 29 Members. Appropriations, with its heavy workload, had 50 Members; Armed Services had 39, including the Delegates from Alaska and Hawaii and the Resident Commissioner from Puerto Rico; Rules had 12 Members; and Un-American Activities had 9.

COMPOSITION OF COMMITTEES

Various criteria have been used in making the committee assignments. The most influential considerations are seniority of service in the Chamber, geography, personal preference, and previous committee service. Seniority is governed by continuous, uninterrupted service; a Member's seniority dates from the beginning of his last uninterrupted service, regardless of previous service in the House, and determines his rank on committees and his place at the committee table. If a veteran Member of the House loses his seat for a single term and returns to his former committee, he begins again at the foot of the committee table despite his previous service. This happened, for example, to Representative Earl C. Michener, of Michigan, who served from March 4, 1919, to March 3, 1933, and enjoyed a long tenure on the Rules Committee, but was defeated for reelection to the 73d Congress. Mr. Michener returned to the House on January 3, 1935, and served until his voluntary retirement on January 3, 1951, but his absence of 2 years during 1933–34 cost him his high place on Rules and the chairmanship of this committee during the 80th Congress.

Party ratios on the standing committees of the House of Representatives are determined by agreement between the majority and minority leadership. Ways and Means is now usually fixed at 15–10, Rules at 8–4 or 10–5. On the other House committees the ratio corresponds roughly, but not with mathematical precision, to the party division in the Chamber.

From the 64th to the 80th Congress, when the Legislative Reorganization Act became effective, the House had 11 major or "exclusive" committees whose chairmen served on no other standing committee of the House while the Democrats were in power. The 11 "exclusive" committees were: Agriculture, Appropriations, Banking and Currency, Foreign Affairs, Interstate and Foreign Commerce, Judiciary, Military Affairs, Naval Affairs, Post Offices and Post Roads, Rules, and Ways and Means.

Under the one-committee-assignment rule adopted in 1946 all the standing committees of the House were "exclusive" committees, except that Members who were elected to serve on the District of

Columbia Committee or on the Un-American Activities Committee might be elected to serve on two committees and no more, and Members of the majority party who were elected to serve on the Committee on Government Operations or on the Committee on House Administration might be elected to serve on two standing committees and no more. These exceptions were made so that the majority party could maintain control of all the committees. In the 83d Congress, however, when the Republicans had a "paper thin" majority of only 7 seats in the House, 18 Republicans were given second committee assignments so as to enable them to control all the standing committees of the House. This necessary departure from the one-committee-assignment rule apparently marked the beginning of the breakdown of that rule, for an examination of committee assignments in the 2d session of the 85th Congress showed that 118 Members of the House had 2 or more committee assignments in 1958. In addition to the four excepted committees mentioned above, five more had been added to the list of those groups upon which some Representatives had second seats: Education and Labor, Interior and Insular Affairs, Merchant Marine and Fisheries, Public Works, and Veterans' Affairs.

The committees of Congress have varied in their representative character, some being fairly representative of the House and the country, others being dominated by members from particular regions or economic interests. It has often happened, for example, that most of the members of the Agriculture Committee were farmers or members from rural districts; that the Interior Committee was largely composed of members from the "public lands" States and districts; and that spokesmen for the coastal districts have sat on Merchant Marine and Fisheries. Congressmen naturally seek assignment to committees that have jurisdiction over matters of major concern to their districts and States. The effect of this practice tends to give a special-interest character to the composition of these panels.

COMMITTEE PROCEDURES

During the time he served as Vice President of the United States and President of the Senate, 1797 to 1801, Thomas Jefferson compiled a *Manual of Parliamentary Practice* in which he acknowledged his debt for information to Hatsell, Clerk of the House of Commons from 1760 to 1797. *Jefferson's Manual* is said to have been his penance to England for the Declaration of Independence. From it we learn, among other things, something of the procedure of congressional committees in those early days. It shows that committee proceedings were not published; that committees were forbidden to receive petitions except through the House, or to sit when notified that the House was in session. When select committees conducted inquiries, only the chairman was to question witnesses; testimony was to be taken in writing for submission to the House.

Committees were to be appointed by the Speaker, but the House was to control their names and number. A bill should be committed only to those friendly to its chief features, for "the child is not to be put to a nurse that cares not for it." Unless the House named the place and the hour, the committee might sit anywhere and at any time. A majority was the committee quorum. Any member of the House could attend the meetings of a select committee, but only its members could vote. It had full power to alter a bill or other paper committed, except the title. Committees themselves could originate bills, resolutions, and addresses. Reports were to be made by the chairman; and when concluded, unless the bill were recommitted to it, the committee was dissolved.

Since Jefferson penned his famous Manual in the days of the stage coach, House procedure has evolved as its business and membership increased until today the parliamentary precedents of that body occupy 11 large volumes. As regards committee procedure we may examine a few significant features of the modern practice: Committee meetings, secrecy versus publicity of their sessions, their rules of procedures and proxy voting, the hearings process, quorums and reports, and discharge.

Under the rules each standing committee of the House (other than the Committee on Appropriations) fixes regular weekly, biweekly, or monthly meeting days for the transaction of its business. Additional meetings may be called by the chairman as he may deem necessary. The committees customarily meet to consider their pending business on their regular meeting days as well as upon the call of their chairmen. Special meetings may be called upon the written request of a majority of a committee if the chairman, after 3 days' consideration, refuses or fails to call a special meeting; but committeemen seldom overrule their chairmen in this way. A committee scheduled to meet on stated days, when convened on such a day with a quorum present, may proceed to the transaction of business regardless of the absence of the chairman. But if the chairman adjourns a committee meeting for lack of a quorum, the committee may not meet again on the same day without his consent. On a typical day of a modern Congress the Daily Digest of the *Congressional Record* will show a score of House committees and subcommittees in session.

SECRECY VERSUS PUBLICITY

Whether committee meetings should be open or closed to the public has long been a controversial question. Although the House galleries have been open from the beginning, secrecy customarily veiled committee sessions during the 19th century and sometimes aroused public suspicions of evil. During the Credit Mobilier scandal after the Civil War it was charged that certain members of Congress [20] had sought to bribe their congressional colleagues with gifts of railway stock. Two House committees set up to investigate these charges in 1872–73 proceeded at first in closed sessions, but the pressure of an excited public opinion forced the House to open these hearings to reporters. Occasional exposures of wrongdoing gave rise to public distrust of star chamber proceedings and to the demand that the searchlight of publicity be trained upon them.

From early days it has been the practice of House committees to print their reports, including minority views, and summaries of these reports often appeared in the public press. During the Civil War, for example, reports of investigating committees were printed and sold by one of the New York daily papers. Committee hearings have usually been open to Members of the House, except those of the

[20] Representative Oakes Ames of Massachusetts and Representative James Brooks of New York.

Appropriations Committee, and it has long been notorious that few secrets are long kept on Capitol Hill. Writing in 1898 of the forces making for greater publicity, McConachie said: [21]

The more important committees have become so large that opportunities for cabal are much lessened. With the reporter going the rounds for interviews, with a diversity of interests represented by committeemen from many States, with a minority on the watch and quick to report to the House and to the public, with the gossipy confidences which pass among public men, and the easy evasions of that antiquated precedent which forbids any mention of committee proceedings in House debates, with the filibuster whose athletics have sometimes called the attention of the country to iniquitous measures, publicity has generally got in some degree its due, though often too late.

During the 20th century the long-run trend has been in the direction of greater publicity for committee activities. Under rule XI, their hearings are now usually open to the public, except executive sessions for marking up bills or for voting or where the committee by majority vote orders a closed session. The schedule of committee meetings is published daily in the *Congressional Record* and in the newspapers and their hearings are printed and sold by the Government Printing Office. Hearings of great public interest, such as those held in 1958 by the Legislative Oversight Subcommittee of the House Commerce Committee into the conduct of the Federal regulatory commissions, are often held in the large Ways and Means Committee room with representatives of the press present. To date, however, the House has not permitted its committee hearings to be broadcast or telecast to the country, as some Senate committee hearings have been; and the press has complained that approximately one-third of House committee sessions are still closed to press and public.[22] Where a committee takes testimony on matters affecting the national security or the reputation of persons, it is sometimes very desirable that the proceedings be secret. During 1958, for example, the hearings of the House Armed Services Committee on the missile and satellite program and the atomic submarine were closed, but it was expected that they would eventually be printed and published after the testimony had been edited "for security reasons" by the Department of Defense. In the modern usage it is for a committee to determine, in its discretion, whether or not its proceedings shall be open to the public. The House has no information concerning the proceedings of a committee not officially reported by the committee, and it is not in order in debate to refer to proceedings of a committee which have not formally been reported to the House.

RECENT DEVELOPMENTS

Several provisions of the Legislative Reorganization Act of 1946 were designed to regularize committee procedure and have since been made a part of the standing rules of the House. Each committee was required to keep a complete record of all committee action, including a record of the votes on any question on which a record vote is demanded. All committee hearings, records, data, charts, and files are to be kept separate and distinct from the congressional office records of the chairman of the committee; such records are the property of

---

[21] L. G. McConachie, *Congressional Committees* (1898), pp. 60–61.
[22] Out of 15 House committee meetings scheduled for March 6, 1958, it was announced that six would be open and nine would be "executive." *Congressional Record*, Mar. 5, 1958, pp. D178–179.

the House and all members of the House shall have access to them. Each committee is authorized to have printed and bound testimony and other data presented at its hearings. It is the duty of the committee chairman to report or cause to be reported promptly to the House any measure approved by his committee and to take or cause to be taken necessary steps to bring the matter to a vote. But no measure or recommendation shall be reported from any committee unless a majority of its members were actually present. So far as practicable, all witnesses appearing before a committee are required to file in advance written statements of their proposed testimony, and to limit their oral presentations to brief summaries of their argument. Digests of such statements are to be prepared for the use of committee members. As noted above, the rule was also adopted in 1946 that all hearings conducted by standing committees or their subcommittees should be open to the public, except executive sessions for marking up bills or for voting or where the committee by a majority vote orders an executive session, an exception that leaves a committee sample authority to hold its hearings in secret.

Since the investigation of the defeat of General St. Clair by the Indians, conducted by a select committee of the House in 1792, hundreds of inquiries have been made by select and standing panels of that body. Perhaps the most important aspect of committee procedure in recent times has been the conduct of investigations. There has been an extraordinary increase in the exercise of the investigative function of Congress in recent years. Most of these inquiries have been carried on with due regard for the rights of witnesses and of parties under investigation. But the activities of a few committees have evoked widespread public and congressional criticism.

The demand for congressional control of committee conduct finally led the House on March 23, 1955, to adopt 10 rules of procedure for its investigating committees that were designed to assure majority control of these groups and to safeguard the rights of witnesses. Under these new rules, not less than two members of a committee shall constitute a quorum for taking testimony and receiving evidence. They direct the chairman to announce the subject of an investigation in his opening statement, to make a copy of the committee rules available to witnesses, and to punish breaches of order and decorum. Witnesses at investigative hearings may be accompanied by their own counsel to advise them concerning their constitutional rights. If a committee determines that evidence or testimony at an investigative hearing may tend to defame, degrade, or incriminate any person, it shall receive such evidence or testimony in executive session; afford such person an opportunity voluntarily to appear as a witness; and receive and dispose of requests from such a person to subpena additional witnesses. Evidence or testimony taken in executive session may not be released or used in public sessions without the consent of the committee. In the discretion of the committee, witnesses may submit brief and pertinent sworn statements in writing for inclusion in the record. And a witness may obtain a transcript copy of this testimony at cost. While this "code of fair play" fell somewhat short of the recommendations of a House Rules subcommittee, its adoption marked a notable milestone in regularizing the rules of House committee procedure.

From the viewpoint of the witnesses modern congressional procedures seem considerably safer than those occasionally employed in the more turbulent past. John Quincy Adams told of an incident that occurred in 1837 while he was serving in the House of Representatives after being President. Adams wrote:[23]

When Reuben Whitney was before a committee of investigation in 1837 Bailie Peyton of Tennessee, taking offense at one of his answers, threatened him fiercely, and when he rose to claim the committee's protection, Mr. Peyton, with due and appropriate profanity, shouted:
You shan't say one word while you are in this room; if you do, I shall put you to death.
The chairman, Henry A. Wise, added: This insolence is insufferable.

Adams commented wryly:

As both of these gentlemen were armed with deadly weapons, the witness could hardly be blamed for not wanting to testify again.

PROXY VOTING IN COMMITTEES

The Rules of the House of Representatives do not permit proxy voting. Members who are not present may announce their stands or "pair" with other absent Members. But these actions do not affect the outcome of the vote.

Another section of the *House Manual* states that the rules of the House shall be the rules of its committees. From this, it has sometimes been argued that use of proxies in committees is illegal.

On the two occasions when the question was raised, however, the Speaker stated an "opinion" that the use of proxies is at the discretion of each committee. On February 16, 1929, Speaker Nicholas Longworth said that a proxy may be voted "only by unanimous consent of the committee itself. * * * A proxy on one particular vote must have the unanimous consent of the committee." On January 26, 1946, Speaker Sam Rayburn was asked to rule on proxy voting. He said—

That is a matter for the committee to determine. The Chair may make this statement: He served on one committee for 24 years (Interstate and Foreign Commerce), and never was a proxy voted on that committee, because the present occupant of the chair always voted against it.

Defenders of proxy voting argue that overlapping official duties make it impossible for Members to attend all meetings of the committees to which they are assigned. Proxies permit them to vote their convictions when circumstances prevent them from attending committee meetings.

Opponents of proxy voting argue that proxy voting actually encourages absenteeism by permitting a Member to disguise his absence from important sessions of committees. Proxy voting encourages irresponsibility; absent Members may not be acquainted with the arguments or even the substance of proposals on which their proxies are cast.

Voting by proxy in legislative committees is the action or practice of voting by means of an authorized agent or substitute. A committeeman authorizes, orally or in writing, another committeeman (the chairman or any other member of the committee) to act for him in his absence. A proxy may be a "general" one, covering all matters before a committee on a specified date; it may be a general and con-

[23] Thomas B. Reed, *Saturday Evening Post*, Dec. 9, 1899. Quoted by DeAlva S. Alexander, *History and Procedure of the House of Representatives*, p. 116.

tinuing one, until revoked by the member authorizing its use, covering all matters before the committee for an indefinite period; or it may be a "special" proxy, limited to a particular bill and/or amendments thereto. In practice, most proxies are in written form, but oral proxies are occasionally (rarely) given and used when time is of the essence.

The use of proxies in House committee voting is regulated either by standing order of the committees or by custom. Seven committees of the House currently have explicit rules on the subject. In other cases it is a matter of customary practice rather than standing rule. A typical rule on the subject is that of the Committee on Agriculture, which reads as follows:

A Member may vote on any matter before the Committee by special proxy. Any such proxy shall be in writing, dated, signed by the Member granting the proxy, shall identify the Member to whom the proxy is given and shall identify the particular bill or other matter under consideration. Proxies shall be filed with the Clerk of the Committee before the vote is taken. No proxy shall be used for the purpose of establishing a quorum. Proxies may be used in subcommittee or in full committee.

In some cases it is committee policy to limit the use of proxies by certain specified conditions. For example, the Post Office and Civil Service Committee allows proxy voting only on a final vote on a measure if its use is authorized by the unanimous consent of the full committee. The Committee on Public Works does not recognize proxies unless, by a majority vote, their use is expressly authorized for a particular meeting when a bill of national importance is being considered. In the Committee on Ways and Means practice permits the use of proxies only on the basis of unanimous consent.

Proxy voting in House committees has raised a number of questions that have been discussed within the committees. There is the question of the limitation of time, i.e., how long shall a proxy be useful? Shall it be effective throughout a congressional session, or must it be limited to a particular committee meeting?

Another problem concerns the pros and cons of general versus special proxies. Some Members object to general proxies on the ground that they have a tendency to promote absenteeism. This objection is reflected in the pertinent rule of the Committee on Interior and Insular Affairs which provides, in part, that "no general proxies shall be given or recognized * * *." On the other hand, the Committee on the Judiciary allows the use of both general and special proxies.

Another objection to the use of proxies, made by some Members, is that they sometimes cause misunderstanding as to the intention of a Member when he authorizes someone else to cast his vote on a matter particularly when unexpected amendments are offered to a bill.

Another interesting question that has arisen in committee is whether a proxy, limited to a special bill and/or amendment thereto, can be used on a vote to send a bill back to subcommittee. If it were a general proxy, no such question could arise. But if the proxy were limited, as stated above, it could not be used in voting on the motion to recommit the bill to subcommittee.

A survey of the rules and practice of all the standing committees of the House of Representatives during the 1st session of the 85th Congress indicated that proxy voting was not permitted in 6 committees and that the use of special proxies was allowed in 13 committees. The 1957 practice is summarized in the table below.

Proxy voting practice in committees of the House of Representatives

Committee	Special proxies permitted	Not permitted
Agriculture	X	
Appropriations		X.
Armed Services	X	
Banking and Currency		X.
District of Columbia	X	
Education and Labor	X	
Foreign Affairs	X	
Government Operations	X	
House Administration		X.
Interior and Insular Affairs	X	
Interstate and Foreign Commerce		X.
Judiciary [1]	X	
Merchant Marine and Fisheries	X	
Post Office and Civil Service	X	
Public Works	X	
Rules		X.
Un-American Activities	X	
Veterans' Affairs		X.
Ways and Means	X	
Total	13	6.

[1] Permits both general and special proxies.

COMMITTEE HEARINGS

"It is not far from the truth to say," remarked Woodrow Wilson in 1885, "that Congress in session is Congress on public exhibition, whilst Congress in its committee rooms is Congress at work." [24] Long located in the Capitol and later also in the House office buildings, the committee rooms have been the chief "workshops" of the House. Here in these spacious chambers with their frescoed domes and swinging chandeliers, their walls adorned with the portraits of former chairmen, the cushioned chairs and long committee table on a raised dias, the visitor sees the fountainhead of the legislative process. Here come the spokesmen for all the competing interests of American society: the lobbyist and the expert, the captain of industry and the labor official, the military men from the Pentagon and the financiers from Wall Street, the Cabinet member and the bureau chief, the merchant and the farmer, the lawyer and the judge—all seeking to influence these "little legislatures" whose reports may prescribe the action of the House itself. Here in the committee room is the meeting ground between the public and the Congress, the citizen and the legislator, where hearings have been held since earliest days on a host of legislative proposals designed to meet the needs of a changing society.

Thousands of bills are introduced in every session of Congress and are referred to the appropriate committees. The committees usually hold hearings on legislative proposals which are administration measures or in which the majority party or the chairmen are sufficiently interested or which are strongly favored by some organized interest group. The hearing on a bill is important because it is practically the only stage in the legislative process in which there is an opportunity to make a critical evaluation of a proposed piece of legislation. Theoretically the floor stage also offers an occasion to debate the merits of a measure, but debate on the House floor is often sparsely attended and is usually "after the fact," so to speak; it is designed to explain

[24] Woodrow Wilson, *op. cit.*, p. 79.

to the country decisions already arrived at in committee rather than to analyze the facts or elucidate the rationale underlying a legislative proposal.

Due notice of the hearings is customarily given, Government officials from the agencies concerned and representatives of interested private organizations are invited to appear, and other witnesses are heard at their own request in favor of or opposed to the pending measure. Notices and brief summaries of committee hearings, with the names of witnesses, are published in the Daily Digest section of the *Congressional Record*. During the first week of March 1958, for example, hearings were held on a score of legislative topics, including tobacco acreage allotments, price supports for dairy products, military pay and reserves, export control and foreign aid, public education, secrecy in government, public works, the conduct of Federal regulatory agencies, weather research and flood control, veterans' fund-raising campaigns, and reciprocal trade agreements. The hearings may run from 1 day to several weeks depending upon the number of witnesses, the controversial character of the subject, and the wishes of the committee. When the hearings have been completed and printed, the committee goes into executive session, reviews the testimony heard, considers amendments, examines the bill and report on it that has been drafted by the staff, and finally decides whether or not to report the revised measure to the House.

Congressional committee hearings as they have developed down through the decades have served a variety of practical uses. Their most important function has been to collect facts so as to enable committee members to make informed judgments regarding legislative proposals. Their printed hearings are a gold mine of factual information about all the public problems of the Nation. A second use of the hearing process is the safety-valve function: an opportunity for individuals and groups that feel strongly about a matter to "blow off steam," so to speak. In this way social tensions are often relaxed even though legislation may not be the end result. A third use of committee hearings is as a political sounding board for the Legislature, furnishing a barometer to gage public opinion and to identify and assess the strength of conviction and relative power of the political forces that are lined up for and against the pending bill. This function helps legislators estimate the political consequences of their votes on a measure when and if the bill reaches the House floor.[25]

In the modern postwar practice the committee hearing has been the scene of some useful innovations. One of these has been to make use of panels of experts to assist committees in clarifying the facts relating to complex legislative problems. During the 84th Congress, for example, when questions arose regarding the safety and efficacy of the Salk vaccine, the National Academy of Sciences cooperated with the House Committee on Interstate and Foreign Commerce in selecting a panel of experts who discussed the scientific problems involved in open hearing before the committee under the guidance of an impartial moderator. This technique was so successful that it was repeated in July 1957, at hearings before the Subcommittee on Health and Science where another panel of experts discussed the scientific problems involved in testing and evaluating the safety of

[25] *Cf.* Julius Cohen and Reginald Robson, "The Lawyer and the Legislative Hearing Process," *Nebraska Law Review*, May 1954, pp. 526–527.

chemical additives. Similarly, panels of leading economists have debated questions of monetary and fiscal policy before subcommittees of the Joint Economic Committee.

Another innovation in committee procedure has been the scheduling of "docket days" at which a committee has invited the authors of bills referred to it to appear at a preliminary hearing early in a session and speak in behalf of their proposals. This procedure serves to give the committee a better understanding of the proposals before it and gives rank and file Members of the House a closer working relationship with the committee and its problems. This sensible experiment was launched by the Committee on Foreign Affairs in 1951 and by the Committee on Interstate and Foreign Commerce in 1953.

At the same time the Commerce Committee adopted the device of holding periodic "question periods" with the heads of the various agencies under its jurisdiction at which they appear before the committee and review their work and the operation of the statutes which they administer. This departure has served the purpose both of acquainting the new committeemen with the scope and composition of the agencies and of bringing the committee up to date on what these agencies are doing. The various persons and industries affected by such legislation and subject to the administrative procedures of these agencies have also been invited from time to time to discuss with the committee the effectiveness of the administration and to suggest any changes that might be desirable in the public interest.

Another technique, occasionally used of late, has been for a committee or subcommittee to hold regional hearings in various parts of the country in order to bring some concrete problem to the attention of grassroots leaders of opinion and to assemble regional thinking on the subject. In the spring of 1956, for example, the Senate Disarmament Subcommittee held a series of regional hearings, some at university centers where college professors and leading citizens gave the results of their studies of armament problems. Another rarity in committee procedure occurred during June 1957, when joint hearings were held by subcommittees of the House Judiciary and Commerce Committees on bills to amend the Packers and Stockyards Act.

The coming of radio and television and the popularity of legislative broadcasts of the Kefauver crime committee hearings, as well as of the proceedings of the United Nations and several foreign parliaments, led to many proposals for putting House committee hearings on the air. But Speaker Rayburn ruled on February 25, 1952, that radio broadcasting and televising of hearings before House committees were not authorized by existing rules.[26]

QUORUMS AT COMMITTEE HEARINGS

A 1949 survey of the modern practice of the standing committees of Congress as regards the presence of a quorum at committee hearings led to the following general conclusions:

1. The committees do not require the presence of a quorum of their members while holding hearings, and testimony is often received with only one or a few members of the committee being present.

2. So far as the presence or absence of a quorum is concerned, it makes no difference whether or not the testimony is sworn.

[26] Cf. George B. Galloway, *The Legislative Process in Congress* (1953), pp. 234–241.

3. It is the accepted modern custom that a committee of Congress, once having convened with a quorum, may without maintaining a quorum, continue to conduct a hearing and take testimony.

4. Some committee clerks recall fairly recent instances when the point of no quorum was raised during committee hearings, but they are not able to give definite citations to such cases. Hinds cites a case in 1862 when the validity of testimony taken when a quorum of a committee was not present was questioned (3 *Hinds' Precedents* 1774). On December 17, 1862, the select committee appointed to investigate Government contracts adopted the following:

Resolved, That inasmuch as certain testimony has been taken by one member of the committee, in the absence of a quorum, touching the official conduct of certain Federal officers in New York, under objection from them, therefore the committee will examine such testimony, and whenever it appears that the testimony of any such witness so taken is found to affect the official character of any such persons, such witness shall be reexamined, and so far as his testimony on reexamination affects the official conduct of any Federal officer in New York, it shall be submitted to him for his inspection (37th Cong., 3d sess., H. Rept. No. 49, pp. 25, 26).

5. The only imaginable motive for objecting to the lack of a quorum during a hearing would be in order to delay the proceedings until some absent committeeman could attend.

Three other more or less pertinent precedents are cited by Hinds and Cannon, as follows:

1. On January 25, 1864, the Joint Committee on the Conduct of the War ordered that less than a quorum should be sufficient for taking testimony (4 *Hinds' Precedents* 4424).

2. In the case of Robert W. Stewart, who declined to answer certain questions propounded by the Senate Committee on Public Lands and Surveys during the 1st session of the 70th Congress, the witness was indicted for perjury and tried in the Supreme Court of the District of Columbia and acquitted on the ground that a quorum of the committee was not present on the occasion of the inquiry which resulted in the indictment. But in charging the jury in this case, Justice Jennings Bailey said in part that, if a quorum be present and subsequently members leave temporarily or otherwise, a quorum is presumed to be present until and unless the question of no quorum is raised (6 *Cannon's Precedents* 345).

3. On June 17, 1922 (67th Cong., 2d sess.) the Chair ruled that no report is valid unless authorized with a quorum of the committee present. The discussion prior to the Chair's decision distinguished between the requirement of a quorum in the House and in a committee. In the course of this discussion, Representative James R. Mann, of Illinois, said in part:

The House does business on the theory of a quorum being present, but it has always been my understanding since I have been a Member of this House that a committee must develop a quorum before it can transact any business. And it is the practice, at least in most of the committees, to call the roll of the committee * * * to ascertain whether a quorum is present (8 *Cannon's Precedents* 2222).[27]

Section 133(d) of the Legislative Reorganization Act of 1946 provides that "No measure or recommendation shall be reported from any

[27] For an interesting discussion of this case, see W. F. Willoughby, *Principles of Legislative Organization and Administration* (1934), pp. 364–366. For a summary of the procedure and practice concerning "quorum of the standing committees," see *Cannon's Procedure in the House of Representatives*, fourth edition, pp. 289–290.

such committee unless a majority of the committee were actually present." This provision relates, of course, to reports and not to hearings.

In the case of *Christoffel* v. *U.S.* (338 U.S. 84), decided June 27, 1949, the U.S. Supreme Court decided, in effect, that a quorum of a committee must be actually physically present when a perjurious offense is committed. In the *Christoffel* case the House Labor Committee was investigating [the [political affiliations of an individual rather than holding a hearing on a piece of proposed legislation. It does not necessarily follow, therefore, from the decision in this case that a standing committee of the Congress is not a competent tribunal unless it maintains a quorum of its members present throughout a hearing held preparatory to reporting legislation as distinguished from a hearing held to investigate individual conduct.

Inquiry among the clerks of the standing committees of the House and Senate indicate (1) that, as a rule, they do not require the presence of a quorum for the taking of testimony, and (2) that they do not consider the holding of a hearing as the transaction of business. Some committee clerks stated that, in practice, a quorum is usually or often present at hearings on important bills, but not at hearings on minor bills, e.g., those which, when reported, are referred to the Consent Calendar.

COMMITTEE REPORTS

Since 1880, a rule of the House has required that all bills, petitions, memorials, or resolutions from the committees shall be accompanied by reports in writing, which shall be printed. A report is not necessarily signed by any or all of those concurring in it, but minority views are signed by those submitting them. Since 1946 another House rule has provided that no general appropriation bill shall be considered in the House until printed committee hearings and a committee report thereon have been available to the Members of the House for at least 3 calendar days. The purpose of this provision is to allow Members time to study the committee hearings and reports on appropriation bills before their floor consideration.

The House has adhered to the principle that a report must be authorized by a committee acting together, and a paper signed by a majority of a committee acting separately has been ruled out. Since 1946, it has been the duty of the chairman of each committee to report or cause to be reported promptly any measure approved by his committee and to take or cause to be taken necessary steps to bring the matter to a vote. But no measure or recommendation may be reported from any committee unless a majority of the committee are actually present. In the modern practice, most committee reports are made by filing them with the Clerk of the House without reading them on the floor, and only the reports of committees having leave to report at any time are made by the chairman or other member of the committee from the floor. While privileged reports are frequently acted on when presented, yet the general rule is that reports shall be placed on the calendars of the House and there await action under the rules for the order of business.

DISCHARGE PROCEDURE

The annals of Congress reveal frequent use of the motion to discharge a committee from consideration of a bill in the early practice of the House.[28] But use of the discharge motion was discontinued in the House at an early date and by the time of the 40th Congress (1867–69) had ceased to be privileged in the order of business. The subject was discussed from time to time and resolutions to reestablish the privilege of the discharge motion were introduced in Congress at intervals. But it was not until June 17, 1910, that the House adopted its first discharge rule.[29]

The 1910 rule provided for filing with the Clerk motions to discharge committees from consideration of bills at any time after reference. Such motions were placed on a special calendar, to be called up on suspension days after the call of the Consent Calendar, and on being seconded by tellers, when called up, were placed on their appropriate calendar as if reported by the committee having jurisdiction. In this form the rule proved ineffective, and it was amended in the revision of 1911 by restricting the presentation of the discharge motion to not less than 15 days after reference and by requiring the reading of the bill by title only when the motion was called up to be seconded. In this form the rule was employed to such advantage in obstructive tactics that it was further amended in the 2d session of the 62d Congress (1911–12) by making it the third order of business on suspension days to follow the call of the Consent Calendar and the disposition of motions to suspend the rules.

According to Clarence Cannon:[30]

This change rendered the rule inoperative, and it remained practically nugatory until the Sixty-eighth Congress, when the Committee on Rules reported a substitute which was agreed to after five days debate and under which motion to discharge a committee when signed by 150 Members was entered on a special calendar and after seven days could be called up under privileged status. This rule was invoked but once and while on that occasion the bill to which it was applied failed to reach final consideration, so much time was consumed, 16 roll calls being had in one day during its consideration, that a further revision of the rule was effected in the succeeding Congress, making it still more difficult of operation. Under this revision the requirement of 150 Members was increased to 218 Members, a majority of the House, and further safeguards were included which rendered the rule wholly unworkable. Only one attempt was made to utilize it during the Sixty-ninth Congress and at the opening of the Seventy-second Congress it was completely redrafted and adopted in its present form with the exception that 145 signatures were sufficient to secure reference to the Calendar. The amendment requiring a majority of the membership of the House was incorporated in the resolution providing for the adoption of the rules of the Seventy-Fourth Congress (1935).

Many petitions to discharge committees have been filed under the discharge rule, but of the 790 petitions filed from 1924 through 1956, only 29 of them obtained sufficient signatures to be printed on the Discharge Calendar. Of these, 21 were granted consideration by the House and 19 were adopted, of which 15 passed the House. In the entire history of the discharge rule, however, only two bills have ever become law by the discharge route: the Fair Labor Standards Act of 1938 and the Federal Pay Raise Act of 1960.

[28] For early examples of discharge action see *Annals*, 4th Cong., 1st sess., pp. 288–290; 9th Cong., 1st sess., pp. 409–412.
[29] For history of the discharge rule see *Cannon's Precedents* vol. 7, sec. 1007.
[30] *Ibid.*

Sentiment in the House varies widely on the discharge rule. Some legislators favor its use as an appropriate means to enable the House to work its will on bills that have been pigeonholed in committees. They believe that, in the last analysis, the legislative power should belong to the whole House and not to any one of its committees. Other legislators believe that taking legislation from the consideration of the properly designated committee disrupts the orderly functioning of the legislative process. Many Members make it a rule not to sign discharge petitions on the ground that floor consideration of bills that have not been fully heard and considered in committee lacks proper safeguards and is a dangerous practice.

EVALUATION OF COMMITTEE SYSTEM

Congress, a microcosm of the Nation, is in turn epitomized in its committees. From a few select panels at the outset, the system has evolved until today there are approximately 300 congressional committees of all types, about equally divided between the Chambers. Congressional government is, in large part, government by committee. Is the House well organized internally for the performance of its lawmaking, supervisory, and informing functions? An objective appraisal suggests that the congressional committee system has both advantages and disadvantages.

At the dawn of the space age, when public problems of bewildering variety and baffling complexity crowd the calendars of the National Legislature, the committee system serves the indispensable function of dividing the labor of screening and digesting the legislative proposals to which these problems give rise. A score of standing committees, subdivided into more than a hundred subcommittees, allows deliberation on many different matters to proceed simultaneously. Thus, the first advantage of the system is that it enables the House to cover a much wider range of subjects than it could in Committee of the Whole, and makes a fuller use of the talents of its Members.

In the second place, the committee system provides invaluable training in the public business by enabling the Members to specialize in a few related subject-matter fields. In Congress the individual Member has a chance to learn the legislative trade more easily than his British counterpart by reason of his continuing service on one or two specialized standing committees. Long service on the same committees develops in the American legislator an expertise that makes him more than a match for the transient department head.

Committee government also facilitates close inspection and review of administrative performance which has become a major activity of the Congress. In practice, legislative surveillance of the executive branch is chiefly exercised by particular committees which operate as overseers and watchdogs of downtown departments. A variety of oversight devices: committee investigations, question periods, departmental reports, the requirement of prior committee approval, concurrent resolutions, and demands for documents and testimony have been increasingly used in recent years to implement the "oversight" function of Congress.

Committee hearings have the further advantage, as we have seen, of serving as political sounding boards for legislative policymakers, enabling them to ascertain the intensity of support for and opposition to legislative proposals on the part of interested groups in the country. In a democracy where preponderant public opinion is supposed to be the source of law, this function of discovering the attitudes of the interested and informed public is obviously an essential one. In cases where a general consensus of opinion has not yet emerged on a legislative proposal or where some regional or sectional group is strongly opposed to a measure, the hearing process will reveal this condition and serve at least as a safety valve for the release of social tensions.

The operation of the committee system is recognized as the heart of congressional activity. Here, in practice, Congressmen organized in "little legislatures" consider legislative and spending proposals, review the operations of administration, and at times themselves initiate new law. Committee work includes hearings as well as discussion in closed meetings. It involves contact with experts and written material. It is the center of legislative activity where criticism of administration and decision upon proposed legislation is largely made.

On the other hand, the congressional committee system is not without some drawbacks that could be corrected. As noted above, these miniature legislatures have acquired such power and prestige over the years that they are largely autonomous of the House itself which created them and whose agents they are supposed to be. Functions which are the constitutional birthright of Congress as a whole—the making of policy and the conduct of investigations—have in practice been delegated by the House and Senate to their standing committees. The role of the House is now largely limited to ratifying decisions made by its committees.

The autonomy of the committees gives rise in turn to the problem of coordination. Since the committees usually have a decisive voice in lawmaking, the committee system makes for the decentralization of legislative policy formation. Jealous of their jurisdictions and acting independently of each other, these little legislatures go their own way at their own pace. Although there is no central or advance planning of the legislative program on a scale comparable with the British practice, the leadership of the House does plan a general outline of the major bills which it hopes to get through at a given session, thus deciding which measures to leave until the second session of the Congress or to a subsequent Congress. This is done informally by the Speaker, the majority leader, the majority whip and the chairmen of the committees handling major measures. Precise, long-range planning as to the exact day or week when a bill is to be voted upon in the House is hardly possible, of course, because of unforeseeable delays in committee action. Closer intercommittee coordination is deemed desirable in order to avoid jurisdictional disputes, promote consistency and coherence between related areas of legislative policy-making, and accelerate the legislative process. The postwar proliferation of subcommittees seems to have carried the process of fission too far—the Committee on Agriculture alone has had 16 standing subcommittees, 1 for each crop—and has further complicated the problem of coordination.

There is also room for improvement in the hearings process. Sometimes committee hearings are held without adequate advance preparation on the part of the members, the witnesses, or the staff. The staff may have failed to choose the witnesses well or coach them wisely; the witnesses may not have filed advance copies of their statements with the committee or their testimony may not be succinct, lucid, and pertinent; the committeemen may lack the requisite background information or fail to study the hearing briefs and ask intelligent questions. In rare instances the committee hearing has been used not to find facts but to suppress them, while the rights of witnesses have not always been fully respected by investigating groups.

The structural defects in the congressional committee system are far from fatal, and they could readily be remedied, as the La Follette Monroney committee recommended, by the creation of majority and minority policy committees in each house, properly composed and effectively operated. On net balance, the manifold advantages of the committee system clearly outweigh its drawbacks.

CHAPTER 7

LEADERSHIP IN THE HOUSE

Political leadership is a fascinating subject for study, and nowhere more so than in nations with democratic forms of government. Such countries are governed in large part by their national legislatures the role of whose leaders excites perennial interest. Writing in 1885, Woodrow Wilson remarked that—

in a country which governs itself by means of a public meeting, a Congress or a Parliament, a country whose political life is representative, the only real leadership in governmental affairs must be legislative leadership—ascendancy in the public meeting which decides everything. The leaders, if there by any, must be those who suggest the opinions and rule the actions of the representative body.

The position of Congress in the American system of government may not be so supreme today as it was when Wilson wrote his little classic on *Congressional Government*. But the leadership of Congress continues to intrigue the interest of scholars and laymen alike. Especially is this true in the House of Representatives where the character and conditions of leadership have had a most interesting history.

In any large assembly leaders must arise or be chosen to manage its business and the American House of Representatives has long had its posts of leadership. Outstanding among them have been the Speaker, the floor leader, the majority whip, and the chairman of the Committee on Rules. The chairmen of Ways and Means and of Appropriations have also long been top leadership positions in the hierarchy of the House, followed by the chairmen of the other great standing committees of that body.

During the first 20 years of congressional history the Speakers were mere figureheads. They presided over the House, to be sure, but actual legislative leadership and control were exercised by the Executive with the aid of trusted floor lieutenants, especially during the Jeffersonian regime. Harlow gives a lucid description of the system of executive control of the legislative process as it operated in that early period.[1]

It is evident that both in methods and in effectiveness the Republican legislative machine differed little from that evolved by the severely criticized Federalists. The president and his Secretary of the Treasury were responsible for the main outlines, and in some cases for the details as well, of party measures. Policies were evolved, programs laid before Congress, and bills passed, all under the watchful eye of the chief executive. Jefferson was so successful that he was called a tyrant, but his methods were more like those of the Tudor kings than of the Italian despots. Everything that he did had to be done through Congress. Congress to be sure was usually ready to follow Jefferson's lead, but the compliance of that body was due to nothing else than the constant and never-ending vigilance of Jefferson and Gallatin.

In one important particular Jefferson improved upon Federalist legislative methods. Hamilton had his followers in Congress, and there was usually some one leader of prominence in charge of the party forces, but this floor leader was not looked upon as the personal representative of the president himself. He was

[1] Ralph V. Harlow, *The History of Legislative Methods in the Period Before 1825* (1917), pp. 176–177.

rather an assistant to the Speaker. From 1801 to 1808 the floor leader was distinctly the lieutenant of the executive. William B. Giles, who was actually referred to as "the premier, or prime minister," Caesar A. Rodney, John Randolph of Roanoke, and Wilson Cary Nicholas all held that honorable position at one time or another. It was their duty to look after party interests in the House, and in particular to carry out the commands of the president. The status of these men was different from that of the floor leader of today, who is given his position because of long service in the House. They were presidential agents, appointed by the executive, and dismissed at his pleasure. * * *.

Thus, in the beginning, "leadership was neither the prerogative of seniority nor a privilege conferred by the House; it was distinctly the gift of the president." During the Jeffersonian period the President kept a recognized leader in the House in order to see that Members "voted right." Party caucus and House floor leader took their orders from the White House.

The infallibility of Jefferson in the political field was like unto that of the pope in the spiritual, and denial of his inspiration was heresy, punishable by political death. Good Republicans such as John Randolph, for instance, who insisted upon the right of independent judgment, were promptly read out of the party. It seemed a far cry to democracy when the President insisted upon doing the thinking for Congress and regulating the actions of its members.[2]

After Jefferson's retirement the balance of power shifted from the President to Congress. Several factors contributed to this transfer: the weakness of President Madison, a rebellion in the House against Executive control, factional fights within the Cabinet, and the appearance on the legislative scene of the "war hawks" of 1812: that famous group of young and energetic men, including Calhoun and Clay, who became the new Speaker. It took some time for Henry Clay and his followers to restore party unity and recover control of the administration, but by the end of the Second War with England they had succeeded in erecting a new system, based on the party caucus, in which legislative leadership was now the prerogative of a group of prominent men in the House of Representatives. No longer subject and submissive to the dictates of a strong President, Congress developed its own internal leadership structure. Under Henry Clay the speakership emerged as an office of greatly enhanced power and prestige. Merely chairman of the House and subordinate in actual influence to the floor leader during the Jeffersonian regime, the Speaker now became both presiding officer and leader of the majority party in the Chamber. Meanwhile, the development of the standing committee system in 1816 and afterwards, with the appointment of their chairmen by the Speaker, completed the transformation. "Thus, by 1825," as Harlow observes, "so far as its organization was concerned, the House of Representatives had assumed its present form."[3]

With the evolution of the committee system during the 19th century, as sketched in the preceding chapter, and with the gradual delegation of functions by the House to these "little legislatures," their chieftains acquired enlarged powers and enhanced importance as leaders in the legislative process. The chairmanships of the great committees called for steering qualities of a high order. Those who demonstrated the most skillful generalship in the arts of floor management were promoted by the Speaker from one committee headship to another, gradually rising in the committee hierarchy to preside over

² *Ibid.*, p. 192.
³ *Ibid.*, p. 208.

Appropriations and Ways and Means, the most prized posts next to the speakership in the leadership structure of the House.

Thus, as the 19th century advanced, the leadership of the House came to be divided among the chairmen of its standing committees. The more numerous the committees, the more was leadership diffused. By 1885 Woodrow Wilson reported that—

the House has as many leaders as there are subjects of legislation; for there are as many standing committees as there are classes of legislation. * * *. The chairmen of the standing committees do not constitute a cooperative body like a ministry. They do not consult and concur in the adoption of homogeneous and mutually helpful measures; there is no thought of acting in concert. Each committee goes its own way at its own pace.[4]

Diffusion is still the characteristic feature of leadership in Congress. In practice, Congress functions not as a unified institution, but as a collection of autonomous committees that seldom act in unison. The system of autonomous committees and the selection of committee chairmen on the basis of seniority render] difficult the development of centralized legislative leadership and the adoption of a coherent legislative program. The function of leadership was dispersed in 1960 among the chairmen of more than 300 committees of all types in both Houses: standing, special, joint, and subcommittees. The chairmen and ranking minority members of the standing committees of the House are described as "seniority leaders" as distinguished from the "elective leaders" who are chosen by their respective party caucuses: the Speaker, floor leaders, party whips, and conference chairmen.[5] Party caucuses or conferences are rarely held to determine the party stand on legislative issues, and they are never binding. And party responsibility for policymaking is weakened by the operation of the seniority system.

Formally, the existence in the House of Representatives of 20 standing committee chairmen, plus the various political committees and elective leaders, gives an appearance of widespread diffusion of leadership functions in the first Chamber. But, paradoxically in practice, leadership in the House is more effectively centralized in the Speaker, the Rules Committee, and the floor leaders than in their senatorial counterparts. Several factors contribute to this result. These include the powers, prestige, and personal influence of the Speaker; the stricter rules of the House; the tighter organization of its business and debates; and the greater discipline of its Members. The larger size of the House and the shorter term of office of Representatives also combine to reduce the Members' comparative independence.

THE OFFICE OF THE SPEAKER

In the American system of government the speakership of the National Legislature is rated as the second most powerful office in the land. Only the Presidency stands higher in the political hierarchy.

The Constitution says that: "The House of Representatives shall choose their Speaker and other officers," but remains silent upon his status and functions. Historians regard him as a direct descendant of the Speaker in the colonial assemblies. Asher C. Hinds, former parliamentarian of the House, held that the Constitution did not

4 Woodrow Wilson, *Congressional Government* (1885), pp. 60–61.
5 David B. Truman, *The Congressional Party* (1959), pp. 198 ff. See ch. 6 of this case study for an intensive analysis of House leadership roles in the 81st Cong.

create the Speaker, but merely adopted an existing officer. His office is thus a colonial heritage whose importance and influence have varied down through the passing years, depending upon the personal force of the incumbents.

SELECTION AND QUALIFICATIONS

We do not know what the intent of the Founding Fathers was with respect to the speakership. They did not say whether he must be a Member of the House, although he always has been. Nor did the framers say how he should be selected. At first he was elected by ballot, but since 1839 he has been chosen by voice vote, on a rollcall. In 1809 it was held that the Speaker should be elected by a majority of all present, and in 1879 that he might be elected by a majority of those present, a quorum voting, a majority of all the Members not being required.

In fact there is a discrepancy between the law and the practice in the choice of the Speaker. For in actual practice the Speaker is really chosen by the caucus of the majority party in the House whose choice is then ratified by the House itself. On the eve of the meeting of each new Congress the congressional parties hold caucuses or conferences at which they nominate their respective candidates for the elective offices in the House. On rare occasions there is a lively contest for the nomination for the speakership. On the eve of the 66th Congress, for example, a spirited campaign was waged between Mr. Gillett of Massachusetts and Mr. Mann of Illinois. Gillett won. The contest is keenest in the caucus of the majority party because its nomination is equivalent to election in the House.

Contests for the posts of party leadership in the House have usually occurred over vacancies, but on rare occasions an incumbent party leader has been forcibly displaced. This happened at the opening of the 86th Congress when Representative Charles Halleck of Indiana was selected as Republican floor leader in place of Representative Joseph W. Martin, Jr. of Massachusetts. Martin had served continuously as Republican floor leader since January 3, 1939, except for the years 1947–48 and 1953–54 when Republicans controlled the House and Martin was Speaker, and Halleck was floor leader. In the Republican caucus on January 6, 1959, Halleck ousted Martin by a 74–70 secret-ballot vote. The Martin-Halleck struggle was not a "liberal-conservative" fight. It reflected, in part, a belief that Halleck, at 58, could provide more vigorous leadership than the 74-year-old Martin, who had been handicapped by a blood clot on his leg. Some Republicans also complained that Martin had cooperated too closely with Speaker Rayburn in the past and had not been sufficiently partisan in his leadership efforts. Martin attributed his defeat in part to GOP election reverses, saying a "fall guy" was needed.

In nominating their candidates for the speakership the congressional parties usually lay stress on length of congressional service, among other factors. Long legislative experience is a criterion that seems to carry more weight in the 20th century than it did in the 19th. Before 1896 the average length of congressional service before election to the Chair was 7 years. Henry Clay of Kentucky and William Pennington of New Jersey were elected to the speakership on their first appearance in the House, something that would never happen in our time. Since 1896, however, the average length of service of Speakers has been about three times as long as before. "Uncle Joe" Cannon was elevated to the Chair in his 31st year in the House of Representatives. Champ Clark was chosen in his 16th year of service, Gillett in his 27th, Longworth in his 21st, and the present Speaker, Sam Rayburn, at the time of his first election was in his 28th year in the House. The increasing rigidity of the seniority system since 1910 is also relevant here, requiring more time to become sufficiently outstanding to be considered for Speaker.

Aside from long congressional service, the modern Speakers are men who have won the confidence and esteem not only of their own party, but also the general membership of the House. They have usually served as chairmen of important committees of the House or as floor leaders. Thus, Speaker Rayburn was long chairman of the Committee on Interstate and Foreign Com nerce and later was the Democratic floor leader.

It has been a longstanding custom of the House to reelect a Speaker to that office as long as his party remains in control of the House and he retains his seat. Both Speaker Cannon and Speaker Clark were reelected consecutively for four terms, until a change of party control took place. Mr. Rayburn was elected Speaker on September 16, 1940, and is now (1960) serving his eighth term in that post, having held the office longer than any predecessor in the chair; he has been his party's top leader in the House for more than 10 terms. Of the 20th century Speakers, three became minority floor leaders when their party lost control of the House: Champ Clark in the 66th Congress; Sam Rayburn in the 80th and 83d Congresses; and Joseph Martin in the 81st, 84th, and 85th Congresses.

When a change in party control of the House occurs, the elective party officers rotate under a system by which the Speaker shifts down to minority leader, the former majority leader becomes the minority whip, and the majority whip returns to the role of a rank-and-file Member. At the same time, when the minority party becomes the majority party, the former minority leader ascends to the speakership, and the minority whip becomes the new majority leader. Thus, when the Democrats captured control of the House in the 52d Congress (1891–93) and retained control in the 53d Congress (1893–95), former Speaker Reed became minority leader during Charles F. Crisp's two terms in the chair. Then, with another switch in party control in the 54th Congress (1895–97), Mr. Reed returned to the speakership. Likewise, Champ Clark served as minority leader of the House in the 61st Congress (1909–11) and, after 8 years in the Speaker's chair (1911–19), became minority leader again in the 66th Congress (1919–21). Similar shifts in the party leadership posts occurred with the changes in party control of the House that took place between the 79th and the 84th Congresses.

POWERS AND DUTIES

The Speaker of the House derives his powers and duties from the Constitution, the rules of the House, previous decisions of the Chair, and general parliamentary law. He presides at the sessions of the House, announces the order of business, puts questions, and reports the vote. He also decides points of order and can prevent dilatory tactics, thanks to the earlier rulings of Speaker Reed. He appoints the Chairman of the Committee of the Whole and the members of select and conference committees. He chooses Speakers pro tem and refers bills and reports to the appropriate committees and calendars. He also enjoys the privileges of an ordinary Member of the House, and may vote and participate in debate on the floor.

When Henry Clay took the chair as Speaker on December 1, 1823, he described the duties of the office in terms that are still apropos today.

They enjoin promptitude and impartiality in deciding the various questions of order as they arise; firmness and dignity in his deportment toward the House; patience, good temper, and courtesy towards the individual Members, and the best arrangement and distribution of the talent of the House, in its numerous sub-divisions, for the dispatch of the public business, and the fair exhibition of every subject presented for consideration. They especially require of him, in those moments of agitation from which no deliberative assembly is always entirely exempt, to remain cool and unshaken amidst all the storms of debate, carefully guarding the preservation of the permanent laws and rules of the House from being sacrificed to temporary passions, prejudices, or interests.

A TRIPLE PERSONALITY

In contrast to his English counterpart, the Speaker of our House is a triple personality, being both a Member of the House, its presiding officer, and leader of the majority party in the Chamber. As a Member of the House he has the right to cast his vote on all questions, unlike the Vice President, who has no vote except in case of a tie. Usually, the Speaker does not exercise his right to vote except to break a tie or when he desires to make known how he stands on a measure. As a Member, he also has the right to leave the chair and participate in debate on the House floor as the elected representative of his district, unlike the Vice President, who may not do likewise in the Senate. The Speaker seldom exercises this right, but when he does, as on close party issues, the House fills up and everyone pays close attention.

As presiding officer of the House, the Speaker interprets the rules that the House has adopted for its guidance. Customarily he performs this duty as a judge, bound by the precedents created by prior decisions of the Chair. But in 1890 Speaker Reed broke with all past practice by refusing to entertain a motion on the grounds that it was dilatory and by including Members physically present but not voting in counting a quorum. With significant exceptions, appeals are in order from decisions of the Chair, but are seldom taken; when taken, the Chair is usually sustained.

The Speaker's power of recognition is now narrowly limited by House rules and conventions that fix the time for the consideration of various classes of bills; require recognition of the chairmen of the Appropriations and Ways and Means Committees when they rise to move the consideration of appropriation and revenue bills; and allow committeemen in charge of other legislation to control all the time allotted for general debate. The Chair still has discretion, however, in determining who shall be recognized while a bill is being debated under the 5-minute rule in Committee of the Whole; but then the Speaker is not in the chair. He still has complete discretion also as to whom he will recognize to make motions to suspend the rules, on days when such motions are in order. The rules of the House may be suspended by a two-thirds vote on the first and third Mondays of the month and on the last 6 days of the session.

As party leader the Speaker prior to 1910 had certain additional powers: to appoint all standing committees and to name their chairmen; to select the members of the Rules Committee; and from 1858 to serve as its chairman. By the exercise of these powers he was in a position to influence greatly the action taken by the standing committees, the order of business in the House, and the character of the action taken by the House itself. His political powers evolved gradually during the 19th century, reaching a peak under the masterful leadership of Speakers Reed and Cannon. Taken together, the powers of the Speaker prior to 1910, as a Member of the House, as its presiding officer, and as majority leader were so far reaching that the speakership was regarded as second only in power and influence to the Presidency, and as supreme in relation to the legislative process. After a long process of evolution the problem of leadership in the House of Representatives seemed to have been finally solved.[6]

In the revolution of 1910, however, a coalition of Democrats and insurgent Republicans, led by George W. Norris, rebelled against the despotism of "Czar" Cannon, dethroned the Speaker from his post of power, and deprived him of most of the great powers he formerly possessed. They removed him from the Rules Committee of which he had formerly been chairman. They stripped him of the power to appoint the standing committees of the House and their chairmen, which he had exercised as a powerful weapon of party discipline. And they restricted his former right of recognition. This revolutionary reversal in the powers of the Speaker was swiftly accomplished and was described as "one of the most remarkable reversions of policy that has ever characterized a political system." The revolt was not so much against the principle of leadership as it was against the concentration of powers in the hands of a single individual who had exercised them in an arbitrary and autocratic manner.

Although the Speaker lost his power in the revolution of 1910 of appointing the standing committees of the House, he still appoints the select committees, the House Members of conference committees, and the Chairman of the Committee of the Whole. Prior to 1910, the Speaker controlled the House in collaboration with a coterie of trusted party lieutenants. Since 1910 the leadership of the House has been in commission. Despite the overthrow of Cannonism, the speakership thus continues to be the most powerful office in Congress.

CONTRAST WITH ENGLISH SPEAKER

The Speaker of our own House of Representatives offers an interesting contrast with the Speaker of the English House of Commons. Formerly the "King's man," and later the majority leader, the Speaker of the House of Commons has been its impartial umpire since 1839. He is elected by the Commons from among its Members, subject to the approval of the Crown. Upon election, he gives up his former political affiliations and becomes the impartial servant of the whole House, its presiding officer, and the protector of its rights and liberties. It seems probable that his role evolved as it did because the Government was present on the front bench as a group of Members,

---

[6] See ch. 9 for a fuller description of the powers of the Speaker during this period.

plus the strength of the leadership and the role of the opposition party in the House.

The English Speaker holds a position of great dignity and authority, enhanced by the wig and gown he wears. Without a bell or gavel to keep order, he rules the House with a firm hand. The English Speaker does not intervene in committee or make political speeches outside Parliament; he keeps aloof from party contacts and does not even enter a political club. After resigning from the Chair, he also retires from the House, being rewarded by the Crown with a peerage. He is not opposed on reelection in the House as long as he wishes to serve.

In his capacity as Chairman of the House of Commons, the English Speaker presides over its deliberations, maintains order in its debate, decides questions arising on point of order, puts the question for decision, and declares the decision. However, like the Speaker of our House of Representatives, he does not act as Chairman when the House is sitting as Committee of the Whole.

RAYBURN AND MARTIN

Sam Rayburn and Joseph W. Martin, Jr., the present and previous Speakers of the House of Representatives, have enjoyed responsibilities beyond those of the typical Speaker of earlier days. Mr. Rayburn was a close friend and trusted adviser of both President Franklin D. Roosevelt and President Harry S. Truman; he was instrumental in starting the regular White House meetings with congressional leaders. Mr. Martin met with President Eisenhower in his weekly conferences at the White House with the Republican leaders of Congress, inheriting a tradition that was continued by his successor, Mr. Charles A. Halleck.

William S. White, who covered Congress for the New York Times, has described the Speaker as "the second most influential elected official" in Washington today.

Officially, his job is in many respects comparable to the job of heading any great corporation or enterprise. He is the ultimate chief of everything in the House, from the nature of its legislative program to the conduct of its dining room, and the direction of its personnel—hired and elected—is his endless concern.

"He performs this job with economy of motion, with scant and infrequent but heady praise for those about him, with a ready and easy delegation of authority and with a somewhat amused deference to perhaps the most temperamental of all men—a politician at work." [7]

COMPENSATION AND ALLOWANCES

For the fiscal year 1960, Congress appropriated $58,510 for compensation for the Office of the Speaker, including $35,000 for his salary, and $9,500 for the Speaker's automobile. In addition, the Speaker receives mileage, stationery, clerk hire, and other expense allowances and is entitled to the franking privilege. He has a suite of rooms in the Capitol Building. Attached to the Office of the Speaker is the Office of the Parliamentarian and his assistants, for which $60,265 was appropriated for the fiscal year ending June 30, 1960.

---

[7] William S. White, "Sam Rayburn—The Untalkative Speaker," *New York Times Magazine*, Feb. 27, 1949, p. 48.

FLOOR LEADER

In the history of the evolution of the office of floor leader the year 1910 marks a major dividing point. For the reform of the House rules adopted in that year brought about a redistribution of the powers of the speakership and a significant change in the position of the floor leader.

During the 19th century the majority floor leader was customarily selected by the Speaker who often designated either his leading opponent within the party or the Chairman of Ways and Means or of the Appropriations Committee or one of his faithful lieutenants. Thus Winthrop appointed his opponent Samuel F. Vinton in 1847; Banks designated Lewis D. Campbell in 1856; Pennington named John Sherman in 1859, and Reed selected McKinley in 1889. Ranking membership of Ways and Means accounted for Clay's appointment of Ezekiel Bacon in 1811; Stevenson's choice of Gulian C. Verplanck in 1822; Polk's selection of Churchill C. Cambreleng in 1835; Orr's promotion of James S. Phelps in 1858; Randall's advancement of Fernando Wood in 1879; Keifer's appointment of William D. Kelley in 1881; Carlisle's designation of Roger Q. Mills in 1887; and Henderson's selection of Sereno E. Payne in 1899. Faithful lieutenants were rewarded by the appointment of James J. McKay by Jones in 1843; Thomas S. Bayly by Cobb in 1849; George S. Houston by Body in 1851; William H. Morrison by Kerr and Carlisle in 1875 and 1883; and William M. Springer by Crisp in 1891.[8]

According to Riddick—

in the House, the early titular floor leaders were at the same time the chairmen of the Ways and Means Committee. Before the division of the work of that committee, the duties of its chairmen were so numerous that they automatically became the actual leaders, since as chairmen of that committee they had to direct the consideration of most of the legislation presented to the House. [Ways and Means handled both the revenue and the appropriations bills down to 1865]. From 1865 until 1896 the burden of handling most of the legislation was shifted to the chairman of the Appropriations Committee, who then was designated most frequently as the leader. From 1896 until 1910 once again the chairmen of the Ways and Means Committee were usually sought as the floor leaders.[9]

Since 1910 the floor leader has been elected by secret ballot of the party caucus. During the Wilson administrations the Democrats resumed their former practice of naming the chairman of Ways and Means as floor leader, but since the 72d Congress (1931–33), when the Democrats recovered control of the House, their floor leaders have not retained their former committee assignments. John W. McCormack, who was elected Democratic floor leader on September 16, 1940, and who has held that office longer than any predecessor, resigned his seat on Ways and Means when he became majority leader. In 1919, when the Republicans captured control of the House, they elected as their floor leader the former chairman of Ways and Means and made him ex-officio chairman of their committee on committees and of their steering committee. He gave up his former legislative committee assignments in order to devote himself, with the Speaker, to the management of the business of the House.

[8] DeAlva S. Alexander, *History and Procedure of the House of Representatives* (1916), ch. VII, "Floor Leaders", pp. 110–111.
[9] Floyd M. Riddick *The United States Congress: Organization and Procedure* (1949), Chapter V, ' The Floor Leaders and Whips", p. 86n.

CHANGES AFTER 1910

As a result of the so-called "revolution of 1910," notable changes were made in the power structure of the House. Under "Uncle Joe" Cannon who had been Speaker since 1903, the Speaker was supreme and all-powerful. He dominated the Rules Committee which made the rules and was a law unto itself. The majority party caucus was seldom needed or used. The Speaker appointed the standing committees which were entirely free from control by a majority of the House, while the floor leader was a figurehead.

After the congressional elections of November 1910, in which the Democrats won full control of the House, they held a party caucus on January 19, 1911, and chose Champ Clark as Speaker and Oscar Underwood as their floor leader and as chairman of the Ways and Means Committee. Under the new system that became effective in the 1911–12 session of the 62d Congress, the Speaker was largely shorn of power and the majority party caucus became the dominant factor. The Rules Committee was controlled by the floor leader and the caucus; it made the rules and retained all its former powers. The Democratic members of Ways and Means organized the House by naming its standing committees.

As floor leader Underwood was supreme, the Speaker a figurehead. The main cogs in the machine were the caucus, the floor leadership, the Rules Committee, the standing committees, and special rules. Oscar Underwood became the real leader of the House. He dominated the party caucus, influenced the rules, and as chairman of Ways and Means chose the committees. Champ Clark was given the shadow, Underwood the substance of power. As floor leader, he could ask and obtain recognition at any time to make motions to restrict debate or preclude amendments or both. "Clothed with this perpetual privilege of recognition, and backed by his caucus," remarked a contemporary observer, "the floor leader had it in his power to make a Punch and Judy show of the House at any time." [10]

After the First World War the party caucus gradually fell into disuse, the Democratic floor leader ceased to be chairman of Ways and Means, the standing committees continued to function as autonomous bodies, and the Rules Committee became a more influential factor in the power structure of the House. After 1937 this powerful committee ceased to function as an agent of the majority leadership and came under the control of a bipartisan coalition which was often able to exercise an effective veto power over measures favored by the majority party and its leadership.

The net effect of the various changes of the last 35 years in the power structure of the House of Representatives has been to diffuse the leadership, and to disperse its risks, among a numerous body of leaders. The superstructure which has come to control "overhead" strategy now includes the Speaker, the floor leader, the chairman of Rules, and the party whip. At a somewhat lower echelon behind this inner "board of strategy" are the chairman and the secretary of the party caucus or conference, the majority members of Rules who have grown from 3 to 10, and the members of the Republican Policy Committee and of the two committees on committees. Thus, the top leaders of the House are no longer "the chairmen of the principal

---

[10] Lynn Haines, *Law Making in America* (1912), pp. 15–16.

standing committees," as Woodrow Wilson described them in 1885, although the chairmen still have large powers over bills within their jurisdiction.

So far as the position of floor leader is concerned, he no longer occupies the post of supremacy that Oscar Underwood held. There is no provision for his office in the standing rules of the House, nor does he receive a special salary. Nevertheless, he stands today in a place of great influence and prestige, the acknowledged leader of his party in the Chamber, its field general on the floor, first or second man in the party hierarchy, and one of the potential successors to the speakership. All the Speakers of the 20th century have been advanced to the speakership from either the minority or majority floor leadership position, except in 1903 and 1919 when Joseph G. Cannon and Frederick H. Gillett, respectively, were chosen as Speaker in lieu of the Republican floor leaders, Sereno E. Payne and James R. Mann.

QUALIFICATIONS AND PREVIOUS EXPERIENCE

After retiring from the House of Representatives where he represented Buffalo from 1897 to 1911, DeAlva Alexander wrote an informative history of that body which contains a series of character sketches of the floor leaders of the House from Griswold in 1800 to Underwood in 1911. Most of these mighty men of old are now forgotten, but to their contemporaries they were men of exceptional capacity. "In interesting personality and real ability the floor leader is not infrequently the strongest and at the time the best-known man in the House."

Alexander went on to give his own evaluation of the characteristics of a good leader as follows: [11]

It certainly does not follow that a floor leader is the most effective debater, or the profoundest thinker, or the accepted leader of his party, although he may be and sometimes is all of these. It should imply, however, that in the art of clear, forceful statement, of readily spotting weak points in an opponent's argument, and in dominating power to safeguard the interests of the party temporarily responsible for the legislative record of the House, he is the best equipped for his trade. It is neither necessary nor advisable for him to lead or even to take part in every debate. The wisdom of silence is a great asset. Besides, chairmen and members of other committees are usually quite capable and sufficiently enthusiastic to protect their own measures. But the floor leader must aid the Speaker in straightening out parliamentary tangles, in progressing business, and in exhibiting an irresistible desire to club any captious interference with the plans and purposes of the majority.

Thirteen men have held the office of majority or minority floor leader of the House of Representatives since 1919. Six of them were Republicans: Mondell, Longworth, Tilson, Snell, Martin, and Halleck. Seven were Democrats: Garrett, Garner, Rainey, Byrns, Bankhead, Rayburn, and McCormack. Elevation to the floor leadership comes only after long service in the House. The Republican floor leaders had served, on the average, 16 years in the Chamber; the Democrats 21 years before their election. The combined average for the whole group was 19 years previous service in the House. The longrun trend in point of previous House experience is downward, both McCormack and Halleck having been elected floor leader after serving only six terms in the House.

All the floor leaders since the First World War have also enjoyed long service on some of the most eminent committees of the House.

[11] Alexander, *op. cit.*, p. 109.

Of the six Republicans, three had served on the Rules Committee, two ranked high on Ways and Means, and one on the Appropriations Committee. Of the seven Democrats, three were high ranking on Ways and Means, two on Rules, one on Appropriations, and one (Rayburn) had been chairman of Interstate and Foreign Commerce.

FUNCTIONS AND DUTIES OF FLOOR LEADER

The standing rules of the House are silent on the duties of the floor leaders who, as we have seen, are selected by the caucus or conference of their respective parties. As his title indicates, the principal function of the majority leader is that of field marshal on the floor of the House. He is responsible for guiding the legislative program of the majority party through the House. In cooperation with the Speaker, he formulates and announces the legislative program, keeps in touch with the activities of the legislative committees through their chairmen, and stimulates the reporting of bills deemed important to the Nation and the party. After conferring with the Speaker and majority leader, the majority whip customarily sends out a "whip notice" on Fridays to the party members in the House, indicating the order of business on the floor for the following week, and the majority leader makes an announcement to the same effect on the floor in response to an inquiry from the minority leader. The legislative program is planned ahead on a weekly basis according to the readiness of committees to report, the condition of the calendars, the exigencies of the season, and the judgment of the party leaders. Advance announcement of the weekly program protects the membership against surprise action.

The role of the majority leader was lucidly summarized in a statement inserted in the *Congressional Record* on May 11, 1928, when the Republicans were in power, by Representative Hardy, of Colorado:[12]

The floor leader, especially the leader of the majority side, has much to do with the legislative program. The majority leader, of course, represents the majority on the floor. Motions he makes are usually passed. He endeavors to represent the majority view and the majority follow his leadership. He leads in debate on administration matters and gives the House and the country the viewpoint of his party on the legislative program.

The leader keeps in touch with proposed legislation, the status of bills in importance, with the steering committee of which he is chairman, and with the attitude of the Rules Committee. He confers with committee chairmen and Members in general. The majority leader often confers with the President and advises with him regarding administrative measures. He takes to the President the sentiment of the party in the House and he brings to the party in the House the sentiment of the President. The majority leader acts also as chairman of the committee on committees and of the steering committee. * * *

The duties of the minority floor leader were described by Representative Bertrand H. Snell in a statement on March 5, 1934, as follows: [13]

The Minority Floor Leader is selected at a conference of the minority members. Usually he is his party's candidate for Speaker. The minority, as now constituted, selects its members to go on committees through a party committee on committees, of which the minority floor leader is ex-officio chairman, and he is its mouthpiece in the House. He is also chairman of a steering committee whose members are his chief advisers. He is spokesman for his party and enunciates its policies. He is required to be alert and vigilant in defense of the minority's rights. It is his function and duty to criticize constructively the policies and program of the majority, and to this end employ parliamentary tactics and give close attention

---

12 *Congressional Record,* 70th Cong., 1st sess., p. 8439.
13 Floyd M. Riddick, *Congressional Procedure* (1941), pp. 345–346.

to all proposed legislation. The minority leader must keep in constant touch with the ranking minority members of committees, he himself not being a member of any committee although indirectly acquainted with the work of all committees.

Through another party functionary called the "whip" the minority leader informs the minority members of the order of business from time to time and secures their attendance when important votes are to be taken. By this method also the attitude of members toward a given proposition is ascertained, looking to unanimity of action.

In fine, the duties of the minority floor leaders are hardly less responsible and exacting than those of the majority leader; such difference being only in kind and degree. The position of minority leader is important, not only from a party standpoint but in the interest of the public business, requiring in its occupant a high degree of alertness and tact combined with parliamentary knowledge; it involves at least three elements—political, parliamentary, and legislative.

Of his party colleagues in the House and of the vast number of constituents whom they represent the minority leader is selected to act as field marshal and as mentor and guide on the floor of the House.

Various parliamentary procedures are employed by the floor leader in directing and expediting the legislative program. Much noncontroversial business on the Unanimous Consent Calendar is disposed of without debate and "without objection." The work of the House is sometimes described as "lawmaking by unanimous consent" because the floor leader uses this device to fix the program of business. Members know that it would be futile to object to his unanimousconsent requests to consider legislation because the same end could be achieved via a simple majority vote on the floor. Similarly, if a Member sought to bring up a matter out of its turn, without prior agreement with the leadership, the floor leader could defeat him by objecting.

The floor leader can also limit debate on a bill, if it tends to get out of control, by making the point of order that debate is not germane to the pending subject or by moving that all debate on the pending bill and all amendments thereto close in a certain time. By his temper and spirit he can also influence the tone of debate.

As the end of a session approaches, with many measures pressing for passage, the Speaker and the floor leader cooperate closely to avoid a last-minute jam. The procedural devices employed at this time are largely unanimous consent, special orders, and motions to suspend the rules which are in order on the last 6 days of a session and require a two-thirds vote.

There is a usual speeding up of the program during the last days. But there is also a tightening of control. In strong contrast to the Senate, the House remains a poised, businesslike body as it approaches adjournment. The men in the cab hold the legislative train ready to the very end of its run." [14]

At the end of each session the floor leader customarily extends his remarks by inserting a record of its accomplishments, showing the major legislative actions taken and the number of public and private laws enacted, viewing with pride the role of the party in the legislative process.

In 1909 the House adopted a rule whereby Wednesdays were set apart for the consideration of unprivileged bills on the House and Union Calendars. Under this "Calendar Wednesday" rule, when invoked, the Clerk calls the roll of the committees in turn and authorized Members call up bills that their committees have reported. At the time of its adoption this rule was regarded as perhaps the most vital of the reforms that the progressives won under Cannonism.

[14] Paul H. Hasbrouck, *Party Government in the House of Representatives* (1927), p. 117.

For it reserved Wednesday as the one day of each week which had to be given to the consideration of bills upon the House Calendar. Before its adoption, the "call of committees" was rarely reached as the result of the accidental or intentional manipulation of privileged matters. To remedy that condition the new rule provided that on one day each week no business, regardless of its privileged character, should be allowed to interfere with the regular routine. In obtaining its adoption the progressives demanded, and thought that they had secured, one day so guarded that nothing could interfere with the consideration and final passage of general legislation.

For many years, however, the Calendar Wednesday rule has been more honored in the breach than in the observance. Session after session passes without a call of the committees. In practice, Calendar Wednesday is usually dispensed with by unanimous consent at the request of the majority leader. If there is objection, it requires a two-thirds vote to dispense with it, but no one ever objects. The leadership has evidently felt that there is little, if any, need for Calendar Wednesday because of the alternative methods by which bills can be brought up and over which they have more control. In the modern practice there are five routes by which bills and resolutions reach the floor of the House: (1) By the leave of certain committees to report at any time; (2) under unanimous consent, on call of the Unanimous Consent Calendar or the Private Calendar; (3) on special days, as on District Day, when particular types of business are privileged; (4) under suspension of the rules on the first and third Mondays and the last 6 days of the session; and (5) under special orders reported by the Committee on Rules.

Since the floor leader is responsible for the orderly conduct of the business of legislation on the floor, it is necessary for him to keep in close touch with the sentiment of the House and with the chairmen of committees that have under consideration bills of interest to the House, the country, and the party. To this end he holds frequent conferences with those concerned with prospective measures in order to compose any differences that may arise, as well as to plan the strategy and tactics of his campaign. Information as to party sentiment on a particular bill is also obtained, with the aid of the party whips, by polls of the State delegations.

WHIP ORGANIZATION

In the practice of the U.S. Congress party whips are used in both Houses and both political parties. The first person officially known as a whip in Congress was Republican Representative James E. Watson, of Indiana, so designated by his party in 1899. In the Senate, the first official Democratic whip was James H. Lewis, of Illinois, named in 1913. Two years later the Republicans designated Senator James W. Wadsworth, of New York, as their whip.

In the modern American practice, the Democratic "whip organization" in the House of Representatives consists of a chief whip, appointed by the Democratic floor leader, and 15 assistant whips selected on a regional basis by the Democratic Representatives. The House Republican "whip organization" includes a chief whip, chosen by his party's committee on committees, a deputy whip, 4 regional and 15 area whips selected by the chief whip. In the Senate the whip machinery is smaller, consisting on each side of a single Senator, elected by his party conference, and a party secretary.

The whips send out weekend "whip notices" to party members about next week's legislative program, conduct polls of party members through a "whip check" to estimate the prospective vote on bills, round up members for the actual votes, arrange "pairs" between opposing Members, and serve as assistant floor leaders in the absence of their leaders. The whips' task has steadily increased since 1900 with the growth of insurgency and factionalism in the congressional parties and the decline of party regularity.

PARTY CAUCUSES

Under the old system (1909–20) the congressional parties held frequent caucuses at which party policies were vigorously discussed and differences settled. Every major measure of a session was considered in party caucus and members were bound to abide by its decisions. The leadership then knew exactly where it stood, whether bills could be passed on the floor without amendment or whether compromises would have to be made. After Champ Clark became floor leader in 1909 the House Democrats held many binding caucuses and much of the success of the legislative program of the Wilson administration was attributed to the effective use of the caucus by the Democratic Party in both Houses of Congress. For many decades House Republicans also held frequent party conferences which, although they were not binding, made for a consensus among the party membership and helped a succession of strong GOP Speakers and floor leaders to hold the party reins tightly.

Under the new system, however, since World War I party caucuses have seldom been held except at the opening of a new Congress to nominate House officers and approve recommendations of the leadership for committee appointments. Perhaps party leaders nowadays consider these meetings too hazardous. The leadership cannot compel Members to vote against their will or conscience nor does it discipline them any more by removal or demotion from committees as the Republican leadership did at the opening of the 69th Congress in 1925 when the Members of the Wisconsin delegation, who had supported Senator La Follette in the presidential campaign of 1924, were barred from the Republican caucus and reduced in rank on the standing committees of the House.[15] In latter years the floor leader has relied for the cooperation of his followers not upon the compulsion of party rules, but upon his own powers of logic and persuasion and considerations of party welfare.

Under the new system the Floor Leader is dependent not upon his power under the rules, but upon his own personality and character, upon the esteem in which he is held in the House for his political sagacity and his wisdom as a statesman, and upon the natural instincts which prompt men belonging to a party, and held together by natural selfish instincts for mutual protection, for his success in harmonizing differences and thus being able to go into the House with a measure assured of sufficient support to secure its enactment * * * the Floor Leader has become the general manager of his party in the House, the counselor of his colleagues, the harmonizer of their conflicting opinions, their servant, but not their master.[16]

[15] A proposal to bar Representative Colmer of Mississippi from his seat on the Rules Committee at the opening of the 87th Cong. in 1961, because he did not support the Kennedy-Johnson ticket in the 1960 presidential election, was not adopted.
[16] George R. Brown, *The Leadership of Congress* (1922), pp. 221–222, 224.

In short, the function of a leader is to lead. In the case of a majority leader of a legislative assembly, leadership involves planning the legislative program, scheduling the order of business on the floor, supporting legislation calculated to implement the party's platform pledges, coordinating committee action to this end, and using his individual influence to keep the members of the party in the House in line with party policies. The majority leader's task is to steer his party in the House toward the formulation and adoption of policies and strategy designed to carry out the administration's legislative program, where the House and the Presidency are controlled by the same political party. As floor leader his function is to employ all the arts of parliamentary procedure to expedite the enactment of that program.

RELATIONS WITH COMMITTEES

During the 19th century, as already noted, the actual floor leader was often the chairman of Ways and Means prior to 1865 when this committee handled both the revenue and appropriation bills. In that year the supply bills were given to the Committee on Appropriations and thereafter the floor leader was often the chairman of Appropriations. When the 62d Congress (1911–13) transferred the power to appoint committees from the Speaker to the Democratic members of Ways and Means, its chairman (Underwood) who was also floor leader, thus acquired an indirect influence over legislation not enjoyed by his predecessors. Today Democratic vacancies on Ways and Means are filled by election by the party caucus which ratifies the choice of the party leadership which is thus able to exercise influence over tax and other legislation reported by that committee.

As already noted, the Republican floor leader always *ex officio* serves as chairman of the Republican committee on committees of the House which has the task of filling its party vacancies on the legislative committees. This involves hearing the claims of interested candidates and deciding who should be chosen.

The floor leader on both sides of the House aisle is also a member of his party's steering or policy committee. The Republican floor leader has been *ex officio* chairman of his steering committee.[17] An interesting account of the role of the Republican steering committee several years ago was given by Representative Hardy of Colorado, as follows:[18]

An influential factor in government is the steering committee. It exerts a powerful influence but makes no effort to exhibit power. It works along diplomatic lines to feel out and consolidate sentiment for administration measures and procedure. It meets at the call of the chairman, and considers the welfare of the Government from the party point of view. It advises with the White House, the chairmen of important committees, the party leaders, and the Rules Committee. It helps to iron out differences, and to formulate the majority program in the House. The chairman of the Steering Committee is the floor leader. When the committee meets the Speaker sometimes and the chairman of the Rules Committee usually are invited in for consultation. * * *

Relations between the leadership of the House and the Rules Committee have varied over the years. From 1890 to 1910 they were merged, for Rules was then a triumvirate composed of the Speaker and his two chief lieutenants, often the chairmen of Ways and Means and of Appropriations. After 1910 the speakership was "syndicated"

---

[17] Representative John W. Byrnes has been chairman of the Republican policy committee since 1959.
[18] *Cannon's Precedents of the House of Representatives*, vol. 8, sec. 3626.

and the leadership was separated from the members of the Committee on Rules who ceased to be the dominant figures in the House, although their chairman continued to be an important personality because of his position.[19] Writing in 1927 Hasbrouck said of the Rules Committee: [20]

It is the trump card of the Floor Leader, but he himself is not officially identified with it. True, he must appeal to the reason of 12 men, and win a majority of them to the support of his proposals. But the mainspring of action is not in the Rules Committee. The impulse comes from the Floor Leader after consultation with his "board of strategy" or, for purposes of more formal and routine action, with the Steering Committee.

In 1939, the leadership lost control of the House Rules Committee, thanks to the seniority custom, when two of its Democratic members joined with the four Republican members to block floor consideration of controversial administration bills. The coalition succeeded in preventing many New Deal-Fair Deal measures from reaching the House floor except by the laborious discharge route. After World War II a rising demand developed for reform of the Rules Committee whose powers were temporarily curbed during the 81st Congress (1949–50) by adoption of the so-called 21-day rule. This rule strengthened the position of the chairmen of the legislative committees of the House vis-a-vis both the Rules Committee and the leadership. While it was in effect, the 21-day rule brought the anti-poll-tax bill to the House floor for a successful vote and forced action on the housing and minimum wage bills. It also enabled the House to vote for the National Science Foundation, Alaska and Hawaii statehood legislation, and other important measures. Altogether, during the 81st Congress eight measures were brought to the House floor and passed by resort to the 21-day rule, while its existence caused the Rules Committee to act in other cases. Repeal of this rule, in January 1951, restored the checkrein power of the Rules Committee which it has since exercised on various occasions.

Today the Rules Committee is regarded as an important arm of the House leadership whose wishes it is expected to respect. Presumably it does so on most occasions. But—

traditions of seniority and tenure have at times made certain of the majority members of the Rules Committee of the House somewhat out of tune with the larger portion of their party colleagues, with the result that there has been something of a cleavage between the actions of the Committee and the wishes of the core leadership of the party.[21]

The influence of the party leadership on the legislative committees of the House is suggestive, not coercive, informal, not official, tactful, not dictatorial. The floor leader seldom appears in person before a committee, but he maintains close and friendly relations with their chairmen on matters of party policy, seeking to mediate between the wishes of the administration and those of the committeemen. Prior to 1947, before the committee structure had been streamlined and jurisdictions clarified, leadership could influence the fate of a bill by referring it to a favorable or unfavorable committee; but freedom of

---

[19] Atkinson and Beard, "The Syndication of the Speakership", *Political Science Quarterly*, Sept. 1911, p. 414.
[20] Hasbrouck, *op. cit.*, pp. 95–96.
[21] Ernest S. Griffith, *Congress: Its Contemporary Role* (1956), p. 165. See also James A. Robinson, "The Role of the Rules Committee in Arranging the Program of the U.S. House of Representatives," *Western Political Quarterly*, September 1959, pp. 653–669.

choice in bill referrals was reduced by the Legislative Reorganization Act of 1946.

The practice of floor leaders regarding their own committee assignments has varied in recent times. Representative McCormack, now the majority leader, voluntarily resigned from Ways and Means in 1940 when he was elected floor leader on account of the strenuous duties of that office. But when the Republicans captured control of the House in the 80th Congress and Mr. McCormack became minority whip, he accepted membership on the Committee on Government Operations and has since continued to serve on that committee. He was also a member of the Committee on Science and Astronautics during the 86th Congress. On the other hand, Mr. Martin, former minority floor leader and former Speaker, has had no committee assignments except Science and Astronautics since 1958, while Mr. Halleck, who was majority leader in the 80th and 83d Congresses, has served on the Rules and House Administration Committees.

RELATIONS WITH THE PRESIDENT

Since 1937, when Franklin D. Roosevelt began the practice, regular conferences have been held at the White House between the President and his party leaders in Congress—the so-called "Big Four": the Speaker and majority leader of the House and the Vice President and majority leader of the Senate, when they belong to the President's party. Inclusion of the majority whips in recent years makes it the "Big Six." When, as during the 85th and 86th Congresses, opposing political parties control Congress and the Presidency, the minority leaders attend these meetings at the White House which are usually weekly while Congress is in session, if the President is in town. These "Big Six" meetings have helped to bridge the gap between the legislative and executive branches of the National Government created by our inherited system of separated powers. Presidents Truman, Eisenhower, and Kennedy continued the practice of holding weekly leadership meetings at the White House.

Mutatis mutandis, they are the American counterpart of what Bagehot, referring to the British Cabinet, described as "the hyphen that joins, the buckle that fastens, the executive to the legislature." They are advantageous to both ends of Pennsylvania Avenue because they give congressional leaders an insight into the President's plans, while affording the President valuable counsel and guidance on the prospects of his legislative program. When of the same political party, the floor leaders are expected to serve as spokesmen for the administration, although there have been a few noteworthy departures from this practice. On the House side, however, during the 83d Congress, Majority Leader Halleck successfully made the transition from opposition to administration leader and became the most effective champion in Congress of Eisenhower's program. In the White House those days "Charlie" Halleck was the best liked man on Capitol Hill.

When President Roosevelt took office in 1933, he launched such a varied legislative program that it was necessary for him to keep in close touch with Congress through the leaders of both Houses. He consulted with his party leaders and committee chairmen with respect to the New Deal measures before they were introduced as administration bills, usually by the majority leaders. Sometimes he called the majority leader of the House or Senate individually to the White House to confer about some problem peculiar to one chamber or the other. After his return from trips abroad he sometimes asked the floor leaders of each House to brief him on legislative developments during his absence.

When opposing parties control the two branches, the President is more likely to discuss domestic legislative matters with the congressional leaders of his own party, although in the early days of the 80th Congress President Truman occasionally conferred with Messrs. Vandenberg, White, Martin, and Halleck, especially on legislation of a nonpartisan nature. In view of the vital role of Congress in the field of foreign relations, the President must sometimes take the leaders of both political parties in both Houses into his confidence. In the days before the Second World War, when President Roosevelt was seeking to strengthen our defenses, he frequently conferred with both Democratic and Republican leaders in both Houses of Congress. Such a conference was the famous night meeting at the White House late in July 1939, when the President and Secretary of State Cordell Hull urged that Congress repeal the Embargo Act. Among those in attendance were the chairmen of the Foreign and Military Affairs Committees, members of the Cabinet, and the majority and minority leaders of the House and Senate.[22]

COMPENSATION AND ALLOWANCES

The Legislative Branch Appropriation Act for fiscal 1960 appropriated $64,340 for the office of the majority floor leader; $50,510 for the office of the minority floor leader; $9,500 for each leader's automobile; and $27,645 each for the offices of the majority and minority whip. Neither of the floor leaders receives a special salary, unlike the recent British practice where, under the Ministers of the Crown Act of 1937, passed by a conservative government, a salary of £2,000 a year is payable to the leader of the opposition in the House of Commons.

---

[22] For further discussion of White House leadership meetings, see Paul T. David *et al.*, *The Politics of National Party Conventions* (1960), pp. 67-69. For a discussion of out-party congressional leadership roles in presidential politics, see *ibid.*, pp. 90-94.

CHAPTER 8

THE BUSINESS OF CONGRESS

The business of Congress in modern times is as varied and multifarious as the affairs of the American people. Once relatively limited in scope, small in volume, and simple in nature, it has now become almost unlimited in subject matter, enormous in volume, and complex in character.

The Founding Fathers had expected that Congress would confine itself, for the most part, to the external affairs of the new Nation leaving the conduct of internal affairs to the States and communities. The National Legislature would have little to do, Alexander Hamilton thought, after the Central Government was firmly established and a Federal code formulated. But with the steady expansion of the national domain, the rapid growth of population, and the development of commerce and industry, this expectation proved to be chimerical. As the new Republic grew greater, the demand for congressional action increased apace. From the opening day of the 1st Congress on March 4, 1789, to the adjournment of the 84th Congress on July 27, 1956, no less than 834,444 bills and resolutions (public and private) were introduced in both chambers: an average of 9,929 for for each of the first 84 Congresses.

Some conception of the enormous expansion of the business of Congress is afforded by a comparison of the work of the 1st (1789–91) and the 84th (1955–56) Congresses.

1st and 84th Congresses compared

Points of comparison	1st Cong.	84th Cong.
Number of bills introduced	268	16,782
House of Representatives	142	12,467
Senate	126	4,315
Number of laws enacted	118	1,921
Public	108	1,028
Private	10	893
Number of Members	91	531
Representatives	65	435
Senators	26	96
Days in session	519	230
Number of committees (standing, joint)	2	45
House of Representatives	1	19
Senate	0	15
Joint	1	11
Committee reports	155	5,801
House of Representatives	85	2,974
Senate	70	2,827
Nominations confirmed	211	82,694
Petitions filed	650	1,205
Presidential messages received	12	85
Executive department communications received	72	2,084

The foregoing figures measure the great growth in legislative business since 1789 and reflect the attendant burdens. The sheer bulk of bills introduced increased more than sixtyfold, while the number of standing committees available to receive and handle the rising flood grew from 2 to 45. Total committee reports jumped from 155 to 5,801 and the number of laws produced by the legislative mills multiplied 16 times. Meanwhile, as the population of the country expanded from 4 to 180 million and 37 new States were admitted to the Federal Union, the membership of Congress available to handle the added workload multiplied almost six times.

Comparative data reflecting the workload and output of single Congresses are available as far back as the 49th Congress (1885–87). The following table gives a comparative statement of the work of five selected Congresses (House only) over the past 75 years.

Congress	Number of bills	Number of reports	Public laws	Private laws	Total laws	Length in days
49th (1885–87)	11,260	4,181	424	1,031	1,455	330
56th (1899–1901)	14,339	3,006	443	1,498	1,941	277
62d (1911–13)	28,870	1,628	530	186	716	500
69th (1925–27)	17,415	2,319	808	537	1,423	297
85th (1957–58)	15,660	2,719	936	784	1,720	469

Source: Final edition, House Calendars, 56th, 70th, and 85th Congresses.

BUSINESS OF FIRST CONGRESS (1789–91)

Such legislative statistics afford no measure, however, of the changes in the range and complexity of public problems facing Congress then and now. The First Congress established the State, War, and Treasury Departments; fixed import and tonnage duties and regulated their collection; appropriated revenue and provided for a public debt; admitted Kentucky and Vermont to the Union and settled certain State accounts; established courts of justice and fixed the compensation of public officers; provided for the census of 1790 and regulated trade with the Indians; and otherwise dealt with the comparatively simple problems of the Federal Government in that remote age. Many problems in the early days of the Republic were State and local in scope, as they still are, and were left to the States and localities or to the private forces of the frontier to settle. Accordingly, the legislative process in Washington was much more leisurely and the life of a Congressman far more tranquil than it is today.

Of the 108 public laws approved by the First Congress, 18 dealt with foreign affairs (including tariff duties), 16 with relations between the Central Government and the States, and 10 with the defense of the infant Nation. Eighteen were concerned with administrative matters (including salaries), 15 with questions of public finance, and 9 with the judiciary. Only three were pension acts and only two were for the relief of private claimants.

WORKLOAD OF THE 84TH CONGRESS (1955–57)

Contrast this with the workload of the 84th Congress. Almost half of the laws it passed—893 out of 1,921—dealt with private and local matters which diverted its attention from national policymaking and with which it need not have been burdened. These included measures relating to the District of Columbia, the settlement of private claims and immigration cases, and other private and local legislation. Much of the work of this Congress was devoted to considering and enacting

33 appropriation bills involving a total of $137 billion: almost two-thirds of it for national defense.

Of the 1,028 public laws enacted by the 84th Congress, the most important dealt with military defense and foreign economic aid, Federal aid to education and social security, the farm program, highways and housing, immigration and labor legislation, public power, industrial health and safety, unemployment compensation, and natural gas regulation.

EXPANSION SINCE 1911

In volume, scope, and complexity the legislative agenda of 1955–56 was obviously a far cry from that of 1790. It was a far cry, too, from the days when Congress struggled with Andrew Jackson over the Bank of the United States and the sale of public lands. It was a far cry even from 1911 when Robert Ramspeck, Democratic whip in the 79th House, came from Georgia to Washington to work in the Capitol Post Office and serve as a congressional secretary. Congress was then in session only 9 months out of 24, and the Members spent the remainder of their terms at home practicing law or attending to their private business. The mail they received then dealt largely with free seed, rural routes, Spanish War pensions, and occasionally a legislative matter. Members had ample time to attend to their congressional duties. "It was a pretty nice job that a Member of Congress had in those days," Representative Ramspeck reminisced when he appeared 34 years later before a joint committee studying the burdens of legislators.

At that time the Government affected the people directly in only a minor way * * *. It was an entirely different job from the job we have to do today. It was primarily a legislative job, as the Constitution intended it to be.

The enormous expansion in the workload of Congress dates back in fact, only to the First World War. A succession of crises in our national life, marked by our participation in two World Wars within a single generation, plus the intervening depression of 1929–33 and the following recovery efforts, imposed vast new responsibilities upon Congress and the administration for the conduct of national and international affairs. Making up as if for lost time, Congress delegated large powers over American economy and society to a score of regulatory commissions, credit corporations, and developmental authorities. Responding to the exigencies of events and the requirements of the times, Congress and the Federal Government took almost all human affairs as their province. So great, indeed, was the gradual expansion of Federal authority and activity from Woodrow Wilson's administration on, that no important field of human interest and endeavor failed to feel its impact.

This past half century has witnessed a striking expansion of public policy into many new fields of activity under the successive impact of Wilsonian and New Deal reforms, two World Wars, and the intervening depression. During the new freedom era an extraordinary series of reforms were enacted into law, including the Underwood tariff, the Clayton Act designed to strengthen antitrust policy, and the Federal child labor laws. Although these measures proved to be short lived or were later diluted or invalidated by the courts, Congress added several important and permanent weapons to the arsenal of Federal control of the economy during the first Wilson administration, including the Federal Reserve Board, the Federal Trade, Power, and Tariff Commissions, and the Federal Farm Loan Board.

World War I saw the creation of numerous emergency wartime agencies in Washington with legislative sanction, such as the War Labor Board which gave Government recognition for the first time to the right of labor organization and collective bargaining, Federal operation of the railroads followed by the Transportation Act of 1920, the activities of the Shipping Board which continued into the postwar period, an industrial mobilization plan of unprecedented scope directed by the War Industries Board, the Food and Fuel Administration, a War Trade Board established to control foreign trade, and the creation of the U.S. Employment Service and the War Finance Corporation to mobilize labor and capital for the war effort.

With the return of peace, most of the emergency wartime machinery was quickly demobilized and a reaction ensued against Government control of economic life. During the decade of the 1920's the political climate of the country was hostile to further experiments in the social control of business, yet this period witnessed the establishment of the Inland Waterways Corporation in 1924 on a permanent basis, creation of the Federal Radio Commission in 1926, and a series of legislative measures designed to help farmers cope with the postwar agricultural depression, including the Packers and Stockyards Act of 1923, the Cooperative Marketing Act of 1926, and the Agricultural Marketing Act of 1929.

With the coming of the Great Depression and the New Deal, Congress collaborated with the Roosevelt administration in a series of novel economic and social experiments designed to promote recovery and conserve natural and human resources. In the agricultural field, steps were taken to increase farm income and expand farm credit facilities. In the labor field, the Walsh-Healey Act and the Fair Labor Standards Act were passed to improve wages and working conditions and the National Labor Relations Board was created to stimulate labor organization. Meanwhile, the range of regulatory authority was widened by the creation of the Securities and Exchange Commission and the Federal Communications Commission, and by expanding the jurisdiction of the Interstate Commerce Commission and the Federal Power Commission. Public enterprise was greatly enlarged in the electrical utility field, in banking and credit, and in the provision of low-cost housing and slum clearance. And Congress approved a broad new program of social security by providing such measures as old-age insurance, unemployment compensation, public assistance, work relief, and long-range public works programs. During the New Deal era, in short, the role of Government in the American economy was vastly enlarged.

During World War II, Congress made many important legislative decisions in major areas of wartime policy. It made decisions respecting the conversion and control over manpower, money, and supplies; labor policy, price control, and monetary policy; military policy and the conduct of the war; foreign policy and postwar commitments; and reconversion to peace after the war. Congress performed three major functions during the war: It made both broad and specific grants of power to the President; it adjusted conflicts of interests; and it supervised the execution of policy. Many difficult decisions were made by the National Legislature on organizing the resources of the Nation and allocating men, money, and materials among competing claimants.[1]

During the postwar period Congress has been called upon to play its essential part in handling many important domestic and international public problems. Passage of the Employment Act of 1946 involved legislative recognition of a new public responsibility for maintaining high production and full employment in the domestic economy. Enactment of the Taft-Hartley Act in 1947 marked a significant reversal of public policy in the labor field and struck a new balance in labor-management relations. Adoption of many of the recommendations of the Hoover Commissions and admission to statehood of Alaska and Hawaii reflected the expanding scope of public activity in the field of Government organization. Passage of the Civil Rights Acts of 1957 and 1960 witnessed the first legislative steps in this field since reconstruction days.

Meanwhile, in the foreign field, Congress and the administration assumed new tasks after the war in organizing and supporting the United Nations, in underwriting the reconstruction of Western Europe by the Marshall plan, in extending aid to Greece and Turkey, in waging the war in Korea, in promoting the fuller development of international trade, in the provisions of the mutual security programs, in the development and control of atomic energy, in the exploration of outer space, and in many other vital areas of international responsibility. In all these and many other areas the developments of the past 50 years at home and abroad have combined with the increasing complexity and technical nature of modern public problems, and with the multiplying interests of constituents in public affairs, to magnify greatly the workload on Congress.

The results of this centripetal, impersonal, and apparently inexorable trend have been seen not only in the astronomical rise of Federal expenditures and debt, in the reduction of once sovereign States to a relatively minor role in American Government and economy, and in the tremendous growth in the power of the President, but also in the mounting burdens upon Congress itself. Still functioning for the most part with the machinery inherited from the simpler days of the 19th century, its calendars and committee schedules became increasingly congested, its councils confused, and its Members bewildered and harassed by multiplying complex problems and local pressures. Under these conditions it was only natural for Congress to place greater reliance upon the President and his well-staffed agencies for guidance and to delegate responsibility for policymaking, economic regulation, and social adjustment to a host of Federal commissions, bureaus, and agencies.

RECENT CHANGES

One of the major objectives of the La Follette-Monroney committee, created in 1945 to study methods of increasing efficiency in the legislative branch, was to reduce the workload on Congress caused by nonlegislative duties and by the consideration of private and local matters. To this end, the joint committee recommended more staff aids for Members and committees, expansion of the bill-drafting and legislative reference services, reduction in committee assignments

---

[1] *Cf.* Roland Young, *Congressional Politics in the Second World War* (1956).

to one or two per Member, delegation of private claims, and home rule for the District of Columbia. Most of these recommendations were embodied in the Legislative Reorganization Act of 1946.

In practice, however, the workload of congressional committees has more than doubled since 1946 in terms of the number of measures referred to and reported by them. The ban upon the introduction of four categories of private bills, imposed by section 131 of the 1946 act, afforded some temporary relief; but has been offset by the rising postwar flood of private immigration bills whose introduction is unrestricted and which crowd the calendars of the Judiciary Committees. During the 84th Congress 1,124 committee reports reached the Private Calendar of the House of Representatives and 893 private bills were enacted into law. Most of these private bills were designed to permit aliens to enter or to remain within the United States, reflecting the efforts of displaced persons to find permanent refuge within our borders.

Despite the effort of the 1946 act to distribute the legislative workload more evenly among the standing committees of Congress, the burden in practice varies within wide limits from committee to committee and from session to session, depending upon the nature of the national and international problems that are paramount at the time. The Appropriations and Foreign Affairs Committees have been among the hardest working because of the importance of their measures and the cold war. The volume of congressional business has inevitably become increasingly onerous in recent decades with the steady expansion of governmental activities at home and abroad. The aim of the streamlining of the committee structure in 1946 was not so much to reduce the workload as it was to effect a more systematic and rational division of labor among the reorganized committees. The reorganization of committee work effected an improvement over the previous situation because it eliminated many duplicating and overlapping jurisdictions and consolidated related functions.

The workload of individual Members of Congress was not lightened by the 1946 act, but more and better staff aids have helped them to keep abreast of it. Administrative assistants to Senators have helped them immeasurably with their departmental business, constituent inquiries, and speechwriting. Enlargement of the Legislative Reference Service has been followed by a great increase in its use by Members. During 1961 the Service handled 84,195 congressional inquiries. The limitation of standing committee assignments to one per member in the House and to two per member in the Senate, with minor exceptions, has been offset in practice by service on subcommittees and on special and joint committees, and appears to have broken down in the House.

Despite these gains, the burden of work imposed today upon the Members and committees of Congress by their legislative and investigative duties and by the importunities of constituents is truly enormous. According to a close observer of the congressional scene, the workload is more than they can handle.

There are now signs that the limits of capacity have been reached * * *. The enormous extension of the activities of the Federal Government generates a volume of detailed and complex business which I believe has gone beyond the capacity of Congress to handle * * *. A law of diminishing returns is actively at work in the field of the Federal Government * * *. The work load is beyond effective legislative control.[2]

Most of the workload of Congress in the 20th century is inescapable, but some of it could be dispensed with. It has been suggested, for example, that the continuing annual flood of private immigration bills could be delegated to the Immigration and Naturalization Service, and that Congress could grant home rule to the District of Columbia and thus get rid of its burden as a city council for the city of Washington. For the fifth time in recent years the Senate passed a District of Columbia home rule bill in 1959, but there has been no House action thus far.

Other proposals designed to expedite the conduct of business include voting by electricity in the House of Representatives, joint hearings by the twin committees of both Houses on the same legislative measures, and the advance planning of the legislative program on a sessional basis with a fixed timetable in the British style. Taken together, these suggested remedies would help considerably to mitigate the rising burden of the congressional business.[3]

---

[2] George H. E. Smith in testimony at hearings on evaluation of the Legislative Reorganization Act before Senate Expenditures Committee, Feb. 18, 1948, p. 172.

[3] *Cf. Activities of the United States Senate:* A Summary and Review of Senate Floor Sessions and Committee Meetings, 84th Cong. Report of the Senate Committee on Government Operations, S. Rept. No. 96, 85th Cong., 1st sess., Feb. 22, 1957.

CHAPTER 9

PARTY GOVERNMENT IN THE HOUSE

Political parties and party leadership found no explicit basis in the American Constitution, but they soon developed as a means both of expressing conflicting sectional and economic interests in the new Republic and of bridging the gap between Congress and the Executive created by the constitutional system of separated branches and shared powers. James Madison with shrewd insight set forth in No. 58 of *The Federalist* the general principle that "in all legislative assemblies, the greater the number composing them may be, the fewer will be the men who will in fact direct their proceedings." And the history of the House of Representatives affords convincing proof of this principle.

PRACTICE IN EARLY CONGRESSES, 1790–1816

Partisanship was noticeably absent from the early deliberations of the First Congress, as we saw in chapter 2. But factional disputes soon dispelled this calm and partisan controversies gave rise behind the legislative scenes to the formation of party groups in the House. The accounts of the time clearly reveal the appearance of an embryonic party organization in the House as early as 1790. Under Alexander Hamilton's masterful leadership the Federalists in Congress were soon holding party caucuses and translating his financial policies into legislation. Later the Jeffersonians, when they came to power in 1801, made similar use of the party caucus and entrusted the conduct of the legislative process to an inner circle of majority leaders. According to Lord Bryce, political parties made their first appearance in Congress in the presidential election of 1796.[1] But Harlow's evidence dates the beginning of party organization in the House back to the First Congress.[2]

During Washington's first administration, James Madison, then a Member of the House, became involved in a struggle with Alexander Hamilton over Treasury domination of Congress. Madison inspired and managed a series of moves against the Treasury forces which led Fisher Ames to write in January 1793:[3]

Virginia moves in a solid column, and the discipline of the party is as severe as the Prussian. Deserters are not spared. Madison is become a desperate party leader, and I am not sure of his stopping at any ordinary point of extremity. We are fighting for the assumption of the balances, which shall be declared due the creditor states. He opposes, *vi et armis*.

[1] James Bryce, *Modern Democracies* (1921), vol. 1, p. 113.
[2] Ralph V. Harlow, *The History of Legislative Methods Before 1825* (1927), pp. 139–145. On Jan. 22, 1941, Representative Clarence Cannon of Missouri, in submitting for the *Record* a partial list of caucus chairmen of both parties, stated that "the caucus had been co-existent with the Congress from its first session; political parties had their origin in the caucus; congressional committees were made up in the caucuses as early as 1797 * * *." *Congressional Record*, 77th Cong., 1st sess., vol. 87, pp. A383–84.
[3] Quoted by Irving Brant in *James Madison, Father of the Constitution* (1950), p. 368.

115

During the Jeffersonian regime (1801-09) the Republicans in Congress followed Federalist precedent and made regular use of the party caucus to determine their attitude on important legislation—

Through the caucus the jarring, discordant elements of the party were reconciled and made to work together, so that concerted policies and harmonious action were no longer the exclusive possessions of the Federalists.[4]

From 1800 to 1824 the most noteworthy caucuses were those that nominated the party candidates for the Presidency.[5] During the Jeffersonian period frequent reference to Republican *caucuses* appeared in the Federalist press—

The Democrats in Congress—

according to an item in the *Washington Federalist*—

are adopting of late quite an economical plan of making laws.—All business is to be settled in *caucuses* before it comes before the House; and the arguments or motives be given in *newspapers* afterwards. The federal members are to be treated as nullities.[6]

It was charged that either Jefferson or Duane (publisher of the Philadelphia *Aurora*) always presided at these meetings. Apparently the first mention of the device on the House floor occurred in 1802 when Representative Bayard referred to the caucus during the debate on the repeal of the act establishing the district courts.[7]

What the Federalists thought of the caucus when it was used by their Republican opponents was reflected in a letter written by Representative Roger Griswold of Connecticut on January 25, 1802:

The Jacobins, finding themselves unable to manage their business on the questions in the House, have adopted the plan of meeting in divan and agreeing on measures to be pursued and passed in the House and then they vote in mass without admitting any alteration in the plan proposed. The wickedness of such a course has never been equalled but by the Jacobin club in Paris; the spirit is intolerant and must lead to ruin.

The way in which the caucus functioned as the "real legislature" was perhaps best described in a speech by Representative Josiah Quincy of Massachusetts in 1809. In speaking of a bill for an extra session he said:

But, sir, with respect to this House, I confess I know not how to express my opinion. To my mind, it is a political non-descript. It acts, and reasons, and votes, and performs all the operations of an animated being, and yet, judging from my own perceptions, I cannot refrain from concluding that all great political questions are settled somewhere else than on this floor.[8]

Some conception of Jefferson's role in developing and controlling his party organization in Congress is afforded by the later observations of Henry Adams in his history of that period.

In ability and in energy—

wrote Adams—

the Executive [Jefferson] overshadowed Congress, where the Republican party, though strong in numbers and discipline, was so weak in leadership, especially among the Northern democrats, that the weakness almost amounted to helplessness * * * the Northern democrats were and always remained, in their organization as a party, better disciplined than their opponents * * * while senators

[4] Harlow, *op. cit.*, p. 184.
[5] In 1828 the State legislatures made these nominations, and in 1832 the present system of national conventions was introduced.
[6] *Washington Federalist*, Feb. 6, 1802. Quoted by Harlow, *op. cit.*, p. 187.
[7] *Annals*, 7th Cong., 1st sess., p. 480.
[8] *Annals*, 10th Cong., 2d sess., p. 1143. Quoted by Harlow, *op. cit.*, p. 189.

had not yet learned their power, representatives were restrained by party discipline * * *.[9]

Madison's first administration was apparently marked by a breakdown of the Jeffersonian system of party organization and strict discipline. But by 1813 Henry Clay and the leaders of the House were in control of the situation; the balance of power had been transferred from the President to Congress; and the party caucus had been revived. Thus, Daniel Webster wrote on June 4, 1813, that all really important business was being carried on outside the House.

In our political capacity we, that is, the House of Representatives, have done little or nothing. The time for us to be put on the stage and moved by the wires, has not yet come. I suppose the "show" is now in preparation, and at the proper time the farce of legislating will be exhibited * * * before any thing is attempted to be done here, it must be arranged elsewhere.[10]

Ten months later Webster's correspondence was reporting the success of Republican party discipline. Writing about the restrictions on commerce in force during the War of 1812, he said that the system had been supported—

because it was attended with a severe and efficacious discipline, by which those who went astray were to be brought to repentance. No Saint in the Calendar ever had a set of followers less at liberty, or less disposed to indulge troublesome inquiry, than some, at least, of those on whom the system depended for support.[11]

Evidence of the effectiveness of Republican party organization in Congress was seen in the enactment during Madison's second term of the bills for the Second Bank and for internal improvements and the tariff of 1816. Party measures were carefully canvassed in caucus before being admitted to the floor of the House where the party edicts were faithfully enforced. Meanwhile, with the establishment of the standing committee system in 1816, the majority party extended its control over these important panels through Speaker Clay who was chosen by the party caucus and who in turn selected the committees.[12]

DEVELOPMENTS DURING 19TH CENTURY

With the development of the committee system in 1816 and thereafter, and with the nomination of presidential candidates by national conventions in 1832 and afterward, the congressional caucus yielded its early preeminence to these new devices. During the period, 1816–60, the standing committee system became the established device for the consideration of congressional business. In 1841 the Rules Committee, which hitherto had lacked special privileges, received authority to report "at all times"; in 1853 its reports were given priority; and in 1858 the Speaker became its chairman. The fragmentary party records of the period show, however, that the party caucus continued to be employed to nominate party candidates for Speaker and other House officers and, occasionally, to shape legislative policy.[13] But party discipline and the power of the caucus were weakened by sectional disputes over the slavery issue as the irrepressible conflict approached.

9 Henry Adams, History of the United States (1889), vol. 1, pp. 264–266.
10 Webster, Private Correspondence, vol. 1, p. 233. Quoted by Harlow, op. cit., p. 203.
11 Annals, 13th Cong., 2d sess., p. 1966, Apr. 6, 1814. Quoted by Harlow, op. cit., p. 204.
12 Harlow, op. cit., pp. 249–251.
13 Clarence Berdahl notes that a Whig House caucus met in 1849 to organize the 31st Cong. "Some Notes on Party Membership in Congress," American Political Science Review, April 1949, p. 311.

The period from 1860 to 1890 was marked by a growing complexity in the economic and social organization of the Nation which was reflected in turn in a more intricate organization of the House. It was a period characterized by intense resistances within Congress both to organizational change and to legislation of any sort. The minority became adept in the utilization of the rules to block the will of the majority, and the end of the period found an extremely decentralized power system prevailing within the House.

The condition of party organization in Congress during the decades after the Civil War was well described by Woodrow Wilson. Writing in 1885, he said:

Outside of Congress the organization of the national parties is exceedingly well-defined and tangible * * * but within Congress it is obscure and intangible. Our parties marshal their adherents with the strictest possible discipline for the purpose of carrying elections, but their discipline is very slack and indefinite in dealing with legislation. At least there is within Congress no *visible*, and therefore no *controllable* party organization. The only bond of cohesion is the caucus, which occasionally whips a party together for cooperative action against the time for casting its vote upon some critical question.

Wilson attributed this condition to the bipartisan composition of the committees.

It is plainly the representation of both parties on the committees—

said he—

that makes party responsibility indistinct and organized party action almost impossible. If the committees were composed entirely of members of the majority * * * committee reports would be taken to represent the views of the party in power" and the leaders of the opposition "could drill their partisans for effective warfare and give shape and meaning to the purposes of the minority. But of course there can be no such definite division of forces so long as the efficient machinery of legislation is in the hands of both parties at once; so long as the parties are mingled and harnessed together in a common organization.[14]

Wilson believed that party government in the United States was complicated by the possibility of party diversity between Congress and the President and that real party government could exist only when Congress possessed complete control of the administration.[15]

During the 48th, 49th, and 50th Congresses (1884–89) the House of Representatives had been reduced to a condition of legislative impotence by abuses of its then existing rules of procedure. Not only was its legislative output small and insignificant, but the use of dilatory motions combined with the disappearing quorum and a series of filibusters to make the House an object of public ridicule and condemnation. For example, during a filibuster against a bill refunding to the States tax collections under the war revenue legislation of 1861, 86 rollcalls were taken, each consuming about half an hour. In January 1889, James B. Weaver of Iowa led a famous filibuster in an effort to compel consideration of a bill organizing the Territory of Oklahoma. The defects of the existing system of congressional procedure were repeatedly demonstrated during these years and evoked widespread public criticism.

For example, on January 19, 1888, the *Washington Post*, in an editorial captioned "Slowly Doing Nothing," observed that the House

---

[14] Woodrow Wilson, *Congressional Government* (1885), pp. 98–100.
[15] *Ibid.*, pp. 267–268.

had passed only four bills, none of them important, in more than 6 weeks, and explained that:

The system of rules is the prime cause of the wonderful inertia of this unwieldy and self-shackled body. * * * In stalling legislation and keeping everybody else from doing anything a few members are all powerful, but when it comes to passing laws little can be done except by what is practically unanimous consent.

In a series of editorials the *New York Tribune* attacked the rules of the House as a system of "Legislative Lunacy" and demanded their amendment as "an absolute and paramount necessity" in order "to permit the majority to control the business for which it is responsible." [16] At the close of the 50th Congress the *Washington Post* denounced the "un-Democratic, un-Republican, and un-American rules of the House of Representatives which have submitted that body to a petty committee of debaters." It was time for a change and "the proper time to establish republican government is at the opening of the next session." [17] The *Post* conducted a nationwide survey of public opinion on the situation, the results of which were extremely critical of the futility, complexity, and wastefulness of House procedure.[18]

Representative Reed of Maine, the minority leader of the House who was destined to be Speaker in the 51st Congress, had observed the parliamentary situation in that body with disgust and indignation. He had repeatedly expressed the view that "the rules of this House are not for the purpose of protecting the rights of the minority, but to promote the orderly conduct of the business of the House," in contrast to the Democratic doctrine, voiced by Representatives Randall and Crisp, that the object of the House rules was to protect the minority's rights from an arbitrary and despotic majority.

To the public discussion of the issue Reed now made two important contributions. In an article on "The Rules of the House of Representatives" in the *Century Magazine* for March 1889, he demanded a check on dilatory motions, a restoration of the "morning hour," and the establishment of majority rule in the House. And in another article on "Obstruction in the National House" in the October issue of the *North American Review*, Reed compared the situation here with that in the House of Commons in 1881 where the Irish obstructionists had forced Speaker Brand to close debate and the Commons to adopt a closure rule in 1882. Reed predicted that an effort would be made at the opening of the 51st Congress—

to establish rules which will facilitate the public business—rules unlike those of the present House, which only delay and frustrate action.

In the September 1889 issue of the same *Review* Henry Cabot Lodge dealt with the same problem. The rules had been so perverted, he said, that—

the American House of Representatives today is a complete travesty upon representative government, upon popular government, and upon government by the majority.

In the coming session drastic changes in the rules would be necessary in order to—

[16] Jan. 7, 11, and 16, 1889, and Feb. 7.
[17] Apr. 8, 1889.
[18] Apr. 22 and May 6, 1889.

change the condition of the House from dead rot to vitality * * *. The people of this country—

continued Mr. Lodge—

are, as it seems to me, thoroughly tired of the stagnation of business and the general inaction of Congress. They are disgusted to see year after year go by and great measures affecting the business and political interests of the country accumulate at the doors of Congress and never reach the stage of action. They have also waked up to the fact that this impotence and stagnation are due to the preposterous fabric known as the rules of the House, and they are prepared to support heartily that party and those leaders who will break down these rules and allow the current of legislation to flow in its natural channel and at its proper rate.[19]

DOMINANCE OF THE SPEAKER

The period, 1890–1910, witnessed an inevitable reaction against the earlier decentralization of power in the House, a reaction that took the form of a tremendous growth in the power of the Speaker of the House. The period began with the elevation of Thomas B. Reed to the speakership in 1889 and ended with a revolt against the concentration of power in that office under Speaker Cannon in 1910.

When the 51st Congress convened on December 2, 1889, Reed was elected Speaker by a margin of 12 votes over Carlisle. The membership of the House then consisted of 170 Republicans and 160 Democrats. On December 3, the rules of the 50th House were referred to the Committee on Rules for consideration and report. Its members were the Speaker, and Representatives McKinley, Cannon, Carlisle, and Randall. For 10 weeks the House operated under general parliamentary law while the Rules Committee drafted a new code which was largely the personal work of Reed himself. On December 19, the Speaker appointed McKinley as chairman of Ways and Means and floor leader, an appointment which proved to be a major steppingstone in McKinley's progress toward the presidency. Reed had defeated McKinley for the Republican nomination for the speakership, but the Ohio member later triumphed over Reed in winning the Republican nomination for the presidency. On December 21, Reed announced the other committee appointments, assigning 25 out of 49 standing committee chairmanships to the North Central States, 15 to the Middle Atlantic States, 7 to New England, 1 to the South, and 1 to the Mountain States.

The opening weeks of the session went quietly, being interrupted by the Christmas recess from December 21 to January 6. But this was only the lull before the expected storm. Several election contests were pending and, in view of the narrow Republican majority, it was anticipated that the election cases would be taken up before the adoption of the rules. Everything depended upon the ability of the leadership to maintain a quorum in a chamber in which the Republicans calculated that they had only 3 more than the quorum of 165. The Democrats caucused on January 24 and the Republicans on the 27th.

Finally the storm broke on January 29, 1890, when the West Virginia election case of Smith versus Jackson was called up and promptly challenged by Mr. Crisp, the Democratic leader. On the ensuing rollcalls the Democrats, though present, declined to vote, thus causing the lack of a voting quorum. Whereupon Speaker

<hr />

[19] For a good account of the situation in the House at this time, see William A. Robinson, *Thomas B. Reed: Parliamentarian* (1930), ch. IX, "Legislative Impotence."

Reed ruled that members present but not voting should be counted as part of the quorum necessary to do business and that a quorum was present within the meaning of the Constitution. This innovation precipitated a great parliamentary battle which continued for 3 days amid scenes of unprecedented turbulence and disorder. The Democrats, led by Carlisle and Crisp, defended the traditional practice of the House, while the Republicans, led by Cannon and McKinley, upheld the Speaker. Reed's ruling was eventually sustained by a straight party vote. During the battle Reed also made his famous ruling that he would deny recognition to members rising to make dilatory motions. Said he:

There is no possible way by which the orderly methods of parliamentary procedure can be used to stop legislation. The object of a parliamentary body is action, and not stoppage of action. Hence, if any member or set of members undertakes to oppose the orderly progress of business, even by the use of the ordinarily recognized parliamentary motions, it is the right of the majority to refuse to have those motions entertained, and to cause the public business to proceed * * *.[20]

Speaker Reed interpreted his victory in the great quorum battle as a verdict in favor of majority rule and party government in the House of Representatives. On February 5, the House Republicans held an extended caucus on the new code of rules that was largely Reed's own handiwork and the next day the "Reed Rules" were reported to the House. The new code revolutionized House procedure by outlawing dilatory motions, which the Speaker was forbidden to entertain, thus setting up safeguards against obstruction; by authorizing a count of Members present in the Hall of the House in determining the presence of a quorum; by reducing the quorum in Committee of the Whole to 100 Members; by authorizing that Committee to close debate on any section or paragraph of a bill under consideration; and by completing revising the order of business. The House debated the new code for 4 days and then adopted it by a vote of 161 to 144, with 23 not voting. Some of the changes were lost in the 52d Congress but were restored in the 53d Congress when the Democrats themselves adopted the new quorum rule.

The net effect of the Reed rules was a great increase in the powers of the Speaker. Reed ruled the House with an iron hand for 6 years.

He established beyond dispute the principle of party responsibility in the lower chamber * * *. As a parliamentary leader he was the greatest ever produced by the Republican party, perhaps by any party in American history.[21]

He created precedents and practices which were continued by Speaker Crisp and later by Speaker Cannon when he assumed the speakership in 1903. Reed's own view of the effect of the reforms of 1890 was summed up in this statement to his own constituents: [22]

Party responsibility has begun, and with it also the responsibility of the people, for they can no longer elect a Democratic House and hope the minority will neutralize their action or a Republican House without being sure that it will keep its pledges.

If we have broken the precedents of a hundred years, we have set the precedents of another hundred years nobler than the last, wherein the people, with full knowledge that their servants can act, will choose those who will worthily carry out their will.

[20] *Ibid.*, p. 215.
[21] *Ibid.*, pp. 388, 389.
[22] *Ibid.*, pp. 233-234.

The period 1890–1910 was characterized by the mastery of the Speaker as majority party leader of the House, operating under the Reed rules. Although the party caucus continued to perform its traditional functions, it was largely replaced by the party hierarchy, i.e., by the Speaker and an inner circle of his trusted lieutenants. In 1883 the Rules Committee was given authority to originate special rules and in 1893 it was allowed to meet at any time. This gave the committee, of which the Speaker was chairman, by far the largest role at the time in the control of the House. After a decade of experience with the new system, Woodrow Wilson described its operation in 1900 as follows: [23]

The power of the Speaker has of late years taken on new phases. He is now, more than ever, expected to guide and control the whole course of business in the House—if not alone, at any rate through the instrumentality of the small Committee on Rules, of which he is chairman. That committee is expected not only to reformulate and revise from time to time the permanent rules of the House, but also to look closely to the course of its business from day to day, make its programme, and virtually control its use of its time. The committee consists of five members; but the Speaker and the two other members of the committee who represent the majority in the House determine its action; and its action is allowed to govern the House. It in effect regulates the precedence of measures. Whenever occasion requires, it determines what shall, and what shall not, be undertaken. It is like a steering ministry—without a ministry's public responsibility, and without a ministry's right to speak for both houses. It is a private piece of party machinery within the single chamber for which it acts. The Speaker himself—not as a member of the Committee on Rules, but by the exercise of his right to "recognize" on the floor—undertakes to determine very absolutely what bills individual members shall be allowed to bring to a vote, out of the regular order fixed by the rules or arranged by the Committee on Rules.

This obviously creates, in germ at least, a recognized and sufficiently concentrated leadership within the House. The country is beginning to know that the Speaker and the Committee on Rules must be held responsible in all ordinary seasons for the success or failure of the session, so far as the House is concerned. The congressional caucus has fallen a little into the background. It is not often necessary to call it together, except when the majority is impatient or recalcitrant under the guidance of the Committee on Rules * * *.

When Speaker Cannon succeeded to the scepter in 1903, he continued and expanded the Reed techniques until by 1909 the power of the Speaker had been extended to a quasi-dictatorship. He had the power to appoint the committees of the House and to designate their chairmen. He had the unlimited power to grant or withhold recognition of Members who might rise to move the consideration of bills. And as chairman of the Rules Committee he could largely determine what business the House should consider. These powers in combination were so far reaching that—

the speaker came to be considered as an officer second only in power and influence to the President of the United States himself, and so far as the enactment of legislation was concerned to exercise powers superior to his.[24]

Such was the situation in the House on the eve of the insurrection of 1909 and the revolution of 1910. Signs of insurgency had appeared, but Speaker Cannon used his great powers to penalize the rebels. For the most part these penalties consisted in unattractive committee assignments and failure to recognize the offending members. As his private secretary and biographer later wrote:

Mr. Cannon * * * believed that parties were necessary in the American form of government; that power must be entrusted to the party having the support of

[23] Woodrow Wilson, *Congressional Government* (1900 edition), pp. ix–xi.
[24] W. F. Willoughby, *Principles of Legislative Organization and Administration* (1934), p. 540.

the majority of the voters of the country, and that without parties a democratic form of government cannot exist. He had an utter contempt for the so-called Independent * * * who refused to submit to party discipline and considered his conscience a safer guide than the judgment of his associates.[25]

KING CAUCUS SUPERSEDES CZAR CANNON

The revolution of March 1910 that dethroned Speaker Cannon has been described elsewhere.[26] It terminated the Speaker's 20-year reign and achieved a certain dispersion of leadership, although by and large sufficient concentration of power remained to insure a measure of party responsibility. The underlying causes of Cannon's overthrow must be sought partly in the background of progressivism under Theodore Roosevelt and partly in the inevitable swing of the pendulum away from too much centralization of power. Cannon's leadership had grown more and more arbitrary, and the contrast between the democratic mood of the Nation and his conduct as Speaker had become too pronounced to be ignored.

The major change effected was in the power of the Speaker himself. No longer was he to be a member of the Rules Committee. A new Rules Committee, composed of 10 members instead of 5, was elected by the House, the chairman to be chosen from this number by the committee members themselves. In actual practice this meant selection by party caucus; and within the party caucuses by a committee on committees of the Republicans and by the Democratic members of the Ways and Means Committee serving for that party.

During the decade, 1910–20, the party caucus functioned as the keystone in the arch of party government in the House of Representatives. Long used to choose caucus officers and to nominate party candidates for the speakership and other House offices, the caucus during this period was also employed to consider matters of legislative policy and to define the legislative program for the session. Thus, on April 1, 1911, the Democratic *Caucus Journal* noted this resolution offered by Mr. Underwood, the floor leader:

Resolved, That the Democratic members of the various committees of the house are directed not to report to the house during the first session of the 62d Congress, unless hereafter directed by this caucus, any legislation except with reference to the following matters.[27]

Two years earlier, in the 61st Congress, the House Democratic caucus had agreed to support the Republican insurgents in their drive to reform the House rules, to discipline those Democrats who had accepted committee assignments from Speaker Cannon without the approval of Champ Clark, the minority leader, and had adopted a set of caucus rules—

or scheme of government for the Democratic party in the House, intended to define more clearly the rights and obligations of Democratic party membership, prevent such breaches of discipline as had just occurred, and thus promote unified and harmonious party action.

This marked the beginning, says Berdahl, of the more formal party organization in Congress.[28]

25 L. White Busbey, *Uncle Joe Cannon* (1927), p. xviii.
26 See ch. 5, pp. 50–52.
27 Wilder H. Haines, "The Congressional Caucus of Today," *American Political Science Review*, November 1915, p. 697n.
28 Berdahl, *loc. cit.*, p. 725n.

Although the Democrats were in control of the House for 8 years during this period—62d to 65th Congresses, inclusive—the Republicans also utilized the party caucus to consider questions of organization, party loyalty, and legislative program. Thus, on January 14, 1910, a White House statement was issued in which an agreement was foreshadowed—

that caucuses should be held from time to time, to which all elected as Republicans should be invited, to take up the various measures recommended by the Administration as performances of party pledges, the subject of each caucus to be announced in advance.

This statement was confirmed by the leaders of both the regular and progressive factions, Representative Dwight, the Republican whip, giving positive assurance that the regular Republicans were prepared to go into caucus upon any proposition and abide by the result.[29] Both factions attended a party caucus on March 23 at which the GOP's six representatives on the new Rules Committee were selected.

After capturing control of the House in the congressional elections of 1910, the Democrats promptly erected on the ruins of Cannonism a new political structure based on the secret caucus. In a caucus held on January 19, 1911, they decided that Champ Clark should be Speaker, that Oscar Underwood should be floor leader and chairman of Ways and Means, that the Democratic members of that committee should organize the House by naming its committees, that the selection of Republican committee members should be left to the determination of the minority party, that the Democratic caucus should not be open, and that their caucus should determine the attitude and legislative action of the majority.[30]

DEMOCRATIC CAUCUS RULES

During the reign of King Caucus, the scope of caucus action was reflected in the preamble to the Democratic caucus rules, as follows: [31]

a. In essentials of Democratic principles and doctrine, unity.
b. In non-essentials, and in all things not involving fidelity to party principles, entire individual independence.
c. Party alignment only upon matters of party faith or party policy.
d. Friendly conference, and whenever reasonably possible, party cooperation.

As adopted in 1909, there were 11 House Democratic caucus rules: [32]

1. All Democratic Members of the House of Representatives shall be prima facie members of the Democratic Caucus.
2. Any member of the Democratic Caucus of the House of Representatives failing to abide by the rules governing the same shall thereby automatically cease to be a member of the Caucus.
3. Meetings of the Democratic Caucus may be called by the Chairman upon his own motion and shall be called by him whenever requested in writing by 25 members [33] of the Caucus or at the request of the Party Leader.
4. A quorum of the Caucus shall consist of a majority of the Democratic Members of the House.

[29] *Ibid.*, p. 317.
[30] Hasbrouck states that the House Republicans gave up the binding caucus after the Cannon regime. but returned to it before the 69th Cong. *Party Government in the House of Representatives* (1927), pp. 31-32.
[31] Hasbrouck, *op. cit.*, p. 34.
[32] The House Republicans have not adopted caucus rules, but have used the rules of the House itself wherever applicable.
[33] Later increased to 50.

5. General parliamentary law, with such special rules as may be adopted, shall govern the meetings of the Caucus.

6. In the election of officers and in the nomination of candidates for office in the House, a majority of those present and voting shall bind the membership of the Caucus.

7. In deciding upon action in the House involving party policy or principle, a two-thirds vote of those present and voting at a Caucus meeting shall bind all members of the Caucus: *Provided*, The said two-thirds vote is a majority of the full Democratic membership of the House: *And provided further*, That no member shall be bound upon questions involving a construction of the Constitution of the United States or upon which he made contrary pledges to his constituents prior to his election or received contrary instructions by resolutions or platform from his nominating authority.

8. Whenever any member of the Caucus shall determine, by reason of either of the exceptions provided for in the above paragraph, not to be bound by the action of the Caucus on those questions, it shall be his duty, if present, so to advise the Caucus before the adjournment of the meeting, or if not present at the meeting, to promptly notify the Democratic leader in writing, so that the party may be advised before the matter comes to issue upon the floor of the House.

9. That the five-minute rule that governs the House of Representatives shall govern debate in the Democratic Caucus, unless suspended by a vote of the Caucus.

10. No persons, except Democratic Members of the House of Representatives, a Caucus Journal Clerk, and other necessary employees, shall be admitted to the meetings of the Caucus.

11. The Caucus shall keep a journal of its proceedings, which shall be published after each meeting, and the yeas and nays on any question shall, at the desire of one-fifth of those present, be entered on the journal.

These rules indicate that Members were bound to follow the party line only in those comparatively few cases where the caucus had declared a matter to be a party measure and had decided by a two-thirds vote of those present to bind the membership upon it, provided such two-thirds vote represented a majority of the entire party membership in the Chamber. On all other matters the individual Member was left entirely free to vote as he pleased. Moreover, even on party measures, Members were allowed freedom of action in cases "involving a construction of the Constitution" or where they had made "contrary pledges to their constituents" prior to their election or when they had received contrary instructions from their constituencies.

OPERATION OF THE CAUCUS SYSTEM [34]

During the Wilson administration a strong system of party government was erected in the House of Representatives. Set up in place of "Cannonism," this system was modeled upon "Aldrichism" in the Senate and was based on the party caucus. The essence of the new system was direct control of legislative action by the caucus itself. This control was effected by the caucus rules quoted above and by binding resolutions through which a majority of two-thirds of those voting at the caucus bound the Democrats in the House (except for rule 7), and hence the action of the House itself. For example, on April 11, 1911, the Democratic caucus adopted a resolution by Mr. Underwood, as follows: [35]

Be it resolved, by the Democratic caucus that we endorse the bills presented by the ways and means committee * * * and pledge ourselves to support said bills in the house * * * with our votes, and to vote against all amendments,

[34] For a detailed description of party organization in the House during the period, 1913–36, see *Cannon's Precedents in the House of Representatives*, vol. 8, ch. 278.

[35] Wilder H. Haines, *op. cit.*, p. 698n.

except formal committee amendments, to said bills and motions to recommit, changing their text from the language agreed upon in this caucus.

Another instrument of caucus control of legislative action was through the standing committees whose Democratic members were chosen by the majority members of Ways and Means, subject to caucus approval. The caucus often controlled the committees by forbidding reports on other than specified subjects, or by other than specified committees, without its express consent; by issuing instructions to the Rules Committee as to the terms of special rules under which bills could be taken up in the House; and even by developing legislation in the caucus itself and bringing it to the floor after formal committee reference.

Under the new regime the majority floor leader, Oscar Underwood, also emerged as a powerful figure. He derived his personal ascendancy from his control of majority committee assignments as chairman of Ways and Means, his chairmanship of the steering committee, and from his right to be recognized at any time on the House floor. He could use this right of recognition to determine the conduct of business in the House, subject to the right of the three privileged committees: Ways and Means, Appropriations, and Rules to report at any time.

In addition to the party caucus and the floor leader, the Rules Committee was a major factor in the new system of party government during the period under review. Under Cannonism this committee had been a "sleeping giant." But after Cannon was dethroned and the majority floor leader succeeded to the scepter, Rules became an active power. Only by the laborious discharge petition procedure could the House force the Rules Committee to act upon any subject over which it had jurisdiction. By the exercise of its powers Rules could function as a steering committee, steering the House in whatever direction the exigencies of the hour seemed to demand.

A contemporary observer of the caucus during this period concluded a description of its organization and operation by remarking that [36]—

* * * the tendency of democratic government seems to be toward a system of party-responsibility; the party program is formulated by the national convention and transformed into legislative form by the congressional caucus; the party is collectively responsible. The legislative instrument of the party is represented in its most highly developed form by the Democratic caucus of the 62d and 63d congresses, the operation of which is based on two principles: strict party-unity on questions of essential party-policy; individual liberty in nonessentials.

This observer felt that the caucus had certain defects which could be remedied by the adoption of reforms in the House itself. And he concluded that—

* * * once the rotten foundations of the caucus—patronage, perquisites, and "pork"—are destroyed, or, rather replaced; the sinister, throttling domination of the caucus will largely disappear of itself, and the institution may be left free to develop as a legitimate instrument of majority control and party-responsibility on the open floor of the house.

By way of summary, it can be seen that during its heyday in the House the party caucus performed the following functions. First, it chose the officers of the caucus: a chairman and a secretary. Then it

---

[36] *Ibid.*, p. 706. The reforms in the House advocated by Wilder Haines included reconstruction of the House rules so as to require the Rules Committee to report within a certain time any proposed amendment to the rules which might be referred to it; reform of the committee system by abolishing dead committees and letting the committees select their own chairmen; self-government for the District of Columbia; voting by electricity; reduction in the size of the House; and the election of Representatives in groups from a few large districts in each State, in place of election by single districts. *Ibid.*, pp. 702–703.

nominated the party's candidates for Speaker and other elective House officers. It selected its floor leader and its Committee on Committees and approved their slate of committee assignments. It considered proposed amendments of the House rules and, occasionally, questions of legislative policy. It elected the party campaign committee and considered matters of Capitol patronage. It was also used by the leadership to test the temper of the House, to "gauge the relative strength of different opinions." [37]   In performing these functions the democratic caucus did not run itself. It was controlled by its own majority which was dominated in turn by the floor leader (Underwood), backed by his power over committee appointments. When necessary the power of the floor leader was reinforced by the other two members of the caucus cabinet: the Speaker (Clark), with the prestige of his position, and the chairman of the Appropriations Committee (Fitzgerald), with his hands upon the purse strings.

Woodrow Wilson credited the Democrats with the invention of this device in early days and gave this perceptive description of its functions.[38]

The caucus is meant as an antidote to the Committees. It is designed to supply the cohesive principle which the multiplicity and mutual independence of the Committees so powerfully tend to destroy. Having no Prime Minister to confer with about the policy of the government, as they see members of parliament doing, our congressmen confer with each other in caucus. Rather than imprudently expose to the world the differences of opinion threatened or developed among its members, each party hastens to remove disrupting debate from the floor of Congress, where the speakers might too hastily commit themselves to insubordination, to quiet conferences behind closed doors, where frightened scruples may be reassured and every disagreement healed with a salve of compromise or subdued with the whip of political expediency. The caucus is the drilling-ground of the party. There its discipline is renewed and strengthened, its uniformity of step and gesture regained. The voting and speaking in the House are generally merely the movements of a sort of dress parade, for which the exercises of the caucus are designed to prepare. It is easy to see how difficult it would be for the party to keep its head amidst the confused cross-movements of the Committees without thus now and again pulling itself together in caucus, where it can ask itself its own mind and pledge itself anew to eternal agreement * * * the silvern speech spent in caucus secures the golden silence maintained on the floor of Congress, making each party rich in concord and happy in cooperation.

DEVELOPMENTS DURING 1920'S

As regards party organization in the House of Representatives, the last 40 years have been characterized by certain long-run tendencies and have witnessed several significant developments. Between the two World Wars the party caucus disintegrated, party discipline declined, and party government was replaced by loose coalitions of voting blocs with shifting leadership. Attempts to bind the party membership to vote for measures designed to carry out platform pledges were rarely made by House Democrats and never by the Republicans. These trends reflected the growing diversity of interests in a pluralistic society, the emergence of deeply divisive political issues such as civil rights, isolationism versus internationalism, and the extent of the "welfare state," the force of localism in American politics, and the decentralized, compromise character of our national parties constructed, as they are, of loose alliances of strong State and local parties.

37 M. I. Ostrogorski, *Democracy and the Party System* (1926), p. 288.
38 Woodrow Wilson, *Congressional Government*, pp. 326-328.

The decade of the 1920's was marked by the diffusion of leadership in the House among a numerous group of men. The inner circle came to include the Speaker, the floor leader, the chairmen of Rules, Appropriations, and Ways and Means, the chairman and secretary of the party caucus, and the members of the steering committee and the Committee on Committees which were enlarged. This tendency toward the dilution of leadership was reflected in a ruling of the Republican caucus in 1919 that no chairman of a major House committee should sit on their steering committee, and in a Republican caucus rule of 1925 that no chairman of a House committee should also serve on the Rules Committee. The development in the same period of "exclusive" committees, whose members were limited to one committee assignment, a practice approved by both party caucuses, illustrated the same trend.[39] On the other hand, the removal of the floor leaders from service on the standing committees of the House helped to strengthen leadership by relieving them from other distractions and giving them time to function as leaders.

Several other developments during the 1920's also affected the distribution of political power in the House. A series of rulings by the Speaker, overruling points of order raised against specific resolutions reported by the Rules Committee, served to clarify the scope of its powers and to expand its jurisdiction. In 1920 the Chair ruled that although the—

Committee on Rules is not permitted to do anything which directly dispenses with Calendar Wednesday or the motion to recommit * * * it can bring in a general rule * * * which indirectly produces that result as a minor part of its operation.[40]

In the same year Speaker Gillett ruled that "the Committee on Rules may report a resolution providing for the consideration of a bill which has not yet been introduced." [41] Another ruling in 1922 held that the Committee on Rules could originate a resolution for the consideration of a bill regardless of whether the subject matter had been referred to it by the House, "because the Committee on Rules is the executive organ of the majority of the House." [42] And in 1933 Speaker Rainey held that the Rules Committee could report a resolution authorizing consideration of a bill on which suspension of the rules had been denied by the House.[43]

Abuses of the powers of this committee led to the adoption of two restrictions in the rules revision of 1924. One provision sought to protect the House from "snap" tactics by providing that the Rules Committee could not call up a report on the same day on which it was presented, except by a two-thirds vote of the House, unless during the last 3 days of a session. The other restriction was designed to prevent the chairman of Rules from defeating the will of his committee by the "pocket veto" method. In the early twenties Chairman Campbell had abused his discretion by pocketing several resolutions which his committee had authorized him to report several weeks before. When Mr. Campbell took this means to suppress an investigation of contracts by the Departments of Justice, War, and Navy in 1922, there were loud complaints, to which Mr. Campbell replied:

[39] Hasbrouck, *op. cit.*, pp. 92–94.
[40] *Cannon's Precedents of the House of Representatives*, vol. VIII, sec. 2667.
[41] *Ibid.*, sec. 3388.
[42] *Ibid.*, sec. 3389.
[43] *Ibid.*, sec. 3392.

"Even though every Member wants this investigation, what will that avail you? I have the resolution in my pocket and shall keep it there." And to the Committee on Rules his language was even stronger. "You can go to * * *;" he said, "it makes no difference what a majority of you decide; if it meets with my disapproval, it shall not be done; I am the committee; in me reposes absolute obstructive powers." [44] Campbell's right to bury the resolution in his pocket was upheld by the Speaker and, on appeal, by the House. As a result of these and other instances of the exercise of autocratic power by the chairman of Rules, the House amended its rules in 1924 by adding the following paragraph: [45]

The Committee on Rules shall present to the House reports concerning rules, joint rules, and order of business, within three legislative days of the time when ordered reported by the committee. If such rule of order is not considered immediately, it shall be referred to the calendar and, if not called up by the Member making the report within nine days thereafter, any Member designated by the committee may call it up for consideration.

As later amended, this rule now provides that if the rule is not called up by the Member making the report within 7 legislative days—

any member of the Rules Committee may call it up as a question of privilege and the Speaker shall recognize any member of the Rules Committee seeking recognition for that purpose. [46]

Dissatisfaction with the Rules Committee during the 1920's also led to a noteworthy amendment of the discharge rule in January 1924. The question was whether access to the House floor should be completely controlled by the majority party leadership or whether a bipartisan coalition could override the leadership and get its bills considered, i.e., whether a majority of the House could work its will. As amended on January 18, 1924, the discharge rule, first adopted in 1910, was changed in several respects of which the most important concerned the number of signatures required on discharge petitions. Mr. Crisp of Georgia favored 100 signatures as sufficient to bring a discharge motion before the House; Mr. Fish of New York favored a majority of the whole House, or 218. The number was fixed at 150 in 1924. The discharge rule of 1924 was another step in the long struggle to strike a balance between centralized leadership and majority rule in the House of Representatives. [47]

In the midtwenties the organization of the Republican Party in Congress was complicated by the defection of the Wisconsin Progressives, as it had been a decade before by the Theodore Roosevelt Progressives. In the Senate, on the eve of the convening of the 68th Congress, six progressive Senators, who held the balance of power in a closely divided body, stayed away from the Republican caucus on December 1, 1923, and conducted a month's fight for the presidency pro tem of the Senate and for the chairmanship of the Committee on Interstate Commerce. After 31 ballots they succeeded in defeating Cummins, the caucus nominee for the committee post, who had been a Progressive 10 years before, and in electing to that office a Democrat, "Cotton Ed" Smith of South Carolina. In the House a progressive bloc of some 60 Members held their own caucus on November 30, 1923,

---

[44] Floyd M. Riddick, *The U.S. Congress: Organization and Procedure* (1949), p. 123.
[45] House Rule XI. clause 22.
[46] This paragraph was amended Dec. 8, 1931, Jan. 3, 1949, and Jan. 3. 1951.
[47] For a searching discussion of this and related questions, the writer is indebted to an unpublished doctoral dissertation at Harvard University by Lewis J. Lapham entitled *Party Leadership and the House Committee on Rules,* April 1953.

and then launched a fight against Mr. Gillett of Massachusetts, the regular caucus nominee for Speaker, putting up Mr. Cooper of Wisconsin as their own candidate for that office. Cooper received 17 votes on the first eight ballots, but Gillett won on the ninth ballot, after an agreement was reached to amend the discharge rule.[48]

In 1925, Mr. Longworth of Ohio, the Republican floor leader who was elected Speaker at the opening of the 69th Congress, raised the question of the party status of some 13 Republican insurgents who had supported LaFollette for President in 1924. The bolters should be disciplined, he thought, for deserting the Republican Party in the presidential election. Ten of the insurgents were from Wisconsin and their leaders, Representatives Frear and Nelson, were ousted from their seats on the Ways and Means Committee and the Rules Committee, respectively, before the new House met in December 1925. Discipline of the other insurgents would depend, Longworth indicated, upon how they voted on the speakership and on restoring the strict discharge rule. When the insurgents failed to satisfy these acid tests of sound republicanism, holding instead their own caucus and voting again for Cooper for Speaker and against the discharge rule, they were excluded from the Republican party caucuses and demoted on their committees to the bottom of the list. Later on, however, on the eve of the organization of the 70th Congress, the insurgents were restored to their party councils.[49]

When Nicholas Longworth became Speaker of the House in 1925, he affirmed his faith in the principles of party responsibility and set forth his conception of the role of the Chair as party leader.

I believe it to be the duty of the Speaker—

he said on assuming his new office—

standing squarely on the platform of his party, to assist in so far as he properly can the enactment of legislation in accordance with the declared principles and policies of his party and by the same token to resist the enactment of legislation in violation thereof.[50]

In some quarters these remarks evoked shades of Cannonism; in others they elicited praise as promising a return to effective party leadership.

EVALUATIONS BY CONTEMPORARY OBSERVERS

During this period a few close observers of the congressional scene offered their evaluations of the dramatic transition from "Czar" Cannon to "King" Caucus and subsequent developments. George R. Brown, who had watched these great events from the House press gallery, deplored the overthrow of Cannonism. It was, he said—

the most tremendous political reaction in the whole history of the American experiment in government, which produced the annihilation of the speakership of the House of Representatives, the second most powerful office in the government.

According to Brown's interpretation—

the ethical impulses which brought about the downfall of the structure of party government in the House of Representatives originated in the country, among the people, and not in the House, nor in Washington. The House itself slowly responded to a demand for reform in general, which finally centered upon the

48 Berdahl, loc. cit., pp. 320–321.
49 Ibid., pp. 497–503.
50 Hasbrouck, op. cit., p. 23.

speakership in particular as the seat of the power in Congress against which the public will, or rather a minority will, had set itself.[51]

In his recollections of these events, written after serving 8 years in the Speaker's chair, Champ Clark took a different view: [52]

It must, in ordinary justice, be written down here that Mr. Speaker Cannon, throughout that bitter contest, bore himself with the utmost dignity and decorum, never appearing to better advantage in his life. * * *.

Neither Underwood nor myself entertained the least ill-will toward Mr. Cannon. We were and are his personal friends. We were not fighting him. We were fighting a system which he had inherited and which was improperly called "Cannonism." We honestly deemed it a bad system, and we destroyed it forever * * *.

In 1909 and 1910, when we made our spectacular fight to overthrow the Cannon system and liberalize the rules, with few exceptions the great metropolitan papers were against us. They criticized, abused, and poked fun at us. They denounced us as a lot of cheap-John demagogues and pestilent disturbers of the Congressional peace. Day in and day out they declared that we were seeking the unattainable and could not accomplish our purpose. When, in spite of their malicious and idiotic chatter, we achieved our great victory, they savagely asserted that we could not keep order, maintain decorum, and transact the public business, and that chaos would come again. All of these wild and preposterous predictions and assertions have been contradicted by the event—by the splendid, the unequaled, record of the House during the last eight years.

Writing in 1922, Robert Luce, scholar in Congress, remarked: [53]

The reformers believed they had put an end to dictatorship. Yet that some few men continued to guide is not to be questioned. What was really accomplished was to lessen the public knowledge of who those men were. Congressmen might know, but since 1910 the public generally has not known who should be rewarded or punished. Irresponsibility has been increased. Perhaps the party caucus has had more chance to commend or scold the men who pull the strings. Perhaps a potential insurgent has had more opportunity to air his views. The Committee on Rules is no longer the organ of the Speaker. But the benefits of the change have not been conspicuous enough to impress anybody as important.

Four years later Representative Luce submitted this additional explanation: [54]

* * * the most striking difference between the old and the new methods is that, whereas leadership was then in the open, it is now under cover. Then the Speaker was the recognized center of authority. Now nobody knows who in the last resort decides. There is a Committee on Rules, the chairman of which evidently has much influence. Behind this is a steering committee of the majority party. which is supposed to advise. And each party has a floor leader who guides in matters of technical detail, though as a matter of fact most of the floor work is handled by committee chairmen as the measures in their charge come along for action. It might be said that nowadays the leadership of the House is in commission, with the membership of the commission more or less fluctuating and shadowy.

* * * Should there be a revival of partisanship in the country at large, with clear-cut issues once more dividing people and Congress into bitterly hostile camps, the present system is not likely to meet the needs of a turbulent House by securing in the majority party the control of its processes and the effective handling of the situation. The division of responsibility between a two-party Rules Committee and a one-party Steering Committee is reasonably sure to make trouble sooner or later. And the same is true of the like division between the Speaker and the floor leader * * * the masterful, dominant leadership of some one man may yet be required.

Probably in such a contingency the party caucus will again amount to something. For a decade it has been of no consequence on the Republican side, rarely meeting and never importantly affecting the action of the House. Results of caucus action have been more evident on the Democratic side, but, at any

[51] George R. Brown, The Leadership of Congress (1922), p. 138.
[52] Champ Clark, My Quarter Century of American Politics (1920), vol. 2, pp. 279, 281–282.
[53] Robert Luce, Legislative Procedure (1922), p. 483.
[54] Luce, Congress: An Explanation (1926), pp. 117–119.

rate in the last six years, have had no serious influence either on House action or on party fortunes. As things stand now, the caucus need not be taken into account when seeking the causes of congressional inefficiency or the sources of congressional achievement.

Hasbrouck concluded his searching study of party government in the House of Representatives during 1909–27 in the belief that the discipline of party control, rather than liberty of individual action, produces a better parliamentary body.

The valid means of enjoining unity in the name of party is action by the caucus, when a proportion greater than a bare majority of party members concur. Such activity of the caucus is a wholesome means of interpreting the campaign platform. The preponderance of agreement necessary * * * to make decisions of the caucus binding upon partisans would in effect narrow the party program to a single policy, or to a few distinctively party principles * * *. Upon measures not endorsed by the caucus, the basis of action must be individual judgment, tempered by instructions from constituents * * *. The aggregate of business on the calendars * * * is so great that deference to party leaders best promotes the everyday activities of the House * * *.[55]

Action in Congress on most legislative proposals is nonpartisan or bipartisan, and the influence of party is also minimized when the two chambers are controlled by different political parties. Allegiance to party is considered closer to the public interest than allegiance to special-interest blocs. Hasbrouck felt that—

party allegiance should grow in meaning, and have more binding force than it does at present * * * [but] that only questions of major importance [should] be advanced as party measures.

The only remedy for the leader's power of suppression was a workable discharge rule, which was rendered necessary, he thought, by the nature of our form of congressional government.[56]

Shortly thereafter Dr. W. F. Willoughby, eminent political scientist of the Brookings Institution, completed a monumental study of Congress by expressing his opinion that the changes effected by the revolution of 1910–11 had resulted in a regrettable weakening of the system of party government in the House of Representatives. Dr. Willoughby, who regarded the binding caucus as an essential feature of party government in the United States, concluded that—

the diffusion of responsibilities that took place [in 1910] * * * in the opinion of the writer was a mistake. The primary objections to the old system were, not so much the centralization of powers in the hands of one agency, as that this agency should be a single individual, the person holding the position of presiding officer. Both of these objections could have been overcome by vesting all of the speaker's powers, other than those of presiding officer, in a single collegiate body, instead of distributing them among a number of agencies.

Such a body, he suggested, might have been either an enlarged Committee on Rules with the duty of selecting the chairmen and members of all the other committees, or a new caucus committee combining the functions of the Committee on Committees and the Steering Committee and chaired by the floor leader.

Under either of these systems—

said Willoughby—

responsibility for party action would have been transferred from the chair to the floor, and from one individual to a collection of individuals, while at the same time all the advantages inhering in a centralization of responsibilities would have been retained. As it is now these advantages are, if not lost, at least greatly attenu-

55 Hasbrouck, op. cit., pp. 236–238.
56 Ibid., pp. 195–198.

ated. Under it, not only is effective leadership made more difficult, but the general public is frequently at a loss to determine where real responsibility for action taken, lies.[57]

After examining the operation of the caucus system during Wilson's administration, Willoughby reached this further conclusion:[58]

While political parties have been definitely accepted as an essential feature of our political system, while the electorate in exercising its function divides strictly along party lines; and while full expression is given to the principle of party responsibility, insofar as the administrative branch of the government is concerned, practice stops short at the point at which the principles of party government are of the most vital importance; that, namely, where legislative policies are determined and put into effect. It may be that there are other ways in which party government may be achieved, but no such other way has, as yet, been brought forward. If party government is deemed to be a desirable feature of our governmental system, and most of our students of politics believe that it is, progress toward its achievement must thus be sought in the definite acceptance and strengthening of the caucus system.

DEVELOPMENT DURING 1930'S

Several developments during the decade of the 1930's bearing upon party government in the House of Representatives are worth noting.

The first of these in point of time was the adoption of the "lame duck" amendment to the Constitution. Ratified in 1933 when the 36th State approved it, the 20th amendment eliminated the short session of Congress which ended automatically on March 4. The House leadership had long liked the short session because it facilitated their control of business and helped them to prevent the consideration or passage of bills they opposed. The amending resolution had passed the Senate three times during the 1920's and had been pigeonholed in the House Rules Committee each time. Finally, the spur of public opinion forced the amendment to the House floor where Representative Snell, chairman of Rules, remarked that:[59]

If it had not been for the significant application of these two words, lame duck, the propaganda that has been spread throughout this country would never have been one-half as effective as it has been, and if it had not been for that propaganda I doubt whether this proposition would be on the floor at this time.

And Representative Kvale observed:[60]

We have waited * * * for eight long years for a chance to vote on this resolution * * * the leadership of the House has denied us the opportunity to express our opinion and our vote on the subject * * *. Three men, the Speaker of the House and the majority floor leader and the chairman of the Committee on Rules * * * have prevented this House from having a chance to vote on this proposition all these years * * * [but] they did not dare block it any longer.

The ratification of the "lame duck" amendment in January 1933, was regarded as a victory over the House leadership by those Members who were seeking to democratize control of the Chamber.

A second development came in March 1933, when the House Democrats set up a steering committee and assigned it the responsibility of watching legislative developments and making day-to-day decisions on party policy and action. This committee was composed of the Speaker, floor leader, chairman of the caucus, party whip, the chairmen of Ways and Means, Appropriations, and Rules, and one Representative from each of the 15 zones into which the country was divided

---

[57] W. F. Willoughby, op. cit., pp. 554-555.
[58] Ibid., pp. 575-576.
[59] 70th Cong., 1st sess., H. Doc. No. 331, Fixing Presidential and Congressional Terms: Proceedings and Debate, p. 43.
[60] Ibid., p. 42. Quoted by Lapham, op. cit., pp. 46-47.

for party purposes, each such Representative being elected by the Democratic delegation in the House from the zone. The committee elected its own chairman, vice chairman, and secretary and cooperated with the party leaders in the planning and execution of party policy. Although this steering committee occasionally played an influential role in the early days of the New Deal, as when it induced the party to adopt the bill to guarantee bank deposits in 1934, it later fell into disuse and disappeared from the political scene.

The role of the Rules Committee as agent of the majority party during the first Roosevelt administration is also noteworthy. During this period that committee used its broad powers to facilitate the achievement of the desires of the Democratic leadership in the House and the enactment of the administration's legislative program. Thus, in the 73d Congress (1933–34) almost all the economic recovery measures of the New Deal reached the House floor under closed rules restricting debate and amendments. Mr. Bankhead of Alabama justified this procedure, stating that "the Committee on Rules is the political and policy vehicle of the House of Representatives to effectuate the party program and the party policy."

Many of the most crucial tests of party loyalty took place on the votes to accept or reject the special rules reported by the Committee on Rules for the consideration of the legislative measures of the administration. Closed rules were used 10 times during the 1st session and twice during the 2d session of the 73d Congress. The House leadership justified their use on grounds of the emergency conditions of the times, the necessity of protecting the coherence of complex bills from confusing amendments, and the requirements of party control over the legislative program. All but one of the closed rules proposed during the 73d Congress were accepted by the House. This record led Lewis Lapham to conclude that—

In the 73d Congress it appears to be a valid conclusion that a sympathetic and cooperative Rules Committee was an instrument by which the leadership of the House exercised a measure of control over the proceedings of the House and the content of legislative measures * * *. The Rules Committee in the 73d Congress operated very definitely as an arm of the leadership and the House generally approved that kind of working relationship.[61]

During the 74th Congress the Rules Committee played a less active role in the management of the business of the House, reporting only three closed rules during 1935–36, all of which were approved. The role of the Rules Committee in 1935 was explained to the House by its chairman, Representative O'Connor, as follows: [62]

To some of you new members I might state in advance that the Rules Committee is an arm of the leadership of this House. It is sometimes called an "arm" of the administration in power in the Nation. Some people have also referred to it as the "political committee", or the committee which shapes or brings before the House the policies of the leadership of the House and the administration.

It is interesting to note that the Rules Committee was then regarded as the agent of both the House majority leadership and the administration. Doubtless it was with a view to strengthening party responsibility, as well as to protecting Members from the pressures of organized interest groups, that the discharge rule was again amended in 1935 by increasing the number of signatures required on discharge petitions from 145 to 218.

[61] Lapham, op. cit., pp. 66–67.
[62] Congressional Record, 74th Cong., 1st sess., p. 13. Quoted by Lapham, op. cit., p. 76.

COALITION CONTROL, 1937-46

During the decade 1937–46 party government in the House of Representatives was seriously impaired by changes that occurred in the composition and tactics of the Committee on Rules. Instead of acting in the traditional manner as the responsible agent of the majority party and its leadership, the Rules Committee came under the control of a bipartisan coalition of southern Democrats and north-central Republicans who used its power to block measures favored by the majority party and the administration. After the 74th Congress this coalition controlled well over half the seats on the Rules Committee, as the table shows:

Party composition of Rules Committee

Congress	Republicans	Southern Democrats	Northern Democrats	Total
75th	4	5	5	14
76th	4	5	5	14
77th	4	1 6	4	14
78th	5	1 6	3	14
79th	4	4	2 4	12

1 Includes 1 from Oklahoma.
2 Includes 1 from Kentucky and 1 from Missouri.

During this period the Rules Committee repeatedly framed rules designed to facilitate its own views of public policy rather than those of the House leadership and the Roosevelt administration by including special provisions in its resolutions granting a "green light" for bills to the floor of the House. The coalition in control of the committee also repeatedly used its powers to obstruct and dilute important measures in the majority party program. Thus, as the decade advanced, this powerful committee became an instrument, not of the majority party and its legislative program, but of a bipartisan majority in the House. Upon occasion, remarked a close student of its activities, members of the Rules Committee "asserted a power independent of any party and almost without responsibility to any political institution." [63]

Domestic labor and public welfare legislation designed to implement Democratic platform planks, such as the wage and hour bill, were pigeonholed in the Rules Committee. Chairman Sabath could not control his own committee whose turbulent meetings witnessed recurring battles between the veteran chairman from Illinois and Representative Cox of Georgia, ranking Democratic member and leader of the coalition. Only the influence of Speaker Rayburn was able to restrain the conflicts between these men.

During the 76th Congress the Rules Committee opposed the majority leadership not by denying major bills access to the House floor, but by making their admission depend upon its own terms which were often distasteful to the leadership. During the early war years (1941–42) the split in the Democratic Party in Congress was partly smoothed over as the Legislature concentrated on defense and war legislation, while the Rules Committee for the most part cooperated with the desires of the majority party leadership and the President.

63 Lapham, *op. cit.*, p. 88.

During the 78th Congress, however, when the party division in the House was very close, the bipartisan coalition frequently succeeded in controlling the fate of legislation. And much of the success of the coalition was attributed to its ability to adapt the rules of the House to its own advantage through its control of the Committee on Rules.[64] After citing several examples of rules granted during the 78th Congress that were deemed objectionable to the Democratic majority, Lapham concludes that—

in each case the majority leadership and the administration could not look to the Rules Committee for action which would assist them in the promotion of the Democratic program or in avoiding outright defeat by coalition forces.[65]

During the 79th Congress the coalition consolidated its control of the legislative process in the House. Lapham summed up the situation when the first session convened.[66]

It is clear that by 1945 the Rules Committee was exercising an increasingly influential role in the development of legislative policy on many of the domestic issues before Congress. Furthermore, this power was exercised in many cases independent of the organized leadership and frequently in opposition to its efforts. The instances in which the Committee facilitated the exercise of responsibility by the leadership or refrained from obstructing it had become almost a matter for comment.

By this time it had become a custom for the committee to examine the substance of bills reported by the legislative committees of the House and to use its powers to force them to amend their bills as the price of getting a "green light" to the House floor. In one instance a rule was reported that would have made it in order to consider a price control bill which had been rejected by the Banking and Currency Committee and had never been reported to the House. This time the House evidently felt that the Rules Committee had gone too far, for it rejected the rule after Speaker Rayburn took the floor and attacked the proposed rule. The Speaker asserted that the Committee on Rules "was never set up to be a legislative committee." If the issue were settled right, he said, there would be "an end to the trespassing of one committee in the House upon the rights, prerogatives, and privileges of other committees."[67]

In another notable instance, after the Senate had passed the full employment bill of 1946, the House Rules Committee granted a rule allowing the weaker House bill to be substituted for the Senate bill. This and other episodes led Lapham to conclude that—

the Rules Committee was simply not at the service of the majority party to assist it in enacting into law the kinds of programs to which it was committed as a party.[68]

While the Committee on Rules failed to function during the decade under review as the responsible instrument of majority party government in the House of Representatives, nevertheless it apparently did faithfully reflect majority sentiment in the House. The rules it granted or denied were calculated to facilitate the expression of the will of a bipartisan majority in the House, which may or may not have reflected majority sentiment in the country, while obstructing adoption of the program of the majority party. The experience of

---

[64] Ibid., p. 124.
[65] Ibid., pp. 130–131.
[66] Ibid., p. 136.
[67] Congressional Record, June 7, 1944, p. 5471. Quoted by Roland Young, Congressional Politics in the Second World War (1956), p. 116.
[68] Lapham, op. cit., p. 151. See also Stephen K. Bailey, Congress Makes a Law (1950), pp. 174–177.

these eventful years raises the fundamental question: Should the Committee on Rules function as the agent of the majority party in the House so as to enable that party to carry out its platform pledges to the American people or should it function as the instrument of a bipartisan coalition which can control a majority of the votes in the House? This question goes to the roots of our two-party system of government.

It is interesting to recall that during the 76th Congress the Democratic Party in the House of Representatives held two party caucuses to deal with the problem presented by coalition control of legislative action. At the first meeting, held on February 14, 1939, the Democratic leaders, including Speaker Bankhead, Floor Leader Rayburn, and Mr. McCormack of Massachusetts, chairman of the caucus, treated the problem as one of absenteeism rather than as a split in the party, urged Members to cooperate with the administration, and threatened, if necessary, "to crack the whip to compel Democratic Members to attend the sessions." When these efforts failed, a second caucus was held on July 28, 1939, at which a resolution was adopted which in effect censured the dissident Democrats who had failed to support the New Deal program and pledged the party in the House to continued support of the Roosevelt program.[69]

The reappearance of coalitions in Congress after the Second World War led observers to comment upon "the looseness of party lines" and the "rather meaningless pattern of our so-called two-party system" and to speculate about the need for a political realinement.

Until the major parties are realigned—

wrote Arthur Krock—

and two parties are formed in each of which there is a common set of political views and principles, these occasional combinations will appear in the House, as they also have in the Senate.   There is both oil and water in the bottle that bears the label "Democrats," and attempts to mix them will be less and less successful as the catalyst of war disappears.[70]

Prof. Clarence A. Berdahl of the University of Illinois, a lifelong student of American politics, completed a 1949 study of party membership in Congress by expressing his belief that the solution of the problem of party government would be found in—

the development of a more genuine and meaningful party system, with fairly precise criteria of party membership, with more closely knit party organizations in Congress, with the House and Senate parties more closely tied together and both closely related to the respective national party organizations, with a keener sense of responsibility as a party, and with a better system of party discipline to keep members mindful of the party position on legislative problems and of their obligations as members of a responsible party group.[71]

LATER DEVELOPMENTS

A few significant developments of later years deserve mention before this chapter is concluded. First was the recommendation for the creation of party policy committees in both Houses, made in the 1946 report of the Joint Committee on the Organization of Congress.

Strong recommendations were made to your committee—

69 Berdahl, loc. cit., pp. 730–731.
70 Arthur Krock in New York Times, Mar. 12, 1946, p. 24, ch. 5. Quoted by Berdahl, loc. cit., p. 732.
71 Berdahl, loc. cit., p. 733.

said the report—

concerning the need for the formal expression within the Congress of the main policies of the majority and minority parties. These representations called for some mechanism which could bring about more party accountability for policies and pledges announced and made in the national platforms of the major political parties.

After referring with approval to the helpful role of party government and party caucuses in Congress, the report continued: [72]

Your committee recognizes the need for freedom of action on the part of the individual Member of Congress and his right to vote at any time against the announced policy of his party. But we feel that if party accountability for policies and pledges is to be achieved, stronger and more formal mechanisms are necessary. The present steering committees, an informal and little-used device, seldom meet and never steer.

We recommend that these be replaced with the formal establishment in the House and the Senate of majority and minority policy committees. The majority policy committees of the two Houses would meet jointly at frequent intervals, as would those of the minority, to formulate the overall legislative policy of the two parties. The majority policy committee of each House would also hold frequent meetings to consider its role in expediting consideration and passage of matters pledged to the people by their party * * *.

We feel that, in the establishment of such policy committees, the Congress chosen at the last general election should be controlling and that the policy committee membership should therefore be chosen at the beginning of each new Congress. Membership on all policy committees would automatically expire at the close of each Congress.

The Senate accepted this proposal and set up its own policy committees which were charged with "the formulation of overall legislative policy of the respective parties" and were equipped with staffs "to assist in study, analysis, and research on problems involved in policy determinations." [73] The proposal was not accepted, however, on the House side.

In January 1949 the Republican Party in the House converted its steering committee, which had been in existence since the 66th Congress, into a policy committee. The House Republican Policy Committee now has 27 members, consisting of the minority floor leader, the whip, the chairman, vice chairman, and secretary of the Republican Conference, the chairman of the Republican Policy Committee, the chairman of the Republican Congressional Campaign Committee, the chairman or ranking minority member of the Rules Committee, the 2 former minority floor leaders, a representative of the last 2 Congressional Clubs,* 8 members elected biennially from regional districts and 7 members at large who are appointed by the minority floor leader.

Under the organizational arrangement in existence between 1959 and 1965, no provisions were made for membership of the conference vice chairman; there were only 3 members at large who were recommended by the Republican Committee on Committees; all 5 of the minority members of the Rules Committee were included; the past 5 Congressional Clubs were represented on the basis of the same formula which applied to the regions; former minority leaders were not included; there were 9 geographic regions represented rather than 8,

---

[72] S. Rept. No. 1011, 79th Cong., 2d sess., pp. 12-13.
[73] See Hugh A. Bone, "An Introduction to the Senate Policy Committees," *American Political Science Review*, June 1956, pp. 339-359. See also George B. Galloway, *The Legislative Process in Congress* (1953), pp. 335-337.
*Congressional Clubs are composed of newly elected Members to each Congress. For example, newly elected Members to the 85th Congress comprise the "85th Club," etc.

each region electing 1 representative for each 20 members or fraction thereof; and the geographic areas of the regions were differently alined.

In December of 1964 a committee was appointed by the Republican Conference to study the organizational structure of the Policy Committee and to report its recommendations to a later conference meeting. Representative Albert H. Quie, of Minnesota, was appointed chairman of this group.

On February 23, 1965, the Quie committee recommendations, with certain amendments offered from the floor, were adopted by the Republican Conference as the resolution establishing the Policy Committee for the 89th Congress. Under this Quie resolution, ex officio and nonvoting memberships were eliminated, and provision was made for the appointment of a Committee on Organizational Structure at the first conference held after each general election to submit recommendations for reapportionment of the geographic regions to the conference.

The number of elected members of the Republican Policy Committee may change from time to time, depending upon the number of Republicans elected to Congress from the various regions.

The Policy Committee is an active branch of the House Republican leadership and meets regularly each Tuesday afternoon while Congress is in session. In the 86th, 87th, and 88th Congresses Representative John W. Byrnes, of Wisconsin, served as chairman. Prior to that time, the minority floor leader (or when the Republicans were in the majority, the Speaker) served as chairman of the Steering Committee and then as chairman of the Policy Committee after it was established in 1949. On February 23, 1965, the conference elected Representative John J. Rhodes, of Arizona, as chairman for the 89th Congress.

At the beginning of the 87th Congress the Policy Committee set up two subcommittees. One was the Special Projects Subcommittee, which was charged with the responsibility of preparing long-range studies of important issues under the chairmanship of Representative John J. Rhodes, of Arizona. The other was the Subcommittee on Minority Employees, which was given the responsibility of supervising the work of the minority employees, with Representative Gerald R. Ford, of Michigan, as chairman.

In 1965 the functions of these two subcommittees were transferred to the newly created Conference Committees on Minority Personnel and on Planning and Research.

The resolution establishing the Policy Committee for the 89th Congress provides:

"The Republican Policy Committee shall be an advisory committee to the Republican membership of this House on day-to-day policy decisions, and as such will meet prior to any important action on the floor, and shall discuss these issues with members of the appropriate regular and special committees, and with such other Republican Members as the chairman may invite to the meetings, and shall report its suggestions for Republican action and policy to the House Members."

The Policy Committee shall be composed of:

"I. One member from each of eight regions apportioned by the conference as equally as possible. At the first meeting of the conference after each general election, the chairman of the conference shall appoint a Committee on Organizational Structure to make reapportionment suggestions in the form of a proposed resolution to the conference. The Republican Members of Congress from the States of each region shall meet in caucus and shall select from their number, by secret ballot, after nomination, a member of the Policy Committee and shall report their selection to the chairman of the conference."

1. West coast region (total, 18), Representative Charles Teague:

Alaska	0	Nevada	0
California	15	Oregon	1
Hawaii	0	Washington	2

(Ranking Republican of this region: Mr. Lipscomb.)

2. Western region (total, 18), Representative Page Belcher:

Arizona	1	Montana	1
Arkansas	0	Nebraska	2
Colorado	0	New Mexico	0
Idaho	1	North Dakota	1
Oklahoma	1	South Dakota	2
Iowa	1	Texas	0
Kansas	5	Utah	1
Louisiana	0	Wyoming	0
Missouri	2		

(Ranking Republican of this region: Mr. Gross.)

3. North central region (total, 16), Representative Albert Quie:

Michigan	7	Wisconsin	5
Minnesota	4		

(Ranking Republican of this region: Mr. O'Konski.)

4. Southern region (total, 17), Representative James Broyhill:

Alabama	5	North Carolina	2
Florida	2	South Carolina	1
Georgia	1	Tennessee	3
Mississippi	1	Virginia	2

(Ranking Republican of this region: Mr. Jonas.)

5. West central region (total, 16), Representative Ralph Harvey:

Illinois	11	Indiana	5

(Ranking Republican of this region: Mr. Arends.)

6. East central region (total, 16), Representative William Harsha:

Kentucky	1	West Virginia	1
Ohio	14		

(Ranking Republican of this area: Mr. Brown.)

7. Mid-Atlantic region (total, 18), Representative Paul Dague:

Delaware	0	New Jersey	4
Maryland	2	Pennsylvania	12

(Ranking Republican of this region: Mr. Corbett.)

8. New England region (total, 22), Representative John Lindsay:

Connecticut	0	New York	14
Maine	1	Rhode Island	0
Massachusetts	5	Vermont	1
New Hampshire	1		

(Ranking Republican of this region: Mr. Joseph W. Martin.)

"2. One member from each of the two latest congressional clubs. The Republican members of each club shall meet in caucus and shall select from their number, by secret ballot, after nomination, a member of the Policy Committee and shall report their selection to the chairman of the conference."

  88th Club:
      Representative Charlotte Reid for first session
      Representative Del Clawson for second session
  89th Club: Representative James Martin

"3. The minority floor leader, the whip, the chairman, vice chairman, and secretary of the Republican Conference, the chairman of the Republican Policy Committee, the chairman of the Republican Congressional Campaign Committee, the chairman or ranking minority member of the Rules Committee, and former minority leaders."

Mr. Gerald Ford, minority leader
Mr. Leslie Arends, minority whip
Mr. Melvin Laird, chairman of the conference
Mr. William Cramer, vice chairman of the conference
Mr. Richard Poff, secretary of the conference
Mr. John Rhodes, chairman of the Republican Policy Committee
Mr. Robert Wilson, chairman of the Republican Congressional Campaign Committee
Mr. Clarence Brown, ranking Republican, House Rules Committee
Mr. Joseph Martin, former minority leader
Mr. Charles Halleck, former minority leader

"4. And a maximum of seven members at large selected by the floor leader to give balance and provide membership from each major committee.

Mr. John Byrnes
Mr. Charles Goodell
Mr. Robert Griffin
Mr. Peter Frelinghuysen

Mr. John Kunkel
Mr. Thomas Pelly
Mr. William Springer

The traditions and privileges of seniority shall not apply to membership on the Republican Policy Committee.

During the 80th Congress (1947–48) the Committee on Rules returned to its traditional role as agent of the majority party, this time the Republican Party which was back in power in the House after 16 years in the wilderness. In sharp contrast to its conduct during the preceding decade, the committee now cooperated with the party leaders to promote the majority party program and to translate its campaign pledges into legislative action. Just as the Democrats in the 73d Congress had relied on closed rules to avoid internal dissension and expedite passage of their measures, so now in the 80th Congress the Republicans did likewise. The Rules Committee reported nine closed rules during the biennium, five in the first session and four in the second. It also made frequent use of the rule waiving points of order on appropriation bills in order to clear the way for the elimination of "wasteful" governmental bureaus and functions. The committee also long tabled rules for the consideration of bills for American membership in the World Health Organization and for selective service, only releasing the WHO bill upon the receipt of a directive so to do from the Republican steering committee and only then after securing restrictive amendments as its price for clearance. The Rules Committee also successfully pigeonholed the UMT bill and the O'Mahoney-Kefauver bill prohibiting the purchase of assets of competitors. After reviewing its performance during the 80th Congress, Dr. Lapham concluded that—[74]

Although the Rules Committee took a lot of abuse during the 80th Congress, the record is pretty clear that the House leadership, including the Speaker, Majority leader, Majority whip, and the Republican Steering Committee, could get a bill out of the Rules Committee if it wanted to badly enough, although occasionally some face-saving was necessary in the form of amendments * * *.

The most exciting development of recent years in this field was the fight that led to the adoption of the so-called 21-day rule in 1949 and to its repeal in 1951. The highlights of this struggle have been described in another chapter.[75] It will be recalled that under this rule,

[74] Lapham, op. cit., p. 183.
[75] See ch. 5, pp. 57–58.

which was adopted by the House on January 3, 1949, the chairman of a legislative committee reporting a bill and requesting a special rule for its consideration could request recognition for the purpose of calling it up if it had been adversely reported by the Rules Committee or if that committee had failed to report the rule for 21 calendar days after reference.   It was in order to call up such special resolutions on the second and fourth Mondays of each month and it was provided that the Speaker "shall recognize the Member seeking recognition for the purpose * * *."   In practice, however, if more than one chairman sought recognition under the rule, the Speaker could exercise discretion as to whom he would recognize.

The 21-day rule, which was in effect during the 81st Congress, was thrice the subject of bitter debate in the House: First at the time of its adoption in 1949, second when an effort to repeal it failed on January 20, 1950, and third when it was repealed on January 3, 1951. The first debate indicated that the new rule was not designed by its framers to strengthen party government in the House, but was conceived rather as a device to deal with a specific situation, that is, the alleged "dictatorship of the Rules Committee."   The second debate, in 1950, was more closely addressed to the problem of majority party responsibility for management of the business of the House and control of the legislative program than the 1949 debate had been.   And a few of the debaters in 1951 considered the effects of the 21-day rule on the exercise of responsible leadership in the House.   But the rationale of responsible party government in Congress and the proper role of the several party agencies in the House of Representatives were never fully spelled out in these debates.

All told, some eight measures reached the House floor and were passed during the 81st Congress by invoking the 21-day rule, while the threat of its use forced the Rules Committee to grant clearance to a few other bills.   But no major measures in the majority party program were actually taken up under this procedure.   Several reasons were advanced for such limited use of the new device: the prestige of the Rules Committee based on a long tradition, fear of retaliation if it were thwarted, the feeling that the new rule should be reserved for use in emergencies, the disinclination of the leadership to develop its potentialities, their desire that certain bills should not be called up, and the availability of other routes to the floor, for example, via suspension of the rules and Calendar Wednesday.[76]

Insofar as the Rules Committee is concerned, the situation following the repeal of the 21-day rule in 1951 reverted substantially to what it had been prior to the adoption of the rule in 1949.   In both foreign and domestic affairs the majority party official leadership and some committee chairmen were often at odds with the majority members of the Rules Committee, except during the first Eisenhower Congress, with the result that a bipartisan coalition on the committee continued to exercise a strong influence on legislation.   Meanwhile, party

76 Lapham, op. cit., pp. 235-237.

leadership in Congress and in the country at large has been the subject of lively public discussion and debate during the past decade.[77]

At the opening of the 86th Congress in January 1959, a group of Democratic liberals in the House contemplated a move to curb the Rules Committee by changing its party ratio and by reviving the 21-day rule. After a conference with the Speaker, however, the liberals called off their drive and issued a joint statement saying:

We have received assurances from Speaker Rayburn that legislation which has been duly considered and reported by legislative committees will be brought before the House for consideration within a reasonable period of time. Our confidence in the Speaker is great, and we believe he will support such procedural steps as may become necessary to obtain House consideration of reported bills from legislative committees.

Despite these assurances, the Rules Committee in 1959 and again in 1960 was criticized for keeping legislation from the House floor. Eventually, however, most of the major bills reported by House committees during the 86th Congress reached the floor of the House either by action of the Rules Committee or by the rarely used Calendar Wednesday route.[78]

As the 87th Congress approached, it became evident that enactment of President Kennedy's legislative program would hinge upon overcoming the conservative coalition's control of the Rules Committee. All signs indicated that a determined effort would be made, when the House met in January 1961, either to curb the powers of the committee or to change its composition so as to enable the House to work its will on such Kennedy measures as medical aid to the aged under social security, a minimum-wage increase, Federal aid to education, and a housing bill. Liberal and conservative forces in Congress and the country girded their loins for the impending test of strength.

On one side was the Democratic study group composed of a hundred or more liberal Democrats led by Representative Chet Holifield of California and Representative Frank Thompson of New Jersey. On the other side was Representative Howard W. Smith of Virginia, powerful chairman of the Rules Committee, the Republican leaders of the House, and many influential southern Democratic Congressmen. Speaker Rayburn kept his own counsel until the eve of the session when he came out on the side of the reformers with a plan to enlarge the membership of the Rules Committee from 12 to 15. His plan called for increasing the number of committee Democrats from 8 to 10, and of Republicans from 4 to 5, thus giving the liberal leadership a close 8 to 7 control of the committee.

---

[77] See a report of the Committee on Political Parties of the American Political Science Association entitled: *Toward a More Responsible Two-Party System*, September 1950, especially pp. 56-65. See also: Stephen K. Bailey, *The Condition of Our National Political Parties* (1959); Clarence A. Berdahl, *Our Two-Party System* (1951); Hugh A. Bone, *Party Committees and National Politics* (1958); James MacGregor Burns, "Two-Party Stalemate: The Crisis in our Politics," *Atlantic Monthly*, February 1960; *ibid.*, "Memo to the Next President," *Atlantic Monthly*, April 1960; Paul T. David, Ralph M. Goldman, and Richard C. Bain, *The Politics of National Party Conventions*, ch. 16 (1960); William Goodman, "How Much Political Party Centralization Do We Want?", *Journal of Politics*, November 1951; Ivan Hinderaker, *Party Politics* (1956); Norton E. Long, "Party Government and the United States," *Journal of Politics*, May 1951; Fritz M. Marx, "Party Responsibility and Legislative Program," *Columbia Law Review*, March 1950; Sigmund Neumann, *Modern Political Parties* (1956); Austin-Ranney, *The Doctrine of Responsible Party Government* (1954); Ranney and Kendall, *Democracy and the American Party System* (1956); Murray S. Stedman, Jr. and Herbert Southoff, "Party Responsibility—A Critical Inquiry," *Western Political Quarterly*, September 1951; Frank Thompson, "The Republican-Southern Democratic Coalition in the House from 1937 to 1959," *Congressional Record*, daily edition, Jan. 27, 1960, pp. 1305-1307; David B. Truman, *The Congressional Party* (1959); Julius Turner, "Responsible Parties: A Dissent from the Floor," *American Political Science Review*, March 1951; U.S. Congress, *Congressional Record*, four memoranda by Legislative Reference Service, Sept. 20-21, 1960, pp. A7088-A7098, A7198, A7199.

[78] For a lucid description of "The Role of the Rules Committee in Arranging the Program of the U.S. House of Representatives" during the 80th-85th Cong., inclusive, see James A. Robinson, *Western Political Quarterly*, September 1959, pp. 653-669.

The issue hung fire for several weeks while the leadership of both parties, the Kennedy administration, and lobby groups brought intense pressures to bear on House Members. Finally, on January 31, 4 weeks after Congress convened, the House approved the Rayburn plan by the close and crucial vote of 217 to 212. Voting for expansion were 195 Democrats and 22 Republicans; against it were 64 Democrats and 148 Republicans. Southern Democrats divided 63 against and 47 for the resolution. Speaker Rayburn rejected last-minute efforts at compromise. Taking the House floor in one of his rare appearances, he said the issue was simple: The Nation had elected a new President who had programs he considered vital to the country's welfare and the whole House should have an opportunity to vote on them. The split in the Democratic vote on enlarging the Rules Committee presumably indicates why the Democratic caucus could not be effective in recent years, especially when dissident members held most of the committee chairmanships.

Subsequently, Representative Carl Elliott, of Alabama, and Representative B. F. Sisk, of California, were appointed to fill the two new Democratic seats on the Rules Committee; while the Republicans named Representatives Katharine St. George, of New York, Elmer J. Hoffman, of Illinois, and H. Allen Smith, of California, to fill their two vacancies and one new place on the committee. After Representative Carroll Reece, second-ranking minority member of the Rules Committee, died on March 9, 1961, he was replaced by Representative William H. Avery, of Kansas.

Behind the scenes a key role in the recapture by Speaker Rayburn of the House Rules Committee was played by one of its Democratic members—Richard Bolling, of Missouri. As described by a close observer, Representative Bolling—

is an occupational, professional anticipator of difficulties; a smoother-out of ruffled feelings; an estimator of the human weaknesses and strengths of other Democrats; a worker of small and sometimes large miracles * * *." [79]

In the 1961 struggle over control of the Rules Committee, he was—

a kind of unsung field commander in a great war between the generalissimos, Mr. Sam and old "Judge" Howard Smith, of Virginia * * *.

An authentic liberal concerned with truly national affairs, a moderate with a long record of responsible performance, Richard Bolling may be destined for a larger role in the leadership of the House.

Another noteworthy development of the past decade has been the activity of the Republican conference of the House of Representatives. Since the beginning of the Eisenhower administration this conference has held more than 40 meetings for the discussion of matters of mutual interest with party leaders, the policy committee, and other Members. The conference promotes a frank exchange of ideas and serves a very useful purpose. Representative Charles B. Hoeven, of Iowa, has been its chairman since 1957. Meanwhile, the Democratic caucus of the House has met infrequently for other than organization matters. It was used during 1949–51 in the struggles over the 21-day rule and has met occasionally on the nomination of Democratic members of the Committee on Ways and Means. But there have been no caucuses of House Democrats on purely legislative matters since 1950.

---

[79] William S. White, "The Invisible Gentleman from Kansas City," *Harper's* magazine, May 1961, p. 84.

In conclusion, mention may be made of the congressional campaign committees. These groups are not agents of party government in the House and have no disciplinary or policy-making functions; they are essentially service agencies that render financial and other forms of assistance to Congressmen regardless of their party regularity. They date from 1866 when the Democratic Members of both Houses, who were supporting President Andrew Johnson against the attempt to impeach him, appointed a committee to manage the campaign of that year. The committee continued as a joint group through succeeding campaigns until the mid-term election of 1882 when separate campaign committees were set up in the House and Senate. Today both the Democratic and the Republican congressional campaign committees are autonomous groups that have no organic connection with the national committees or conventions and are primarily concerned with electing party members and maintaining party majorities in the House. Both committees maintain offices in Washington, employ a permanent secretariat, and are supported by voluntary contributions.

The congressional campaign committees are each composed of one Member of the House from each State having party representation in the Chamber. They are chosen at the opening of each Congress by their respective State delegations. Each committee elects a chairman, several vice chairmen, a secretary, a treasurer, and other officers; and carries on its activities through standing subcommittees. Thus, the Democratic congressional committee has four standing subcommittees: Executive, finance, research, and speakers. According to the *Democratic Manual*—

the Committee does not participate in primary campaigns for the party nomination but supports the officially chosen Democratic candidate for election to the House by supplying reports on issues and candidates, campaign literature, party speakers, and routine campaign facilities.[80]

As described by Hugh Bone, the congressional campaign committee is—

a device for catering to certain of the congressman's needs in campaigning, in his constituent relations, and in his work at the Capitol * * *. The lawmaker can be an isolationist or an internationalist, for or against the Bricker Amendment, for or against rigid farm price supports; but as long as he wears the party label, asks for help (and presumably needs it), and has an outside chance of election he will be served * * *. As far as these committees are concerned, party platform and program are clearly subordinate to organization.[81]

[80] *Democratic Manual for the Democratic National Convention of 1960*, by Clarence Cannon, p. 12.
[81] For a full and informative account of the congressional campaign committees, see Hugh A. Bone, *Party Committees and National Politics* (1958), ch. 5, "The Capitol Hill Committees."

CHAPTER 10

PERFORMANCE OF THE LEGISLATIVE FUNCTION

Knowledge of the various steps in the enactment of a law is part of the stock in trade of experienced Members of Congress. But the nature of the legislative process is more or less of a mystery to the general public.

Let us suppose that a matter comes to congressional attention with the suggestion that it would be desirable to pass a law relating to it. There are at least a dozen steps that might be taken to translate a legislative proposal into a statute. Let us list these steps first and then try to explain each one in some detail.[1]

1. Research and factfinding.
2. Drafting the bill.
3. Getting sponsors.
4. Timing its introduction.
5. Planning the campaign.
6. Organizing group support.
7. Propaganda and pressure.
8. Staging committee hearings.
9. Getting the bill to the floor.
10. Floor debate and passage.
11. Getting the President's approval.
12. Implementation of the statute.

RESEARCH AND FACTFINDING

Considerable research is ordinarily required in order to determine, first, that some governmental action is desirable; second, that there is no legislation already on the statute books which covers the situation; third, that the problem could not be better handled by appropriate administrative action or at the State or local level or by resort to the judicial process.

When it appears that no suitable legislation exists and that the problem calls for congressional action, despite all the risks and disadvantages involved in this procedure, then the next step will be to collect and comprehend the principal facts relating to the problem so that the author may be sure that the legislative proposal has merit. For law is subsequent to the facts, as Woodrow Wilson once remarked, and the facts are precedent to all remedies. In gathering the facts the interested Congressman may call upon his own staff and/or committee staff and the experts in the administrative agencies concerned and in the Legislative Reference Service of the Library of Congress, as well as those who are acquainted with the matter at firsthand in the community or the industry involved. He may also call upon

---

[1] A vivid and profusely illustrated description of most of these stages may be found in Bertram M. Gross, *The Legislative Struggle* (1953), *passim.* This chapter is based both upon my own observations and on this excellent book by Mr. Gross.

146

representatives of the State or local governments for their comments and recommendations regarding the proposal.

Of course, he is not under the illusion that legislation is, or can be made, a strictly scientific business or that facts alone can solve our political and economic problems. But he appreciates that it is essential to obtain the basic facts with respect to an important problem so as to establish an area of agreement from which to proceed to consider their meaning for policymaking.

DRAFTING THE BILL

Then, with all the relevant facts at hand, the next step is that of drafting a bill which, in appropriate legal terms, will carry out the intended purpose of the law. For this purpose the Congressman may call upon the Office of Legislative Counsel, a group of skilled lawyers who are experts in the art of bill drafting. This Office has a branch on the House side and another branch on the Senate side. First established in 1918, it has today a combined staff of some 30 lawyers and law clerks whose services are of the highest quality.

The Chief Legislative Counsel of the House will send one or more members of his staff to the Member's office to confer with him about the form and substance of his bill. Depending upon the scope and complexity of the proposal, they will have a series of conferences. The Congressman will tell the draftsmen what he is driving at, what objectives he has in view, what problem he would solve by legislative action. The draftsmen will incorporate his ideas into appropriate legal language, but they will not advocate any particular policy.

The drafting of a major measure is a complicated and time-consuming process that requires decisions regarding the distribution of costs and benefits, the assignment of functions to Federal agencies, the creation or reorganization of governmental machinery, relationships with private organizations, judicial review and congressional oversight, administrative discretion, and the delegation of power. The form of a bill also raises important questions for author and draftsmen.

GETTING SPONSORS

The steps enumerated thus far may, in the case of comprehensive legislation, consume weeks or even months, before the Member is satisfied that he has come up with a proposal suitable for the purpose at hand. Sometimes, of course, there are occasions where the facts are clear from the start, where the remedy needed is a simple one that may be accomplished with the passage of a short, concise bill.

In any event, once the bill is drafted, the next step is the choice of sponsors. The rules of the Senate permit multiple sponsorship of bills which has the advantage of mobilizing mass bipartisan support. In the House of Representatives, however, multiple sponsorship is forbidden by the rules which provide that the name of only one sponsor can appear on a bill. This rule is evaded, however, by the introduction of identical bills by several Members.

In order to improve the prospects of his bill, the Member will try to get identical measures introduced in the House by influential members of the majority party and by members of the committee, preferably the chairman, to which the bill will be referred. Unless he is a member of the committee to which the bill will be referred, it might not even get a hearing in the absence of good committee connections. He will also try to get some influential Senator to introduce a companion bill in the Senate and to fight for its passage by that body.

The sponsor of a bill is not necessarily the author of it. "In 1890 a bill was passed," wrote Senator Hoar in his autobiography, "which was called the Sherman Act for no other reason that I can think of except that Mr. Sherman had nothing to do with framing it whatever." [2]   Many measures are drafted in the executive departments and agencies or by private parties outside the Government and then are introduced in Congress by sympathetic Members who often play an important part in their eventual enactment.

TIMING THE INTRODUCTION

After the Member has lined up his sponsors, the next step in the legislative strategy is the choice of time for the introduction of his bill. Several alternatives are available in the matter of timing. Shall the bill be introduced in the first or the second session of a Congress? Shall it be put in at the beginning of the session, or in the middle, or toward the end of the session? Shall it be introduced simultaneously in both Houses of Congress, or in one House only, or in one House first and then in the other?

The answer to these questions depends upon a variety of factors: the climate of opinion in the country, the legislative program of the administration and the congressional leaders, the condition of the economy, the state of the Nation and the world, the character of the legislation, and other factors. It is wise to wait until the time is ripe before dropping the bill in the "hopper." For example, a presidential election year is usually considered a favorable time for introducing a tax-reduction bill, but a bad time for raising taxes.

Early introduction is usually the best strategy for a big complicated measure like a farm bill or a civil rights bill that is likely to encounter a filibuster in the Senate or dilatory tactics in the House. Sometimes it is deemed best to take up a controversial bill in one House during the first session and in the other House during the second session. That strategy was followed in the 84th Congress by Speaker Rayburn and Senator Lyndon Johnson in the case of the natural gas bill. The end-of-the-session legislative jam is ordinarily not a propitious time for the introduction of major measures. But the suspension-of-the-rules procedure during the last 6 days of a session in the House of Representatives, when debate is limited to 40 minutes, is sometimes used to rush through controversial bills without serious amendments. This technique was frequently used by the Roosevelt administration in obtaining extensions of price-control and war-powers legislation.

It is interesting to watch the ebb and flow of legislative tides. Times of crisis during the 20th century produced the great reform legislative achievements of the New Freedom and New Deal eras, and the legislation granting the President vast powers after the Japanese bombed Pearl Harbor, while the calmer days of the con-

[2] George F. Hoar, *Autobiography of Seventy Years* (1903), vol. II, p. 363.

servative administrations of Harding, Coolidge, and Hoover were comparatively barren of this type of legislation.

PLANNING THE CAMPAIGN

If the Member's bill is a major measure that affects the vital interests of some powerful group in the country, such as the veterans or the farmers or the trucking industry, then it will be necessary to develop a basic plan of campaign. Planning a legislative campaign calls for the definition of objectives, the determination of priorities, and attention to strategic positions such as committee chairmen and party leaders. It also involves the use of weapons of propaganda and pressure, the development of sources of intelligence on the progress of the battle, and the arts of compromise in negotiating legislative settlements. Effective legislative campaigns require skilled and experienced leaders who are familiar with every phase of the legislative process and with all the tricks of the legislative trade.

Legislative campaign planning also involves cooperative arrangements with the "legislative departments" and "legislative representatives" or lobbyists of the private interest groups that are back of the bill. Most of the great organized interest groups in this country have their legislative units and agents who work with the Congress and with the administrative agencies that function in their field of interest. The Congressman who is trying to get a bill passed will be in close and constant touch with the functional representatives of the organized interest groups and with the officials in the administration. During recent debates on farm bills, for example, agents of the Department of Agriculture and of the National Grange, the Farmers Union, and the Farm Bureau Federation were much in evidence on Capitol Hill.

Sometimes special campaign organizations are retained for a fee. Law firms may be hired to help on bill drafting and the development of Government support; while public-relations firms may be utilized for propaganda purposes and to develop the support of private groups. Legislative campaigning costs money for advertising, radio, and television, and grass-roots lobbying; so that fund raising is an essential part of the total effort. The Buchanan committee—a select House committee that investigated lobbying during the 81st Congress—estimated that lobbying in all its ramifications had become a billion dollar industry.

ORGANIZING GROUP SUPPORT

The next step in the legislative battle is that of lining up the support of the groups in the country that are friendly to the bill. Much persistent effort is required to arouse the sustained backing of friendly groups. Not only the national and regional leaders of private organizations must be lined up, but also the officials of the executive agencies that have a stake in the legislation. In the campaign which led to the passage of the Employment Act of 1946, according to Stephen K. Bailey—

the lining up of a strong phalanx of political forces was considered to be politically necessary and in truth it is doubtful if [the bill] would ever have passed, even in modified form, without active support of these liberal organizations.[3]

---

[3] Stephen K. Bailey, *Congress Makes a Law* (1949), p. 76.

The mobilization of group support also involves the effort to win over neutral groups who are not directly affected by the bill and have only a secondary interest in it. On most legislative issues the national political parties remain neutral in order to avoid alienating large segments of the electorate. But the chances of getting the bill enacted will be greatly enhanced if the author can secure the support of one or both of the political parties.

In trying to get his bill passed, a Congressman will also resort to the venerable strategy of "divide and conquer" by splitting the opposition. For example, the friends of the original full employment bill tried to split the business opposition to the measure. Where a legislative proposal has originated in an executive department, a time-honored tactic of private opponents of the bill is to try to promote internal dissension within the executive branch or to create a conflict between Congress and the executive.

Other tactics sometimes used in legislative campaigns are to hold an ad hoc conference on the subject of the measure and to organize an advisory committee to aid in the formulation of the proposal and to provide a center for the development of public support. From time to time, for example, White House Conferences on Education have met in Washington, and advisory committees have been used by the finance committees of Congress to assist them in the preparation of revenue and social-security bills.

PROPAGANDA AND PRESSURE

The next step in the legislative campaign, if the Member is working on a major bill for which public opinion is not yet fully prepared, is the distribution of propaganda and the application of pressure. Congress will not adopt a legislative proposal until it is convinced that it expresses the general will of the people and until there is sufficient public steam behind it. In an interest-group society Congress yields only to the strongest influences that play upon it. It becomes necessary, therefore, for the sponsors of the legislation to employ all the arts of modern propaganda and publicity in order to build a convincing case and to disseminate it through all the media of mass communication.

We are all familiar with the techniques of publicity and propaganda that have been perfected in the world of advertising. They include the indirect methods of grassroots lobbying that seek to influence public opinion through the mass distribution of books and pamphlets, full-page advertisements in the newspapers and periodicals, radio broadcasts, and literature for use in schools and churches. The development of institutional advertising in which particular business, labor, and other groups set forth their views on public issues in the form of full-page ads and illustrated pamphlets is a modern method of influencing public opinion on legislative questions.

Meanwhile, the old-style direct techniques of contacting legislators are still employed. Interested groups will make their views known to Members of Congress by letters, telegrams, and telephone calls. Congressmen will be personally contacted in their offices, their homes, and in the corridors and lobbies of the Capitol itself. Delegations will march en masse on the Capitol, a method sometimes used in recent years by the Civil Rights Congress. Senators and Representatives will receive personal letters from influential friends in their

States and districts, a technique perfected, for example, by the National Association of Real Estate Boards.

In this stage of the campaign the Member will endeavor to show that his proposal will promote the interests of this group and that group by indicating the exact benefits that will flow from its enactment. A full bill of particulars on the probable consequences of the proposal will be presented, directed at the special interests of different groups in the country, but embraced in terms calculated to promote the general welfare. Long-range objectives of unquestionable value will be avowed, such as peace, prosperity, and the preservation of the private-enterprise system; and the bill will be dressed up in all the accepted symbols of "democracy," the "public interest," and "the American way of life." In short, all the devices of propaganda and all the weapons of pressure: patronage, campaign contributions, chances for gain, the social lobby, petitions and memorials, letters and telegrams, will be employed to turn on the heat behind his bill.

STAGING COMMITTEE HEARINGS

The next step in the legislative campaign is the committee stage. As sponsor of the bill, the Member will have sought its reference to a friendly committee. Prior to the 80th Congress there was often some choice in the matter of bill referrals. But the Legislative Reorganization Act of 1946 considerably narrowed the Parliamentarian's discretion as regards the reference of bills by its more precise definitions of committee jurisdiction.

Of the various steps in the legislative process the committee stage is by far the most important. For it is through the committee hearings that Congress is informed of the merits of the measure. Here the friends and opponents of the bill marshal their arguments pro and con. Here the members of the committee interrogate the witnesses in a long and intensive study of the proposal. And here in executive sessions the committee amends the bill, seeks to compromise conflicting interests, and reaches a decision to report if favorably to the House. In the modern practice a committee will seldom report a bill without a hearing that may last for several weeks. But the mere holding of a hearing does not guarantee a favorable report.

In staging committee hearings several questions of strategy must be answered. Shall the hearings be held soon after the introduction of the bill before its opponents can marshal their resources? Or shall they be postponed for several months so as to allow ample time for the mobilization of friendly support and for the advance planning of the hearings? If companion bills have been introduced in both houses, shall the House or the Senate committee hold the first hearings?

Shall the hearings be short or long? For example, the House Subcommittee on District of Columbia Home Rule and Reorganization in the 80th Congress held hearings from June 30 to July 25, 1947, and from February 2 to 10, 1948, and heard 159 witnesses before reporting a home rule bill. Shall the hearings be open to the press and public so as to publicize the proceedings, or shall closed hearings be held so as to prevent unfavorable publicity and external criticism? Shall hearings be held in Washington only or also in the field? What witnesses shall be heard, in what order shall they appear, and how shall the available time be divided among them? Shall joint hearings be held with the twin committee of the other House and shall the power of subpena be used?

In planning the presentation of testimony, the author will sit down in advance of the hearings with his friends and allies among the organized groups which have persuaded him to sponsor the bill. In a series of conferences they will develop and document the case for their proposal. They will select the best witnesses they can find and will brief them in advance of the hearings on their testimony and on the attitudes of the committeemen. They will utilize all the techniques of modern research and fortify their case with elaborate charts, tables, and statistics. In this event, the hearings may take on the atmosphere of an economic seminar—something that has actually happened in recent years in the case of hearings held by the House Committee on Interstate and Foreign Commerce.

GETTING THE BILL TO THE FLOOR

When at last the committee is satisfied that no new facts will be brought to light, the hearings are terminated and the committee goes into what is called executive session. At this stage the committee will examine the merits of the proposal and perhaps vote to report the original bill pretty much in the form in which it was introduced, with a recommendation that the House approve it. Or the bill may be revised in committee and be reported out with majority and minority reports or by unanimous agreement. These reports usually outline the provisions of the bill, giving a section-by-section analysis of it, and summarize the committee's reasons for recommending passage of the measure. A minority report may call attention to sections of the bill that the minority does not endorse and give the reasons for its opposition.

Of course, it is possible that the committee may decide to report out no legislation at all, thus bottling up the bill in committee and, in effect, killing it. When this happens, all the author can do is to circulate a petition in the House to discharge the committee from further consideration of his bill. Under the discharge rule, first adopted in 1910, it now takes the signatures of 218 Members of the House, a simple majority of the entire body, on a discharge petition to take a bill away from a committee and bring it to the floor of the House.

Once the bill has been reported out of committee, it is placed upon the appropriate calendar of the House. The calendars are simply lists of bills upon which committee work has been completed and that are ready for floor action. The House has five calendars; the Senate has one. Getting the bill from the calendar to the floor is easier said than done. Shall they try to get it called up for floor consideration early or late in a session? In the House or Senate first? Enough time must intervene between the committee stage and the floor stage for the friends of the bill to get ready for the floor debate, prepare floor statements, and map their floor strategy.

Then there is the more perplexing problem of how best to reach the floor. In the House of Representatives there are five routes by which bills and resolutions can reach the floor: (1) By the right of certain committees to report at any time—a privilege enjoyed, for example, by the Appropriations and the Ways and Means Committees; (2) by unanimous consent on the call of the Consent Calendar or the Private

Calendar; (3) on special days when certain bills have the right of way, for example, District Day when District of Columbia business is considered; (4) under suspension of the rules on the first and third Mondays and the last 6 days of the session, when debate is strictly limited and no amendments may be offered; and (5) under special rules reported by the Committee on Rules. Most major bills depend upon a "green light" from the Rules Committee for access to the floor of the House. The Committee on Rules is the instrument of the majority leadership for determining the order of business in the House.

Since the hypothetical measure under consideration is a major, controversial one, the leadership will probably try to get it to the House floor via a special rule from the Rules Committee. To this end, the chairman and ranking minority member of the legislative committee that has favorable reported the bill will ask the chairman of the Rules Committee for a hearing. Their request will probably be granted and the chief sponsor of the bill may be invited to attend. The members of the Rules Committee, of whom there are 15—10 for the majority party and 5 for the minority—will question them closely about the background and merits of the measure. It is possible that they may disapprove of certain provisions of the bill and require the reporting committee to amend it to suit their predilections as a condition of its admission to the floor of the House.

FLOOR DEBATE AND PASSAGE

The floor stage of the bill is a story that need not long detain us, for it is short-lived and "after the fact" in the sense that the key decisions have already been made in committee. If strong opposition to the bill develops on the floor, it may be recommitted or postponed or become the victim of dilatory tactics, or be killed by having its enactment clause struck out, or be emasculated by amendments. But its fate will soon be determined, for debate in the House is strictly limited and rarely lasts more than 1 or 2 days per bill.

Assuming that the bill passes the House, it will then be messaged over to the Senate where it will repeat its long journey through the same stages of the legislative process that it took on the House side. All told, there are 28 stages in the enactment of a law, including its final approval by the President.

If our bill is approved by the Senate without amendment, it will be enrolled. signed by the Speaker and Vice President, and sent to the White House for the approval of the President. But if the bill is passed by the Senate with amendments, and if there is disagreement between the two Houses on any amendment, a conference is asked by one House and agreed to by the other. In this case, a conference committee is appointed by the Speaker and the Vice President composed of members of the appropriate committees in each House that handled the legislation.

In the appointment of House conferees, the chairman of the committee which reported the bill recommends the majority party conferees to the Speaker while the ranking minority member of the committee recommends the minority conferees. In most cases the chairman and the ranking minority member will honor requests to serve on the conference committee according to the seniority of the applicants. The Speaker may or may not agree with the recommendations of the committee chairman either as to the names or the number of the conferees for the majority party. It may make a great deal of difference as to the outcome of the conference whether there are three or five majority party conferees from the House. The chairman may recommend five because he wants to achieve a certain objective and he knows the views of the five, while the Speaker may wish another result from the conference and so insists on having only three conferees, or vice versa. If the chairman resists the Speaker's suggestions, the Speaker may tell the chairman: "You must remember that I am the one who has the final say on conferees. If you will not agree to have three, then I will simply name them myself, but that may be an embarrassment to you." This power to select conferees who represent the wishes of the leadership is a little-noticed but powerful weapon in the hands of the Speaker who, to be sure, rarely uses it, but it is a telling weapon in reserve.

The conferees, as they are called, meet and endeavor to compose the differences between the two Houses. If they succeed, as they usually do, they prepare a conference report embodying their recommendations and submit it simultaneously to House and Senate. The report of the conference committee is almost always accepted by both Houses. This done, the bill is enrolled, signed by Speaker and Vice President, and sent to the White House for the consideration of the President.

CONCLUSION

Such in sketchy outline are the major steps that a Member of Congress takes to get a bill passed. Several months or even years may elapse between the original conception of a legislative proposal and its final birth as a statute. After its enactment and approval by the President, the implementation of the statute with adequate funds, competent personnel, and effective administrative action is another story—a sequel to this biography of a legislative campaign—that would require another chapter to tell.

CHAPTER 11

PERFORMANCE OF THE OVERSIGHT FUNCTION

In the course of exercising its constitutionally delegated powers, the Congress impinges in many ways upon the administration of the laws. Congress can limit administrative discretion by detailed prescription of legislative standards, or by the adoption of resolutions otherwise limiting administrative action or subjecting it to some form of congressional approval or veto. It can fix the location of administrative responsibility and the form of organization; enact legislation affecting administrative personnel and procedures; itemize its appropriations; provide for review and audit of expenditures; require periodic and special reports from administrative agencies; and conduct investigations of the conduct of administration.

It would not be feasible to attempt to review even in summary fashion the history of the part played by the House of Representatives in these varied aspects of congressional surveillance of administration. This chapter will focus rather on three major areas of inspection and review: The selection of administrative personnel, the expenditure of public funds, and the economy and efficiency of administrative management. The specific role of the House of Representatives is stressed, but it cannot always be sharply differentiated from the actions of the Congress as a whole.

CONTROL OF APPOINTMENTS

From the earliest days Members of the House have sought to influence appointments to Federal office by corresponding with the President and department heads in favor of their friends and constituents. In important cases State delegations have acted as a group in submitting their recommendations. While the Constitution conferred upon the Senate the power to confirm nominations to superior offices, it had become customary by the end of John Adams' administration for Representatives to be consulted concerning nominations to inferior Federal offices in their districts. The annals of the Federalist period record numerous examples of attempts by Representatives to influence the appointment of postmasters, revenue officers, land-tax commissioners, and Army officers.[1]

Several examples of congressional influence on appointments during the Federalist period are given by Leonard White.[2]

On August 12, 1789, Representative Jeremiah Wadsworth of Connecticut wrote to Oliver Wolcott, offering him the support of the state delegation if he would apply to the President for an office in the Treasury. Wolcott sent his application to the President through Wadsworth's hands and was eventually appointed Auditor. In his diary under date of February 5, 1790, Washington wrote, "Received from Doctr. Williamson, of North Carolina, a list of names he thought would be proper to fill the Revenue offices in that State. Submitted the same to the Sena-

---

[1] Leonard D. White, *The Federalists* (1948), pp. 82–87.
[2] Leonard White, *ibid.*, pp. 84–85.

155

tors of that State for their inspection and alteration." In June, 1790, Jefferson consulted members of the North Carolina delegation on candidates for district judge and attorney and gave Washington notes of their opinions. In November, 1790, Hamilton consulted with the North Carolina representatives on behalf of Washington. On December 2, 1790, he reported to the President the recommendations of Representative Nicholas Gilman of New Hampshire, and suggested that the President might wish to await "the arrival of the eastern members" before making an appointment. In 1791, we find Representatives Gerry and Ames intervening in the Boston postmastership at the instance of the incumbent postmaster who was about to be displaced * * *. In 1794 the Georgia delegation offered a nomination for the vacant post of Attorney General.

Congressional influences continued to be strong during Jefferson's presidency. According to Carl Russell Fish—

The New Yorkers, already becoming adept at businesslike politics, agreed upon a slate, to be submitted to the president by Burr in the name of the whole delegation in Congress. This was accepted, but with a few changes. Although this form was not always followed, the successful candidate seems generally to have been the one who had the support of his state delegation; and if congressmen did not take the initiative, the president usually consulted some of them in regard to names presented.[3]

During the Jeffersonian period, writes White—

local claims to local offices of the federal government, buttressed by the political interests of Congressmen in their constituents, became well-nigh irresistible * * * Congressmen hovered around the executive offices to gain what they could for their friends. * * *[4]

In 1821 John Quincy Adams declared:

About one-half the members of Congress are seekers for office at the nomination of the President. Of the remainder, at least one-half have some appointment or favor to ask for their relatives.[5]

The low salaries of Congressmen at that time stimulated their appetite for more lucrative public offices, and the indebtedness of the President to the congressional caucus for his nomination during this period encouraged the feeling that his partisans in Congress were entitled to "an interchange of good offices," as Representative Quincy phrased it.

Toward the end of this period portents of the spoils system were seen in the Tenure of Office Act of 1820. This act embodied the concept of rotation in office and provided that the principal officers concerned with the collection or disbursement of money should henceforth be appointed for fixed terms of 4 years and that the commissions of incumbents should expire at stated intervals.

During the age of Jackson, which was marked by historic battles between the President and the Senate over the control of appointments to Presidential offices, department heads tended to defer to Congressmen in the appointment of inferior officers in their districts. Democrats in Congress actively solicited appointments to these offices for their friends and constituents during the Jackson and Van Buren administrations, while Members of Congress sought Executive appointments and military commissions for themselves during the Polk administration and the Mexican War. The adoption of an apportionment rule in 1853 for clerical jobs in the Washington agencies increased the potential influence of Representatives over local appointments. By the time of the Civil War they had acquired control over inferior appointments in the field services.[6]

[3] Carl Russell Fish, *The Civil Service and the Patronage* (1904), p. 47.
[4] White, *The Jeffersonians* (1951), pp. 362, 365.
[5] Adams, *Memoirs*, vol. V, p. 238. Quoted by White, *The Jeffersonians*, p. 92.
[6] Leonard D. White, *The Jacksonians* (1954), pp. 115–118.

According to Paul Van Riper, Congressmen themselves sought office during the period before the Civil War.

The information is most complete for Jackson's administration, though the tendency antedated his term. One list shows fifteen ex-senators and twenty-six ex-representatives as recipients of presidential appointments between 1829 and 1834. Nor did all of these appointments represent "lame ducks." [7]

Local Federal appointments to inferior positions continued to be regarded as the patronage of House Members in Lincoln's Presidency and in succeeding administrations. Adherence to the patronage system was accepted as the price the President had to pay for congressional approval of executive measures. The conflict between President Hayes and Senator Conkling over the New York customhouse is the best remembered of the period, but famous episodes involving the President and Members of the House are not lacking.

Lincoln had hardly entered the White House before he was besieged by an army of office seekers anxious to participate in the spoils of Republican victory. Among the applicants for Federal jobs, Carl Sandburg cites two Wisconsin Congressmen who went to see Secretary of State Seward in behalf of the appointment of Carl Schurz to be Minister to Spain. Sandburg also describes an interview that Lincoln had with Congressman William Kellogg, of Illinois, who called at the White House to solicit an appointment for one Major Hinshaw. Congressman White, of Indiana, asked Lincoln to give the job of postmaster at Lafayette, Ind., to a certain man. And Speaker Grow visited the Executive Mansion to seek an appointment for a friend in the Treasury Department. [8]

In an attempt to transfer control of the Federal patronage from the executive branch to Congress, that body passed the famous Tenure of Office Act of 1867 over President Johnson's veto. Henry Adams wrote in 1870 that "the success of any executive measure must now be bought by the use of the public patronage in influencing the action of legislators." [9] And John Sherman declared in 1871 that—

the position in which the President is now placed with regard to Congress is a constant source of irritation. Members of Congress, especially of the House of Representatives, claim the right to dictate local appointments, and if their wishes are not yielded to in every case it creates at once a cause of quarrel, which finds its outlet in some legislation or other * * *.[10]

Increasing recognition of the limitations of the patronage system, accelerated by the assassination of President Garfield by a disappointed officeseeker, led to the passage of the Civil Service Act of 1883. From this point on political influence in appointments to public office declined and the merit system was steadily expanded by congressional and Presidential action, notwithstanding occasional countermovements. In 1883, 10 percent of the positions in the executive civil service were under the merit system; in 1959, 86 percent. A series of Executive orders and of major laws, including the Classification Act of 1923, the Postmaster Act of 1938, and the Ramspeck Act of 1940, have marked the evolution of a Federal career service during the present century.

7 Paul P. Van Riper, *History of the United States Civil Service* (1958), p. 49.
8 Carl Sandburg, *Abraham Lincoln: The War Years* (1936), vol. 1, pp. 168, 175, 373, 375.
9 Henry Adams, "The Session," *North American Review*, vol. CXI, p. 58.
10 *Congressional Globe*, 41st Cong., 3d sess., p. 293 (Jan. 4, 1871).

The total number of positions subject to political or patronage appointment is still substantial. Moreover, Members of the House continue to have many requests for help in obtaining civil service posts. With the increasing acceptance of the merit system, however, the impact of the House on Federal personnel has largely shifted from direct influence in appointments to participation with the Senate in the enactment of legislation covering varied aspects of personnel policy, and in surveillance of administration of these policies through the Committee on Post Office and Civil Service and through the investigative power, discussed later in this chapter.

CONTROL OF PUBLIC EXPENDITURE

The second main area of congressional oversight of administration has been in the field of finance. During the Federalist period (1789–1801) the prevailing practice was to pass annually two general appropriation acts granting lump sums, one for the civil list, the other for the Military Establishment. The Federalists favored general grants and broad executive discretion, while the Republicans, especially under the leadership of Albert Gallatin who served in the House from 1795 to 1801, sought to limit administrative discretion in public expenditure by making specific appropriations. The Republicans had little success in their efforts during the 1790's, when the form of the supply bills was typically cast in very general terms. The pros and cons of executive discretion versus legislative restraint in fiscal affairs—a perennial issue in legislative-executive relations down through the decades—were clearly set forth in the debate on the resolutions of censure of Alexander Hamilton offered by Representative William B. Giles, of Virginia, in 1793. Giles sought to censure the Secretary of the Treasury for not strictly observing the laws making specific appropriations, but the House rejected the Giles resolutions and confirmed, at least for the time being, the Federalist viewpoint on administrative discretion.[11]

During the Jeffersonian period (1801–1829) the concern of the House with spending manifested itself in the creation of a standing Committee on Public Expenditures in 1814 and in the establishment in 1816 of six standing committees on expenditures, one each for the State, Treasury, War, Navy, and Post Office Departments, and one on public buildings. These committees were set up under the leadership of Henry Clay and reflected the intention of Clay and his friends "to take control of the Government." They were mainly concerned with checking up on administrative economy and efficiency rather than with substantive policy, and they operated sporadically.

As regards the control of expenditure, the struggle continued throughout this period between the theory of executive discretion and that of congressional control, the Federalists favoring the former concept and the Republicans urging the doctrine of specific appropriations. The actual practice at this time was for Congress to pass three annual appropriation bills: the civil list for the support of the Government, which was fully itemized and closely controlled; and the Army and Navy supply bills which granted lump sums with ample room for administrative discretion. Beginning in 1809 Congress sought to restrict the transfer of funds between branches of expenditure and in

11 Leonard D. White, *The Federalists*, pp. 326–334.

1817 certain types of transfers were forbidden. During the depression of 1819–20 Congress undertook a widespread program of retrenchment in public expenditures reducing the size of the Army, Indian outlays, the construction of ships, and the erection of forts. By the end of the period, White concludes—

the tug of war between Republicans in Congress and Republicans in the executive branch thus ended in a clear-cut victory for neither * * *. The balance in fiscal affairs between the executive and legislative branches remained about where the Federalists had left it.[12]

The struggle for power between Congress and the several executive departments over the control of public expenditures, which has gone on from the beginning of the Republic down to the present day, gained momentum during the age of Jackson. Congress now became more specific in its expectations as to the form and breakdown of the estimates and tended to demand better justifications for the funds requested. During this period the financial struggle involved five major issues: the form and detail of the estimates, the itemization of the appropriations, limitation of authority to transfer funds from one appropriation head to another, the control of deficiencies, and the prevention of expenditures or commitments not authorized by Congress. In the long fight for full control of Federal expenditures the guiding principle of Congress was expressed by Representative John Sherman of Ohio, who sat in the House from 1855 to 1861, as follows:

The theory of our government is, that a specific sum shall be appropriated by a *law* originating in this House, for a specific purpose, and within a given fiscal year. It is the duty of the executive to use that sum, and no more, especially for that purpose, and no other, and within the time fixed.[13]

Such full control does not appear to have been achieved in practice. Leonard White sums up his illuminating account of the battle over the control of Federal expenditures during the period 1829–61 by saying that:[14]

Congress never succeeded in making such a rigid interpretation of the Constitution a reality. It did not appropriate specific sums for the armed services; it regularly held appropriations open for two years; it did not punish executives for using more money than had been appropriated nor for requiring more time than had been planned.

The executive branch, on its side, found means, where necessary or useful, to avoid or to evade many of the fiscal limitations that Congress deemed it proper to impose. It drew the teeth out of some requirements by interpretation, it pleaded necessity in other cases, it confused Congress by its accounts, it made commitments that Congress had to honor, and it spent more than Congress had appropriated. In all of this there was a ready acquiesence on the part of individual Congressmen or party factions that wanted some particular payment made or task undertaken. The interests of the Congressmen were often different from and contrary to the interests of Congress. So also the interests of administration were often contrary to the requirements of an appropriation act.

After the depressions of 1837 and 1857 the House set up select committees on retrenchment in public expenditures which reported lack of cooperation from the departments and failed to achieve substantial results.

In the decades following the Civil War, Congress was described by Woodrow Wilson as "the central and predominant power of the system." One of the reasons for this impression was the nature of the postwar major supply bills. They followed a uniform pattern of

---

12 White, *The Jeffersonians*, pp. 110–116.
13 John Sherman, *Recollections*, vol. I, p. 155.   Quoted by White, *The Jacksonians*, p. 141.
14 White, *The Jacksonians*, p. 141.

detailed itemization for the civil establishments specifying the objects and amounts for which money could be spent down to the last dollar, severely restricting executive discretion in the use of available funds; combined with lump-sum appropriations for the basic operations of the Army and Navy, based, however, on itemized estimates which were subject to congressional oversight and required departmental justification.

Restrictions on the spending power, which had been largely relaxed during the Civil War, were soon restored. Power to transfer funds from one purpose to another was repealed. Unexpended balances were recovered into the Treasury. Contract obligations in excess of appropriations were forbidden. The only escape for the departments from these limitations was to incur coercive deficiencies, a long-standing practice in which Congress acquiesced until it enacted the Antideficiency Act of 1905 which apportioned expenditures at monthly or quarterly intervals.

Oversight of both revenue and spending was concentrated in the House in the Committee on Ways and Means down to 1865 when the Committee on Appropriations was created in order to divide the workload of handling both revenue and supply bills which had become very burdensome. During this period the House Committee on Appropriations was chaired by a succession of three strong men: James A. Garfield (1871–75), Samuel J. Randall (1875–77, 1883–87), and Joseph G. Cannon (1889–91, 1895–1901). Reacting to the dominant role acquired by the Appropriations Committee over both supply and general legislation, the House dispersed jurisdiction over the supply bills among half a dozen committees during the period 1879–85. The Committee on Appropriations lost control of the rivers and harbors bill and the Agriculture, Army, Navy, Indian Affairs, and foreign affairs bills. As a result of this decentralization of fiscal control among several spending committees, the House of Representatives lost an overall coordinated view of income and outgo and the several appropriation committees tended to become protagonists rather than critics of the fiscal needs of their departmental clientele.

The fiscal situation during the last three decades of the 19th century has been neatly summarized by Leonard White.[15]

Whatever the constitutional pretensions of Congress over appropriations, its record in the years from 1869 to 1901 did not suggest a high sense of responsibility on its part. A Democratic Congress refused to pass the great appropriation bills under Hayes in order to compel removal of federal troops from southern polling places. An unreasonable parsimony often controlled Congress when faced with the major supply bills, and departmental operations were often seriously handicapped by lack of adequate resources. On the other hand, Congress was open-handed in authorizing large sums for local improvements, until the annual rivers and harbors bill became a public scandal. Executive leadership was almost, if not indeed entirely, lacking. The President was not consulted on the preparation of the estimates; he was not consulted except sporadically on their disposition by the committees handling appropriations; and the Secretary of the Treasury was merely a compiler, not a minister of finance. To make matters worse, the volume of fiscal business dispersed responsibility among a number of appropriations committees to the point that coordination and unity were illusory. The Budget and Accounting Act of 1921 was finally to move in the direction of both executive and legislative responsibility in fiscal programs.

The 20th century has been replete with developments in the arena of fiscal control. A major change occurred in the House in 1920 when jurisdiction over all appropriations was consolidated in a single com-

---

[15] Leonard D. White, *The Republican Era* (1958), pp. 66–67.

mittee. Of great significance also was the Budget and Accounting Act of 1921, which provided for a budget system and an independent audit of Government accounts, the latter by the General Accounting Office. Further improvements in financial administration were provided by the Budget and Accounting Procedures Act of 1950.

In 1945 the House Appropriations Committee was authorized to conduct studies and examinations of the organization and operation of executive departments and agencies, and it has made numerous such studies since. The Legislative Reorganization Act of 1946 contained several sections designed to strengthen congressional power of the purse. Outstanding among them was that for the creation of a Joint Budget Committee which was to formulate a legislative budget and fix a ceiling on expenditures. However, the Joint Budget Committee failed to function after 1949. A short-lived attempt at coordination in the fiscal field was the consolidation of all the general supply bills in a single package in 1950. In the 1955 session the House Appropriations Committee established a special Subcommittee on Budget Reform. Chairman Clarence Cannon of the full committee described its creation as aimed at exploring all fields and proposals relating to improving procedures for balancing the budget.

With respect to control of expenditures, the General Accounting Office, its original authority considerably strengthened by the Government Corporation Control Act of 1945 and the Budget and Accounting Procedures Act of 1950, audits the financial transactions of executive departments and agencies. It has submitted several hundred audit reports to Congress and its committees which have been reviewed and analyzed by the staff of the Committee on Government Operations which has held numerous conferences with representatives of the General Accounting Office and with agency officials to assure appropriate action.

In recent years several changes in appropriations and budgetary procedures have been proposed by Members of the House of Representatives and have been considered by the appropriate committees. They include the following measures: A Presidential item veto on appropriation bills, further use of the performance budget, expanded use of the General Accounting Office by the Committee on Appropriations in considering budget requests, record votes on appropriation bills, a requirement that bills authorizing appropriations be accompanied by cost estimates, a resolution that Federal expenditures shall not exceed Federal revenues except in time of war or grave national emergency, and the creation of a budget office in the legislative branch. None of these proposals, however, has gone beyond the committee stage.[16]

OVERSIGHT OF ADMINISTRATION

The conduct of administration in its multifarious aspects has been a third major focus of legislative oversight since the founding of the Republic. The House early asserted its right to supervise the executive branch by the investigation in 1792 by a select committee of the defeat of General St. Clair by the Indians, by the Baldwin committee investigation of the Treasury in 1794, and by frequent calls

---

[16] For a comprehensive history of financial legislation. see *Financial Management in the Federal Government*, prepared by staff of Senate Committee on Government Operations, a committee print, Dec. 30, 1960.

upon department heads for information. In 1793–94 a House committee conducted an inquiry into Hamilton's management of the public debt and exonerated him from any misuse of power.

The St. Clair investigation, which was the first formal inquiry into the conduct of executive officers, raised at the beginning of our national history deep constitutional issues that are still rife in Washington. When the House committee called upon Secretary of War Knox for the St. Clair documents, President Washington conferred with his Cabinet and laid down the rule that has stood ever since as executive policy in response to congressional requests for executive papers, i.e., that—

the Executive ought to communicate such papers as the public good would permit, and ought to refuse those, the disclosure of which would endanger the public.

The St. Clair inquiry was highly successful in its primary purpose of informing the Congress, but it failed to determine who was to blame for St. Clair's defeat.[17]

During the Jeffersonian period congressional supervision of the executive manifested itself through calls for papers, the requirement of regular annual departmental reports, requests for special reports on alleged cases of maladministration or malfeasance, and by frequent ad hoc investigations of executive conduct after 1815. White reports that—

in the decade from 1815 to 1825 the power to investigate became well fixed as an important means by which Congress discharged its duty of supervising the conduct of administration.[18]

The first comprehensive administrative reorganization was achieved during 1815–17 after the War of 1812 had demonstrated the need of administrative reform. Important changes were made in' the organization of the State, Treasury, War, and Navy Departments. Congress cooperated in effecting these necessary reforms by providing the legislative basis wherever it was needed.[19]

The evidence leaves no doubt—

says White—

that a new spirit of enterprise and a different sense of responsibility animated Congress after the close of Jefferson's administration, and notably after the achievement of peace in 1815 gave the country opportunity to look at its domestic institutions.[20]

By 1829 the House had become very active in its exercise of the oversight function, thanks not only to the vigorous conduct of legislative inquires into administrative behavior but also to the development of factionalism within the Republican Party and a sense of responsibility on the part of the House to hold the Executive responsible for its performance of public affairs. Suspicious critics of the Executive like William B. Giles and John Randolph of Virginia were also a contributing factor.

After Jefferson's administration, select and standing committees of the House conducted a series of investigations of the economy and efficiency of administrative affairs which were unprecedented in scope and which reflected a growing congressional sense of responsibility

---

[17] Telford Taylor, *Grand Inquest: The Story of Congressional Investigations* (1955), ch. II.
[18] Leonard D. White, *The Jeffersonians*, p. 100.
[19] *Ibid.*, pp. 117–119.
[20] *Ibid.*, p. 106.

for supervision of the administration. A fairly complete list of the topics and years of these inquiries follows: [21]

1810—Conduct of General Wilkinson.
1815—Expenses of the State militia.
1816—Charges against Colonel Thomas.
1816—Army expenditures on the northern frontier.
1816—Fiscal affairs of the Post Office Department.
1818—Conduct of General Jackson in the Seminole War.
1818—Conduct of clerks in the executive departments.
1818—Fees exacted by a district attorney.
1819—Application of Army appropriations.
1819—Embezzlement by a clerk of court.
1819—Failure of a judge to hold court.
1820—Illegal loans of powder to private persons.
1821—Administration of the Post Office.
1822—Conduct of the Post Office Department.
1822—Accounts and expenditures of the War Department.
1823—Refusal of a judge to admit an attorney to practice.
1823—Alleged suppression of documents by Gales and Seaton.
1823—Conduct of superintendent of Indian trading houses.
1824—Charges against Secretary of the Treasury Crawford.
1825—Navy contingent fund.
1826—Conduct of Calhoun as Secretary of War.

Many of these investigations were conducted by select committees of the House which were frequently given power to send for persons and papers. Others were carried on by the new standing committees on expenditures in the executive departments, six of which were established in 1816. These and other inquiries during this period indicated that the House was conscious of its role as overseer of the public business.

During the Jacksonian era Congress extended its requirements for departmental reports to include annual reports on finances, contracts, and personnel and payrolls. Beginning in 1836 each House of Congress also required its Clerk to prepare an annual statement of all appropriations, a list of all new offices with their salaries, and a statement of all pay raises. This period was also marked by frequent congressional investigations of executive agencies including the Post Office Department, the New York customhouse, public buildings, the Brooklyn Navy Yard, and political corruption under the Buchanan administration. One of the outstanding inquiries at this time was that in 1842 by the House Select Committee on Retrenchment under the chairmanship of Thomas W. Gilmer of Virginia. If the achievements of these investigations were not conspicuous, they at least succeeded, as Leonard White remarks, in turning the spotlight of publicity on wrongdoing and in arousing public indignation over official misdeeds. [22]

The annals of Congress reveal that at least 36 investigations were conducted by committees of the House during the years, 1829–61, 32 of them by select committees and 4 by standing committees. The agencies most frequently examined were the executive departments in general (seven times), Treasury (six), the Post Office Department (three), War Department (five), and Navy Department (four).

---

[21] Compiled from 3 *Hinds' Precedents*, ch. LIV, and Leonard White, *The Jeffersonians*, pp. 99–100.
[22] White, *The Jacksonians*, pp. 148–154.

The following list shows the subjects and dates of most of these inquiries.[23]

1830—Post Office Department.
1832—Bank of the United States.
1832—Conduct of Secretary of War Eaton.
1834—Post Office Department.
1834—Bank of the United States.
1936—New York customhouse.
1837—Management of deposit banks.
1837—Condition of the executive departments.
1839—Conduct of Captain Elliott.
1839—New York customhouse.
1842—Economy in public expenditures.
1842—New York customhouse.
1846—Charges against Daniel Webster.
1848—Administration of Indian affairs.
1850—Party patronage.
1850—Galphin claim.
1850—Secretary of Interior Ewing.
1850—Activities of office holders in elections.
1855—Smithsonian Institution.
1856—Affairs in Territory of Kansas.
1857—Charges of congressional corruption.
1859—Brooklyn Navy Yard.
1860—Control of public printing.

During the Civil War period the House of Representatives continued to be active on the investigative front. In the 37th Congress (1861–63) it set up select committees to investigate Government contracts, the defenses of the Great Lakes and rivers, on emancipation, and on the confiscation of rebel property. In the 38th Congress (1863–65) select committees were appointed to investigate certain charges against the Commissioner of Patents, on emancipation, on the Northeastern defenses, on the rebellious States, on immigration, the Pacific Railroad, and on the railroad from New York to Washington. This period also witnessed the establishment of one of the most important joint select committees of the two Houses Congress has ever known. This was the so-called Wade Committee on the Conduct of the Civil War. It originated primarily to investigate the disaster of Ball's Bluff, but exercised a roving commission thereafter to look into all sorts of matters connected with the war effort. This committee was given wide powers and played an important part in the successful prosecution of the war. Commencing its labors at a time when the Government was still engaged in organizing its first great armies, it continued them until the rebellion had been overthrown. Ten distinct reports were submitted by the Wade committee between December 1862 and May 1865. Its investigations filled eight volumes.

During the post-Civil War period congressional committees, stimulated by constituent complaints of delay and waste in the executive branch of the Government, conducted a series of investigations into the organization and operation of the administrative departments with a view to promoting economy and efficiency, from the inquiry of the Joint Select Committee on Retrenchment (1869–71) to that of

[23] Compiled from 3 Hinds' Precedents, ch. LIV, Marshall E. Dimock, Congressional Investigating Committees (1929), and Ernest J. Eberling, Congressional Investigations (1928).

the Dockery-Cockrell Joint Commission of 1893-95. Their voluminous reports produced valuable basic data on departmental organization and methods of administrative management and effected substantial economies, but they contributed little in the way of general principles for the guidance of practitioners of the administrative arts. While successive Presidents prior to Theodore Roosevelt remained aloof from such mundane matters, Congress took the initiative in seeking specific improvements for particular administrative problems. But it was too preoccupied with individual cases to be able to modernize the administrative system as a whole. It remained for later studies by a series of Presidential commissions on economy and efficiency to pave the way for widespread administrative reform.[24]

During the years from the Civil War to the end of the century some 70 investigations were conducted by select and standing committees of the House of Representatives, many of them into various aspects of administrative management. The scandals of Grant's administration (1869–77) provoked upward of 30 House inquiries alone. Among the outstanding investigations of this era were the Credit Mobilier inquiry of 1872–73 and the investigation of the real estate pool and Jay Cooke in 1876.

The sensational Credit Mobilier investigation was conducted by two House and one Senate committees. It involved the financing of the Union Pacific Railroad. A principal stockholder in both companies was Oakes Ames, a Representative in Congress from Massachusetts. Charges appeared in the press that Ames had bribed men prominent in public life by distributing shares of stock in the Credit Mobilier. Among those involved in the alleged speculation were Speaker Blaine and Vice President Colfax. One House committee was appointed, on motion of James G. Blaine, himself, to investigate the charges that Members of the House had been "bribed by Oakes Ames, or any other person or corporation, in any matter touching his legislative duty." Representative Luke Poland, of Vermont, was named chairman of this five-man select committee. A few weeks later, another five-man select committee, chaired by Representative Jeremiah M. Wilson, of Indiana, was set up to determine whether the Government had been defrauded, because of possible conspiracy in high places, by the Credit Mobilier. Meanwhile, the Senate appointed its own committee, under the chairmanship of Senator Lot M. Morrill, of Maine, to determine if any of its members were implicated. Each committee was empowered to send for persons and papers.

The Poland committee recommended that both Oakes Ames and James Brooks, a Representative from New York, be expelled from the House. The committee held that Ames had been—

guilty of selling to members of Congress shares of stock in the Credit Mobilier of America, for prices much below the true value of such stock, with intent thereby to influence the votes and decisions of such members in matters to be brought before Congress for action.

Brooks was found guilty of procuring stock for his son-in-law, intended for and used for his own benefit. In the final event, both Ames and Brooks were censured by the House, but not expelled.[25]

²⁴ White, *The Republican Era*, pp. 84–92.
²⁵ 2 Hinds' *Precedents of the House of Representatives* 1286.

The Wilson committee found that the profits of the Credit Mobilier had been grossly exorbitant and recommended that the Attorney General bring suit against all who had ever received stocks or bonds in the railroad without paying for them, or who had received dividends unlawfully declared from the profits made in the construction of the road.[26]

The Morrill committee found that Senator James W. Patterson, of New Hampshire, had purchased stock from Mr. Ames at below its "esteemed" value in the knowledge that such sales are in the nature of bribes. The committee recommended that he be expelled from the Senate.[27] But the Senate permitted Patterson, whose term was about to expire, to retire without having the expulsion resolution brought to a vote and without formal censure.

No evidence was found that Speaker Blaine had any dealing with the Credit Mobilier or with Ames other than to decline offers of stock. The political career of Vice President Schuyler Colfax, however, was ruined by the investigations.

A second major investigation of this era was that by a House select committee in 1876 which was authorized to investigate financial dealings between Jay Cooke's banking firm, in which Federal funds were deposited, and a "real estate pool" in the District of Columbia which was managed by one Hallett Kilbourn. The committee subpenaed Kilbourn who refused to answer questions or produce documents on the ground that the House lacked power to investigate his private business. The House cited Kilbourn for contempt and committed him to the District jail. At the request of the Speaker, the District grand jury indicted Kilbourn under the criminal statute of 1857, but when the District marshal tried to take custody of Kilbourn from the House Sergeant-at-Arms, the House decided to keep Kilbourn in custody for contempt. Kilbourn then sued out a writ of *habeas corpus* which the House ultimately honored. Chief Justice Cartter, of the District of Columbia court ruled that, by passing the 1857 statute, Congress had deprived itself of the power to punish contempts by imprisonment, and that prosecution under that statute was the only way to deal with recalcitrant witnesses. And so he ordered Kilbourn's release. Kilbourn at once seized the initiative and sued the Speaker, the members of the investigating committee, and the Sergeant-at-Arms for false imprisonment. The case went to the U.S. Supreme Court where it was decided in 1880 in the famous decision of *Kilbourn* v. *Thompson*. The Court held, in effect, that the investigating function and contempt powers of Congress, like its lawmaking and other powers, are subject to constitutional limitations, and that the courts will review congressional exercise of all these powers. Kilbourn finally received $20,000 in damages for false imprisonment, paid by a special legislative appropriation; while Justice Miller's opinion raised doubts about the investigative powers of Congress that were not dispelled until the Supreme Court's decision in 1927 in the celebrated case of *McGrain* v. *Daugherty*.

Woodrow Wilson wrote in 1885 that "quite as important as legislation is vigilant oversight of administration * * *." But he added that:[28]

---

[26] H. Rept. No. 78, 42d Cong., 3d sess.
[27] S. Rept. No. 519, 42d Cong., 3d sess.
[28] Woodrow Wilson, *Congressional Government*, p. 270–271.

* * * it is quite evident that the means which Congress has of controlling the departments and of exercising the searching oversight at which it aims are limited and defective.   The intercourse with the President is restricted to the executive messages, and its intercourse with the departments has no easier channels than private consultations between executive officials and the committees, informal interviews of the ministers with individual members of Congress, and the written correspondence which the cabinet officers from time to time address to the presiding officers of the two Houses, at stated intervals, or in response to formal resolutions of inquiry. * * *

And then follows this famous passage: [29]

Even the special, irksome, ungracious investigations which it from time to time institutes in its spasmodic endeavors to dispel or confirm suspicions of malfeasance or of wanton corruption do not afford it more than a glimpse of the inside of a small province of federal administration.   Hostile or designing officials can always hold it at arm's length by dexterous evasions and concealments.   It can violently disturb, but it cannot often fathom, the waters of the sea in which the bigger fish of the civil service swim and feed.   Its dragnet stirs without cleansing the bottom. Unless it have at the head of the departments capable, fearless men, altogether in its confidence and entirely in sympathy with its designs, it is clearly helpless to do more than affright those officials whose consciences are their accusers.

Wilson concluded on this question of controlling the administration that—

members of Congress ought not to be censured too severely, however, when they fail to check evil courses on the part of the executive.   [For] they have been denied the means of doing so promptly and with effect.[30]

Since Woodrow Wilson wrote these words, the problem of effective supervision of administration has been greatly magnified by the steady growth of Executive power induced by recurring economic and political crises, two World Wars, the emergence of the United States as a world power, the perils of the postwar period, and the growing complexity of our economic, political, and social activities, both nationally and internationally.   Meanwhile, there has also been a notable increase in the means of legislative liaison with the Executive and in the techniques of congressional control of administrative action.

Liaison with the President, while still not entirely satisfactory, has been improved by the weekly meetings at the White House with the leaders of Congress; the personal delivery of the state of the Union messages before joint sessions, a practice revived by Wilson himself; and by the designation of a deputy assistant to the President to handle congressional relations.   President Eisenhower's practice of inviting each Member of Congress to a meal at the White House has increased the social intercourse between them.

Meanwhile, liaison with the departments has been improved by the appointment in a few cases of Assistant Secretaries for Congressional Relations, by the opening of branch departmental offices on Capitol Hill, and by some recent experiments with question periods at the committee stage.   In recent years a few House committees have developed the practice of holding periodic or sporadic question-and-review sessions with the officials of executive agencies under their jurisdiction, especially at the beginning of each session.   These meetings afford an opportunity for the review of administrative action, the discussion of citizen complaints, and the reaching of informal understandings concerning administrative policies and procedures.

Even more significant than these steps toward closer liaison between the legislative and executive branches has been the extension of the

[29] Ibid., p. 271.
[30] Ibid., p. 302.

function of standing committees from the consideration of bills to the study and control of administration. "Committee government," as Wilson described it in the middle 1880's, was a system primarily if not entirely concerned with "digesting schemes of legislation." Occasional investigations of the executive were conducted by select committees. The annals of the House reveal only eight such inquiries between 1885 and 1925, and nine between 1925 and 1946, as follows: [31]

Administration of Government Printing Office—50th Congress (1887–89).

Reform in the civil service—50th–52d Congresses (1887–93).

Soldier's Home in Leavenworth, Kans.—54th Congress (1895–97).

Purchase of the Danish West Indies—57th Congress (1901–3).

Prevention of fraud in public service—60th Congress (1907–9).

Operation of U.S. Shipping Board and Emergency Fleet Corporation—66th Congress (1919–21).

Contracts and expenditures by War Department—66th Congress (1919–21).

Operations of U.S. Air Service—68th Congress (1923–25).

Shipping Board—69th Congress (1925–27).

Government organization—76th Congress (1939–41).

National Labor Relations Board—76th Congress (1939–41).

Acts of executive agencies beyond scope of their authority—78th and 79th Congresses (1943–46).

Seizure of Montgomery Ward & Co.—78th Congress (1943–44).

Federal Communications Commission—78th Congress (1943–44).

National defense program in re small business—78th Congress.

Postwar military policy—78th and 79th Congresses.

Disposition of surplus property—79th Congress (1945–46).

Today "legislative oversight" has become a, if not the, principal activity of the standing committees of both Houses. There has been an extraordinary increase in the exercise of the investigative function of Congress in recent times. As many inquiries have been conducted by each Congress since 1950 as were carried on in the whole 19th century.[32] This development has been due, at least in part, to the directive in section 136 of the Legislative Reorganization Act of 1946 that "each standing committee of the Senate and the House of Representatives shall exercise continuous watchfulness of the execution * * * of any laws" by the administrative agencies within their jurisdiction. The expansion of the investigative function has also been facilitated by the increase in standing committee staffs which have doubled in the Senate and tripled in the House during the past decade.

After 1885 the House made comparatively few inquiries into the conduct of executive departments, while the Senate assumed the leading role as "grand inquest" of the Nation. The House shifted its inquiring eye, especially after the turn of the century, to studies of

[31] *Records of the U.S. House of Representatives*, 1789–1946. 2 vols. Preliminary Inventories. National Archives and Records Service, General Services Administration, Washington, 1959.

[32] Nelson McGeary reports that House committees conducted 50 investigations during 1929–38, and Floyd Riddick states that 107 inquiries were carried on by House committees during 1942–50. M. Nelson McGeary, *The Developments of Congressional Investigative Power* (1940), p. 8. Floyd M. Riddick in his review of the session articles in the *American Political Science Review* and the *Western Political Quarterly*.

economic and social problems. Among its major inquiries in this area during the past 50 years have been the so-called "Money Trust" (Pujo) investigation of banking and finance in 1912–13, the investigations of fascism and communism by the Committee on Un-American Activities since 1945, the examinations of the Federal regulatory commissions by the so-called Legislative Oversight Subcommittee since 1957, and the widespread investigations by the Committee on Government Operations since 1947.

Early in 1957 a Subcommittee on Legislative Oversight was appointed by Representative Oren Harris, chairman of the House Committee on Interstate and Foreign Commerce. This subcommittee was set up—

to examine the execution of the laws by the administrative agencies, administering laws within the legislative jurisdiction of the committee, to see whether or not the law as the Congress intended in its enactment has been and is being carried out or whether it has been and is being repealed or revamped by those who administer it.

The subcommittee listed some 16 regulatory boards and commissions that it proposed to examine, and some 8 subjects that it was going to consider, in what promised to be the most sweeping investigation of the organization and operation of the regulatory agencies of the Federal Government in American history. Late in 1957 the scope of the initial inquiry was limited to the "big six" regulatory agencies: Civil Aeronautics Board, Federal Power Commission, Federal Trade Commission, Interstate Commerce Commission, Securities and Exchange Commission, and the Federal Communications Commission.

Representative Morgan M. Moulder, of Missouri, was named chairman of the special subcommittee and Prof. Bernard Schwartz of New York University Law School was retained as chief counsel and staff director. Originally designed to determine whether the agencies had followed the intent of Congress, the investigation became in 1958 a probe of charges of influence peddling by representatives of the regulated industries, commissioners, Congressmen, and members of the White House staff. Later, Schwartz was dismissed as subcommittee counsel. Representative Moulder resigned as subcommittee chairman and was replaced by Representative Harris, chairman of the parent committee. The subcommittee then held hearings on charges of misconduct by members of the Federal Communications Commission, which led to the resignation of Commissioner Richard A. Mack. Subsequently an inquiry into the affairs of Bernard Goldfine, Boston industrialist, led to the disclosure of his gifts and financial assistance to Presidential Assistant Sherman Adams and to some Congressmen. Later, Goldfine was indicted for contempt of Congress for his refusal to answer subcommittee questions, and Adams resigned his White House post.[33]

In its final report the Legislative Oversight Subcommittee recommended the establishment of a permanent Subcommittee on Regula-

[33] For a full account of this episode see *Congressional Quarterly Almanac*, vol. XIV, 1958, pp. 687–701. See also report of the Subcommittee on Legislative Oversight, H. Rept. No. 2711, 85th Cong., 2d sess.; Bernard Schwartz, *The Professor and the Commissions* (1959); J. Sinclair Armstrong, "Who's Overseeing the Oversightors?" *Congressional Record*, Feb. 2, 1959, pp. A707–710. For a critique of legislative participation in the administrative process, see Frank C. Newman and Stanley S. Surrey, *Legislation: Cases and Materials* (1955), ch. 4, sec. 2.

tory and Administrative Commissions to serve as an adviser to the full committee concerning administrative process problems.[34]

Another recent important development was the revival in 1946 of the long-moribund Committee on Expenditures in the Executive Departments. As redefined by the Legislative Reorganization Act of that year, this committee was given the duties of (1) receiving and examining the reports of the Comptroller General and of reporting to the House thereon; (2) studying the operation of Government activities at all levels with a view to determining their economy and efficiency; (3) evaluating the effects of laws enacted to reorganize the legislative and executive branches of the Government; and (4) studying intergovernmental relationships. It was thus designed to be a public accounts and machinery of Government group. In 1952 its name was changed to the Committee on Government Operations. It has 30 members and has established subcommittees on executive and legislative reorganization, Government activities, military operations, intergovernmental relations, foreign operations and monetary affairs, donable property, and Government information.

This committee has held hearings on a wide range of subjects and has published numerous staff studies and reports. It handled most of the Hoover Commission legislation and has reviewed the audit reports of the General Accounting Office. The committee has become the principal investigative agency of the House in the field of Government operations. Among the wide ranging subjects of inquiry by this panel have been Government information policies and practices, military procurement, the operations of Federal Prison Industries, of the Institute of Inter-American Affairs, of the Maritime Commission, of the General Accounting Office, of the Rural Electrification Administration, of the Veterans' Administration, and of the Office of Education, Federal supply management, U.S. relations with international organizations, and many other matters.

With a mandate to watch continuously, equipped with staffs and funds, "committee government" in our time has thus acquired new significance as a system of inspection and review of administrative performance. The 83d Congress alone authorized upward of $7.5 million for various probes. Various oversight techniques are employed, some of ancient usage, some of recent vintage. They include question periods at the committee stage, field inspection trips at home and abroad, interim supervision of agency activities, and demands for documents and testimony, all of which have been increasingly used in recent years to strengthen the oversight function of Congress. And they have had many far-reaching effects, of which one of the most spectacular was the forced resignation of Secretary of the Air Force Talbott.

A comparatively novel weapon in the oversight arsenal is the provision, found in several statutes of recent years, vesting in standing committees the power to approve or disapprove proposed actions of executive officials. Prior committee clearance is now required by law for military real estate transactions, contracts for the development of naval petroleum reserves, construction of military public works, the erection of veterans' hospitals, and the purchase of public buildings.

---

[34] Independent Regulatory Commissions. Report of the Special Subcommittee on Legislative Oversight. H. Rept. No. 2238, 86th Cong., 2d sess., Jan. 3, 1961, pp. 41–42.

In one case the control of administrative action is placed solely in the hands of the chairman of the House Appropriations Committee. A section of the Defense Appropriation Act of 1956 provided that no business enterprises of the Armed Forces could be closed if the Appropriation Committee of either House disapproved, but this section was struck from the new Defense money bill by a record vote in the House. These instances indicate an apparent gradual trend toward the participation of Congress in the actual administration of the laws.

In 1920 President Wilson vetoed an act making appropriations for the legislative, executive, and judicial expenses of the Government for the fiscal year 1921 because it contained a section giving the Joint Committee on Printing control over the printing of all Government publications. In his veto message Wilson said in part:

> I do not concede the right, and certainly not the wisdom, of the Congress endowing a committee of either House or a joint committee of both Houses with power to prescribed "regulations" under which executive departments may operate * * *. I regard the provision in question as an invasion of the province of the executive and calculated to result in unwarranted interferences in the processes of good government, producing confusion, irritation, and distrust. The proposal assumes significance as an outstanding illustration of a growing tendency which I am sure is not fully realized by the Congress itself and certainly not by the people of the country.[35]

Another major development of the past 75 years, as regards congressional control of administration, has been in the field of administration regulation. Beginning with the Interstate Commerce Commission in 1887 and continuing through every decade to the Atomic Energy Commission in 1946, 10 regulatory Commissions have been created and granted rulemaking powers. Congress exercises oversight of these "floating ribs of Government" through statutes prescribing the terms and qualifications of their members, through the power of the Senate to reject nominees to them, through the annual appropriation hearings and interim amendments of the basic statutes, through sporadic committee question periods and occasional full-dress investigations of their work, and by requiring them to submit periodic and special reports.[36]

Despite the variety of weapons in the armory of congressional oversight of delegated powers, these methods of inspection and review apparently proved inadequate, especially under the emergency conditions of depression and war. Recurring complaints of the abuse of the rulemaking power, finally led, after long study, to the Federal Administrative Procedure Act of 1946. This act laid down a series of procedural safeguards for the guidance of the rulemakers, prescribing the minimum requirements of fair administrative procedure.

In the area of administrative review it has been suggested that oversight of administrative regulation and delegated powers could be strengthened by: (a) The creation of a Joint Standing Committee on Delegated Legislation, to scrutinize quasi-legislative administrative rules and regulation, to draw the attention of Congress to any of them, and to advise as to their affirmation or annulment, or alternatively,

[35] Richardson, *Messages and Papers of the Presidents*, vol. XVII, p. 8845–8849.
[36] For a description of the behavior of members of a congressional committee in their role as overseers of an independent regulatory commission, see Seymour Scher, "Congressional Committee Members as Independent Agency Overseers: A Case Study," *American Political Science Review*, December 1960, pp. 911–920.

(b) the establishment of a Standing Committee on Administrative Procedure in each House, as Representative Smith of Virginia has proposed (H. Res. 462, 84th Cong., 2d sess.). At hearings in May 1956, on the Smith resolution, witnesses representing the American Bar Association testified that:

the proposed committee would evaluate the effects of laws enacted to regulate the procedures of administrative agencies. It also would study the procedure and practices of administrative agencies with a view to determining whether they were in accordance with law, adequately protected public and private rights, avoided undue delay and unnecessary expense, and comported with principles of fair play. No standing committee presently appears to be vested with the jurisdiction to inquire into such matters on an overall basis throughout the entire executive branch.

The legislative veto procedure is another safeguard of delegated powers that Congress has repeatedly used in latter years in authorizing reorganizations of the executive branch. Under this procedure, resembling the British system of provisional orders, the President is required to submit reorganization plans before a given date that will take effect after a specified period unless they are rejected meantime by a simple resolution approved by a constitutional majority of either House.

Such control of executive or administrative action by congressional resolution is a comparatively recent innovation. Since 1939 many Federal statutes have provided that a resolution passed by one or both Houses of Congress, without the President's signature, may veto, terminate, or compel Executive action. Five types of control of administrative action by simple or concurrent resolution of Congress have received statutory sanction in recent years, as follows: [37]

1. Veto of action proposed by the President or an executive officer pursuant to a statute, as in the Executive Reorganization Acts of 1939, 1945, and 1949, and the alien deportation statute.

2. Terminations of statutes or statutory powers, as in the Lend-Lease Act of 1941 and many other statutes.

3. Termination of executive action carried on pursuant to statute, as in the foreign-aid statutes.

4. Direction of Executive action pursuant to a statute, as in the Neutrality Act of 1939, and

5. Removal of executive officers, as in the Tennessee Valley Authority Act.

In recent years Congress has expanded its exercise of the oversight function by attempting to secure for its committees some degree of continuing influence in the exercise of powers delegated to the Executive, especially as regards emergency and defense legislation. The control techniques employed have included the requirement of periodic reports to both Houses or to specified committees, consultation with committees, and on occasion committee approval before action may be taken. Some examples of recent requirements to consult with congressional committees are:

1. The Economic Cooperation Act of 1948, in which a joint committee of Congress was set up to consult with the administrators.

---

[37] Cf. Robert W. Ginnane, "The Control of Federal Administration by Congressional Resolutions and Committees," Harvard Law Review, February 1953, p. 570.

2. The Defense Production Act of 1950, in which a joint committee was established to study continuously the programs authorized by the act and officials were ordered to "consult with the committee from time to time."

3. The Immigration and Nationality Act of 1952, which established a joint committee to receive all "regulations, instructions, and all other information as requested by the committee relative to the administration of this Act" and also provided for consultation of the administrators with the committee.

Recent acts in which congressional committees actually participate in decisions delegated to administrators include the Defense Appropriations Act for fiscal 1956 and the Atomic Energy Act which order the Executive to inform the Joint Committee on Atomic Energy of any arrangements with other nations concerning atomic secrets 30 days before the arrangement would be consummated and while Congress is in session.[38]

---

[38] J. Malcolm Smith and Cornelius P. Cotter, "Administrative Accountability: Reporting to Congress," *Western Political Quarterly*, June 1957, p. 405-415.

CHAPTER 12

ROLE OF HOUSE IN FOREIGN AFFAIRS

The relations of the House of Representatives to the foreign affairs of the United States stem from the days of the American Revolution. During that conflict the Continental Congress conducted and controlled the foreign relations of the 13 States. Colonial experience with the English King and royal Governors had produced a deep distrust of executive authority. So Congress appointed our diplomatic agents abroad and referred their instructions and correspondence to a series of select committees. On November 29, 1775, a Committee of Secret Correspondence was set up to correspond "with friends in Great Britain, Ireland, and other parts of the world" and to seek foreign aid; after April 1777 it was known as the Committee for Foreign Affairs. In January 1781 the drawbacks of the committee system induced Congress to establish the office of Secretary of Foreign Affairs, but the Legislature continued to deliberate on foreign relations in Committee of the Whole and to refer particular problems to select committees.

During the period of the Confederation (1781–89) congressional control of foreign affairs continued with little change. The Articles of Confederation gave Congress exclusive power over war and peace (unless a State were invaded), the right to send and receive diplomatic agents and embassies, and the right to make treaties. Robert Livingston and John Jay served as Secretary of Foreign Affairs during this period, but Congress inspected their correspondence, issued detailed instructions concerning their negotiations, and kept a tight rein on the conduct of foreign affairs. Historians have assigned credit, however, for the treaty of 1783 with Great Britain less to the Congress than to the able American negotiators: John Adams, John Jay, and Benjamin Franklin.

It was thus against a background of congressional control of foreign affairs that the Constitutional Convention met in Philadelphia in May 1787. Its discussions concerning the conduct of foreign relations dealt largely with the power to make treaties and to appoint ambassadors, functions which, in the first draft of the Constitution, were assigned to the Senate. This draft also provided that treaties as well as the acts of the Legislature should be "the supreme law of the several States, and of their citizens and inhabitants," and it forbade the States to make any treaties or alliances save with the consent of Congress. These proposals evoked an amendment that no treaty should be binding on the United States unless "ratified by a law," thereby requiring concurrence of the House of Representatives.

This amendment was rejected, but after a revised draft of the Constitution assigned control of foreign relations to the President *and* the Senate, it was proposed that the advice and consent of the House as well as that of the Senate should be required in the treaty process. In the closing debate of the Convention James Wilson discussed the treaty clause and moved to add after the word "Senate" the words "and House of Representatives". Treaties, he said, were to have the sanction of laws and should therefore be ratified by both houses. But his proposal was not adopted. In the final draft the framers assigned to Congress the other important powers in the field of foreign affairs, i.e., the powers to regulate foreign commerce and to declare war, while the House of Representatives received a share in the treaty power through the commerce clause and through its power to originate appropriation bills needed to implement a treaty.

Whatever the expectations of the framers may have been with respect to the control of foreign affairs, in the perspective of history it appears, as Prof. Edward S. Corwin has written, that—

the Constitution, considered only for its affirmative grants of power which are capable of affecting the issue, is an invitation to struggle for the privilege of directing American foreign policy. * * * The verdict of history * * * is that the power to determine the substantive content of American foreign policy is a *divided* power, with the lion's share falling usually to the President, though by no means always.[1]

FROM 1789 TO 1800

During the first decade of the new Republic, the House of Representatives participated in several decisions affecting the foreign relations of the United States. It helped enact the act of July 27, 1789, which established a Department of Foreign Affairs whose name was changed to the Department of State some weeks later. By the Appropriation Act of July 1790, a lump sum of $40,000 was made available to the President for the support of our embassies abroad. In establishing the Post Office by the act of February 20, 1792, the Second Congress authorized the Postmaster General to make arrangements with the postmasters in any foreign country for the reciprocal receipt and delivery of letters and packets which, according to Wallace McClure, was the first use of the executive agreement under the Constitution.[2]

President Washington's famous proclamation of neutrality of April 22, 1793, during the war between France and Great Britain gave rise to a public controversy and a lively pamphlet debate between Hamilton and Madison over the powers of President and Congress. Both Houses subsequently approved the President's actions, and in June 1794 Congress passed the first neutrality law, prohibiting certain acts and imposing penalties. These developments established the precedent that the President has power to determine a policy of neutrality toward foreign nations, and that Congress has legislative authority to enforce neutrality within the domestic jurisdiction of the United States. Meanwhile, Congress placed a temporary embargo by joint resolution on all ships in American ports bound for foreign ports and authorized the President to lay an embargo pending the next session: The first uses by Congress of its commerce power as a lever in foreign relations.[3]

The question of the role of the House of Representatives in the implementation of treaties arose as early as 1796. John Jay had

[1] Edward S. Corwin, *The President: Office and Powers*, third edition revised (1948), p. 208.
[2] Wallace McClure, *International Executive Agreements* (1941), p. 38.
[3] Dorothy B. Goebel, "Congress and Foreign Relations Before 1900," *Annals of the American Academy of Political and Social Science*, September 1953, pp. 28–29. I have made extensive use of Dr. Goebel's excellent article in this and the following sections.

gone to England to negotiate a commercial treaty with Great Britain. Publication of the treaty after the Senate ratified it in June 1795 was followed by an outburst of popular resentment against Jay's surrender of American neutral rights.   After President Washington sent a copy of the Jay Treaty to the House, a prolonged debate ensued in that body concerning the constitutional obligation of Congress to supply the appropriations required to carry the treaty into effect.   When a bill was introduced in the House to vote the needed funds, supporters of the treaty—Hamilton, Chief Justice Ellsworth, and others—argued that the House must make the appropriation willy-nilly; that the treaty, having been ratified by and with the advice and consent of the Senate, was "supreme law of the land," and that the legislative branch was bound thereby no less than the executive and judicial branches.   James Madison, a Member of the House, opposed this thesis in a series of resolutions that asserted the traditional doctrine:

When a Treaty stipulates regulations on any of the subjects submitted by the Constitution to the power of Congress, it must depend for its execution, as to such stipulations, on a law or laws to be passed by Congress. And it is the Constitutional right and duty of the House of Representatives, in all such cases, to deliberate on the expediency or inexpediency of carrying such Treaty into effect, and to determine and act thereon, as, in their judgement, may be most conducive to the public good.

The upshot of the matter was that the House adopted Madison's resolutions, while at the same time it voted the required funds.[4]

As the 18th century approached its end, our relations with France reached a crisis induced in part by French annoyance over American neutrality and Senate ratification of the Jay Treaty.   In 1798 the fifth Congress enacted the alien and sedition laws and abrogated all existing treaties with France.   This was congressional regulation of foreign policy with a vengeance and, after 2 years of an undeclared naval war, the convention of 1800 confirmed congressional action.

NINETEENTH CENTURY DEVELOPMENTS

During the 19th century the House of Representatives was largely preoccupied with domestic affairs, but on at least a dozen occasions it played a prominent part on the international stage.

The first occasion occurred in 1803 in connection with the Louisiana Purchase.   After Spain retroceded the Province of Louisiana, as it was then called, to France in 1800, President Jefferson sent James Monroe to Paris to negotiate with Napoleon for the cession of New Orleans to the United States.   Napoleon was getting ready to renew his war with England; he needed money, and he feared that England or the United States might seize New Orleans.   So he offered to sell the entire Province of Louisiana.   Monroe and the American Ministers to France and Spain, Robert Livingston and Charles Pinckney, accepted the offer and the treaty of cession was signed at Paris on April 30, 1803.   The price finally paid for the territory was $27,627,622 and has been called "the most gigantic real estate transaction of all times."   News of the acquisition of Louisiana, which more than doubled the area of the United States and gave us complete control of the Father of Waters, produced a sensation in this country.   At a special session of Congress in October 1803 the Senate promptly rati-

---

[4] *The Constitution of the United States* (1953).   Corwin annotated edition, p. 418.

fied the purchase, and both Houses passed the necessary appropriation bills. The sentiment of Congress had been foreshadowed early in 1803 when it had appropriated $2 million for the purchase of New Orleans and the land around the Mississippi River.

After the renewal of the Napoleonic Wars and the ensuing invasion of American neutral rights and damage to our foreign trade, Congress, and especially the House of Representatives, employed its foreign commerce power to retaliate against Britain and France. From 1806 to 1812 a series of nonimportation and embargo acts were passed in an unsuccessful effort to win respect for our neutral rights and to keep the United States out of war. Finally, the activities of Henry Clay and his band of "war hawks" in the House forced the hand of President Madison and led to the second war with England. Although referred to derisively as "Mr. Madison's War," it was largely a war of Congress own making. The Treaty of Ghent, which terminated the conflict, was effectuated by the act of February 5, 1816, in which the House, conscious of its commerce power, enacted the clauses of the treaty seriatim after debating at length the issue of legislative power in relation to the status of a treaty.

A few years later the House for the first time challenged the authority of the President with regard to the recognition of the insurgent Republics of Latin America. In 1818 Henry Clay proposed to appropriate funds to pay the salary for a Minister to one of the new Republics, although the President had not requested the money. Clay's proposal was defeated, but on February 10, 1821, the House passed a resolution giving its "constitutional support" to the President whenever he should consider it expedient to recognize the new states. Finally, in May 1822, the congressional viewpoint prevailed when the President asked for and received $100,000 for diplomatic missions to Latin America.

In his annual message of December 2, 1823, President Monroe inserted the passage which became famous as the "Monroe Doctrine." He asserted—

that the American continents, by the free and independent condition which they have assumed and maintain, are henceforth not to be considered as subjects for future colonization by any European power.

This doctrine was purely an Executive declaration of principle, and although it was favorably received by the American people, it was never adopted or sanctioned by Congress. In 1824 Henry Clay tried unsuccessfully to persuade the House of Representatives to pass a resolution embodying the doctrine. However, its basic principle had been foreshadowed by a congressional resolution of January 9, 1811, relating to East Florida, which stated that the United States could not see—

with indifference, any part of the Spanish provinces adjoining the said States eastward of the River Perdido pass from the hands of Spain into those of any other foreign power.

French intervention in Argentina and Uruguay in 1838 prompted Caleb Cushing, chairman of the House Committee on Foreign Affairs, to sponsor a House resolution based on the Monroe Doctrine questioning French intentions. But that and later attempts to secure the formal sanction of Congress for the doctrine all proved ineffectual.[5]

⁵ Goebel, *loc. cit.*, p. 32.

After Texas declared its independence of Mexico in 1836, the House of Representatives played an important part in the developments that ultimately led to the recognition and annexation of the "Lone-Star State." Popular sentiment strongly favored westward expansion of the growing Nation and Texas became the first goal of the advocates of "Manifest Destiny." On July 1, 1836, the Senate adopted a resolution favoring the recognition of Texas, and the House did likewise a few days later. President Jackson reasserted Executive power in the recognition of new States, but extended recognition to Texas soon after Congress appropriated funds for the salary of a diplomatic agent to the new Republic. For 9 years, however, the annexation of Texas was delayed both by the Mexican threat that this would lead to war and by the rising agitation against the extension of slavery. Texas twice applied for admission to the American Union, first during Jackson's administration and then during that of President Van Buren, but both applications were refused.

Finally, in April 1844, President Tyler submitted a treaty of annexation to the Senate which rejected it in June. Tyler then took the unprecedented step of sending the rejected treaty to the House, hoping to obtain favorable action on the annexation project by joint resolution, which would require a simple majority vote in both Houses. No action was taken on the joint resolution until after the presidential election of 1844 in which James K. Polk, an outspoken advocate of annexation, defeated Henry Clay who opposed annexation without the consent of Mexico. Interpreting the election as a popular mandate, Congress passed a joint resolution on March 1, 1845, expressing its consent to the admission of Texas as a State and specifying the conditions of admission, and by joint resolution of December 29, 1845, Texas was admitted into the Union. Within a few months Senator Benton's prediction of war with Mexico came true, and the House approved the declaration of war by a vote of 174 to 14. "The war with Mexico," remarks Carroll, "was a presidential war, but the House, supported by public opinion, had found a way to circumvent senatorial stubbornness." [6]

The War Between the States was marked by serious complications in our relations with England and France in which the House of Representatives was involved. Both these countries had recognized the Confederates as belligerents and England especially had helped the South by allowing cruisers and blockade runners to be equipped and to discharge their cargoes at her ports. The Confederate Government appointed James M. Mason and John Slidell as Commissioners to England and France, respectively. After reaching Havana safely in a blockade runner from Charleston, they sailed for England in the British mail steamer *Trent*. On November 8, 1861, the *Trent* was overhauled at sea by Capt. Charles Wilkes in command of the U.S. warship *San Jacinto*, and Mason and Slidell were taken prisoners of war and confined at Fort Warren in Boston Harbor. The people of the North greeted this action with joyous approval, although it was a direct violation of the neutral rights for which we had fought England in 1812. On December 2, 1861, the House of Representatives passed a joint resolution extending the thanks of Congress to Wilkes, but it was pigeonholed in the Senate. And the *Trent* affair ended when Secretary of State Seward wisely released the Confederate envoys to

[6] Holbert N. Carroll, *The House of Representatives and Foreign Affairs* (1958), p. 11.

England.   In approving this decision President Lincoln remarked that "one war at a time is enough."

During the Civil War Congress became aroused by the intervention of Napoleon III in Mexico and tried to force President Lincoln to adopt a more vigorous policy toward France.   On April 4, 1864, the House unanimously passed a joint resolution offered by Henry Winter Davis, chairman of the Committee on Foreign Affairs, which declared that—

The Congress of the United States are unwilling, by silence, to leave the nations of the world under the impression that they are indifferent spectators of the deplorable events now transpiring in the Republic of Mexico; and they therefore think fit to declare that it does not accord with the policy of the United States to acknowledge a monarchical government, erected on the ruins of any republican government in America, under the auspices of any European power.

In a dispatch to the U.S. Minister at Paris shortly after the House adopted this resolution, Secretary of State Seward instructed him to explain to the French Government that this was purely an Executive question beyond the constitutional power of the House which had no authority in the determination of American recognition policy.   After Seward's dispatch had been communicated by the President to the House at its request, Representative Davis offered another resolution which was adopted by an overwhelming vote on December 21, 1865, and which declared that—

Congress has a constitutional right to an authoritative voice in declaring and prescribing the foreign policy of the United States, as well in the recognition of new powers as in other matters; and it is the constitutional duty of the President to respect that policy, not less in diplomatic negotiations than in the use of the national forces when authorized by law; and the propriety of any declaration of foreign policy by Congress is sufficiently proved by the vote which pronounced it; and such proposition while pending and undetermined is not a fit topic of diplomatic explanation with any foreign power.

The tempest subsided, but the controversy over the respective roles of the Executive and the Congress in foreign affairs under the Constitution remained unresolved.[7]

The House again asserted its legislative power over foreign relations following the Senate's ratification of the treaty with Russia for the purchase of Alaska on April 9, 1867.   Considerable opposition to the purchase was displayed in the House, which finally passed an appropriation bill on July 14, 1868, with a preamble asserting the authority of Congress over the subjects covered in the treaty and giving its "assent" thereto.   The Senate balked, of course, at this presumption but finally conceded in the compromise bill that certain clauses of the treaty could not be executed "except by legislation, to which the consent of both Houses of Congress is necessary."[8]

The relation of congressional legislative power to treaties arose again in this period when the House challenged the traditional practice of governing relations with the Indian tribes by treaty.   It refused in 1870 to make an appropriation for the execution of certain Indian treaties and succeeded in removing the regulation of Indian affairs from the field of foreign relations by a provision in the Indian Appropriation Act of 1871 that prohibited future recognition of an Indian tribe by treaty.[9]

[7] Goebel, *loc. cit.*, pp. 34–35.
[8] *Ibid.*, p. 35,
[9] *Ibid.*, p. 36.

During the closing decades of the 19th century Congress was largely preoccupied with domestic matters, but in the final years of the century it played an active part in three foreign episodes. In 1893 Queen Liliuokalani of Hawaii was deposed, but Congress resisted efforts to use American troops to restore the monarchy. In 1894 both Houses passed resolutions of noninterference in the Hawaiian situation; on July 4 Hawaii became a republic and was formally recognized by President Cleveland. Treaties for the annexation of the Hawaiian Islands failed during the Harrison and McKinley administrations, but after Admiral Dewey's electrifying victory at Manila, Congress approved the annexation of Hawaii by joint resolution which passed the House by a vote of 209 to 91.

In 1895 the longstanding boundary dispute between Great Britain and Venezuela came to a climax. By joint resolution Congress backed up President Cleveland's demand that the dispute be submitted to arbitration. When Britain refused, Congress, in a burst of anti-British feeling, quickly granted the President's request for an appropriation for a commission to investigate the boundary controversy. The episode led the two countries to the brink of war, but Britain finally agreed to arbitration.

At the end of the century congressional action led to the Spanish-American War. A vivid account of the role of Congress in this fateful conflict is given by Dr. Goebel: [10]

The Cuban revolution led to a complete reversal of the roles of President and Congress in our foreign relations. While in the Venezuela dispute, the President led with Congress close on his heels, in the case of Cuba, Congress dragged an unwilling Executive into an armed conflict. Throughout the nineteenth century, Cuba had been a subject of concern to the United States; American political, strategic, and commercial interest in the island was of long standing. On various occasions public anger had flared up over Spanish policy. By the early nineties, heavy American investments in Cuba reinforced traditional interest. The revolt of February 1895 evoked a rising tide of American sentiment, curiously compounded of the idealism of Don Quixote and the motives of a traveling salesman.

As the revolution continued, the spreading desolation in Cuba (trumpeted by the "yellow press") brought a nationwide demand for American action. The pugnacious mood evoked by the Venezuela crisis found in Spain a fresh target. Congressional humanitarian feeling and wrath erupted in a concurrent resolution (April 6, 1896) declaring in favor of recognition of the belligerency of the insurgents, and urging that the United States should tender its good offices to obtain from Spain recognition of the independence of Cuba. Cleveland and McKinley, in turn, refused to adopt this course and sought to restrain the Congressional temper.

The sinking of the *Maine* in Havana harbor (February 15, 1898) was a fuse that set off a charge of pent-up emotion. Cries for war against Spain and for American intervention to liberate Cuba echoed in the halls of Congress. While diplomatic negotiations with Spain dragged to an unsatisfactory conclusion, McKinley surrendered to Congressional pressure. Following the Presidential message of April 11, 1898, Congress passed the famous joint resolution (April 19) declaring the independence of the Cuban people, authorizing American intervention for the liberation of the island, renouncing any intention of annexation. A few days later, Congress passed an act declaring that, as of April 21, war existed between the United States and Spain.

By its action, Congress abandoned the historic American principle of nonintervention, and set the United States on a new and uncharted course. The span of the Spanish-American War was brief; its results were both unanticipated and momentous, for the war was carried into the Pacific. Admiral Dewey's attack upon the Philippine Islands resulted, successively, in the annexation of Hawaii (endowed with a new strategic importance) by joint resolution of Congress, July 7, 1898, and in the somewhat reluctant American decision at the close of the war to retain the Philippine Islands. The treaty with Spain (ratified

10 *Ibid.*, pp. 37–38.

by close vote in the Senate in February 1899) recognized the independence of Cuba, transferred the Philippines to the United States for the sum of $20 million, and ceded Puerto Rico and Guam to American possession. A by-product of the crusade for the liberation of Cuba was, thus, the creation of an American overseas empire and the emergence of the United States as a world power. Not since the days of the American Revolution had Congress exercised so fateful on influence on American foreign policy.

Thus it will be seen in retrospect that Congress, and especially the House of Representatives, participated intermittently in the foreign affairs of the United States during the 19th century and that at times—as in the War of 1812, the annexation of Texas, and the intervention in Cuba—it exercised a decisive influence upon our foreign policy. But at the end of the century the longstanding disputes between the House and Senate over the rival powers of legislation and treaty, and between Congress and the President over the right to recognize foreign states, remained unsolved.

TWENTIETH CENTURY TRENDS

While the 20th century was destined to witness a remarkable growth in the influence of the House of Representatives in the foreign field, its role in foreign affairs was a comparatively minor one down to the end of World War I. It participated in the passage of a bill for reciprocity with Canada during the special session of the 62d Congress, which that country promptly rejected; it approved the Underwood tariff bill in the 63d Congress by a vote of 281 to 139; and on April 6, 1917, it voted for war with Germany by 373 to 50. President Wilson dominated the foreign relations of the United States during the First World War. After the Senate rejected the Versailles Treaty in 1919, both Houses adopted a joint resolution "declaring peace," but President Wilson vetoed this measure on May 27, 1920, on the ground that it did not seek to accomplish any of the objects for which the United States had entered the war, and the House declined to override his veto. Later a similar resolution was adopted and signed by President Harding on July 2, 1921. Meanwhile, on the issue of naval disarmament, both Houses adopted the Borah amendment which was designed to remove the danger of Anglo-American naval rivalry.

During the interwar years (1920–40) the House of Representatives played a noteworthy part in legislative consideration of adherence to the World Court, proposals to prohibit the exportation of arms, and in neutrality legislation.

Adherence by the United States to the World Court was repeatedly urged by the President, but the Senate was slow to act. Finally the House, in 1925, by a vote of 303 to 28, took the unprecedented step of adopting a resolution declaring its approval of such a course and its willingness to make the necessary appropriations. Whereupon the Senate, on January 27, 1926, adopted a resolution of adherence by a vote of 76 to 17, but attached reservations which proved unacceptable to other members of the Court. In 1932 Chairman Linthicum of the Foreign Affairs Committee of the House sponsored a joint resolution authorizing an appropriation as our share of the Court's expenses for that year, but the resolution of adherence was rejected by the Senate on January 29, 1935, by a vote of 52 to 36, seven short of the required two-thirds majority. The United States finally became a member of the World Court on October 24, 1945, when the Charter of the United Nations and the statute of the Court became effective.

In 1922 Congress, at the request of the State Department, extended the arms embargo resolution of 1912 to prevent the shipment of arms to nations engaged in civil war. During the ensuing decade the House Committee on Foreign Affairs had arms embargo bills on its agenda on which extensive hearings were held. Finally, in May 1933, the McReynolds arms embargo resolution passed the House by a vote of 254 to 109. An amended version of this resolution passed the Senate on February 28, 1934, but was not called up in the House. But the long study of the subject by the House was not without some influence, for on April 19, 1934, the Senate set up the special Nye committee to investigate the international traffic in arms, and in May President Roosevelt asked the Senate to give its advice and consent to the Geneva Convention of 1925.[11]

Meanwhile, as the clouds of war were gathering in Germany under Hitler, in Italy under Mussolini, and in the Far East, Congress turned its attention to measures designed to keep the United States out of war. These included credits to belligerents, restrictions on travel by Americans in war zones, on the use of ports by submarines, and on the shipment of raw materials to belligerents. Between 1935 and 1939 the Committee on Foreign Affairs and the House itself considered a flood of bills and resolutions that sought to prevent American involvement in any conflict. For 5 years or more Congress engaged in a futile quest to find neutrality in a world bent on war. The upshot of this effort was a series of five neutrality laws: The joint resolutions of August 31, 1935, February 29, 1936, January 8, 1937, May 1, 1937, and November 4, 1939. When World War II broke out in 1939, the country embarked upon a defense program and Congress responded generously to Executive requests for grants of money and power to safeguard the Nation. As part of the defense program Congress enacted the Lend-Lease Act of 1941 which passed the House by a vote of 260 to 165.[12]

Thus, the two decades prior to the outbreak of the Second World War were marked by expanding congressional activity in the foreign field. This activity found expression in committee hearings and inquiries, in extended floor debates and the adoption of resolutions, and in the legislative consideration of a wide range of international problems. Albert Westphal concluded his survey of the role of the House in foreign affairs down to 1940 by observing that it was still inferior to that of the Senate for various reasons, including qualities inherent in the composition and organization of the House; that the Senate was "less amenable to Presidential leadership in foreign affairs than the House"; and that the Foreign Affairs Committee, which had long been regarded as an "ornamental committee" whose members were "relatively obscure in the national scene" and had been apathetic toward obtaining a large role in foreign policy, had come since 1935 into public and legislative prominence with the increasing importance of legislation on foreign affairs.

---

[11] For a detailed account of the role of the House Committee on Foreign Affairs in arms embargo legislation during these years, see A. C. F. Westphal, *The House Committee on Foreign Affairs* (1942), ch. VI.
[12] For a full account of the part played by the Committee on Foreign Affairs and by the House in shaping the various neutrality laws and the lend-lease bill, see Westphal, *op. cit.*, ch. VII.

EXPANDING ROLE OF HOUSE SINCE 1935

While the House of Representatives up to the midthirties had upon occasion played an important part in specific foreign policy issues, its emergence as a major force in the field of foreign affairs on a continuing basis dates from that period. It found expression, first, in the neutrality legislation of the latter half of that decade and, second, in the active participation of the House in the legislative underwriting of the Second World War. President Roosevelt set forth the goals of a new foreign policy for the United States in the form of the Atlantic Charter and the four freedoms. The war period was marked by the establishment of bipartisan and bicameral consultations between Congress and the State Department during the Hull-Welles regime, the extension of the lend-lease legislation in 1943, 1944, and 1945 which the House approved by votes of 407 to 6, 334 to 21, and 354 to 28; creation in 1943 of the United Nations Relief and Rehabilitation Administration by means of an executive agreement which the House approved by a vote of 287 to 57 on the conference report; House adoption of the Fulbright resolution by a vote of 360 to 29, indicating, together with the Connally resolution, congressional support for the postwar establishment of an international organization to keep the peace; and congressional participation at either the preparatory or conference stages in international conferences at Dumbarton Oaks, Mexico City, and San Francisco. Desiring to participate in the control of postwar policy, the House in 1945 passed a resolution amending the Constitution by giving itself equal power over treaties with the Senate by a vote of 288 to 88, but the Senate was unwilling to share its treaty power with the House and took no action on the resolution.[13]

Any President must depend upon congressional support in order to implement his foreign policy, for Congress has power to regulate foreign commerce, to raise armies and maintain navies, to lay and collect taxes for the common defense, and to declare war. Moreover, it has the added power "to make all laws which shall be necessary and proper" for effectuating its own powers and those of the Government of the United States. Before and during World War II the foreign policy of the Roosevelt administration was implemented and sustained by a series of legislative acts of which the Lend-Lease Act of March 11, 1941, was the classic example. Under this act, as extended, the United States entered into mutual aid agreements whereby our allies received $40 billion worth of munitions and other supplies. According to Professor Corwin, the Lend-Lease Act was "the most extensive delegation of authority ever made by Congress to the President to enter into executive agreements. * * *"[14] Corwin further comments that—

the relations of President and Congress in the diplomatic field have, first and last, presented a varied picture of alternate cooperation and tension, from which emerge two outstanding facts: first, the overwhelming importance of Presidential initiative in this area of power; secondly, the ever increasing dependence of foreign policy on Congressional cooperation and support.[15]

The enhanced role of the House of Representatives in the foreign affairs field was seen during the Second World War in the composition of the Committee on Postwar Foreign Policy on which the House was

---

[13] For a fuller account of these wartime developments see Roland Young, *Congressional Politics in the Second World War* (1956), ch. 7.
[14] Corwin, *The Constitution of the United States*, p. 443.
[15] *Ibid.*, p. 470.

represented by Representative Sol Bloom, chairman of the Committee on Foreign Affairs, Representative Charles A. Eaton, ranking minority member of the committee, and Representative Luther A. Johnson, of Texas. It was also reflected in Secretary Hull's consultations with various Members of Congress prior to the Dumbarton Oaks Conference and in the presence of two representatives on the U.S. delegation to the San Francisco Conference. After the Senate ratified the United Nations Charter, it was implemented by the United Nations Participation Act of 1945, thus invoking the national legislative power to accomplish the objectives of the charter.

The increasing importance of the role of the House in the international scene has also been shown in recent years by the submission to the Congress of international agreements which require legislative implementation to become effective and which Congress has approved by joint resolution. The original UNRRA legislation (Public Law 267, 78th Cong.) was an early example of this procedure. During the 79th Congress both Houses approved U.S. membership in the International Monetary Fund and the International Bank (Public Law 171, 79th Cong.) and in the Food and Agricultural Organization of the United Nations (Public Law 174, 79th Cong.). During the 80th Congress the same procedure was employed to secure U.S. membership in the International Refugee Organization (Public Law 146, 80th Cong.), the World Health Organization (Public Law 643, 80th Cong.), the revised International Labor Organization (Public Law 843, 80th Cong.), the Caribbean Commission (Public Law 431, 80th Cong.), and the South Pacific Commission (Public Law 403, 80th Cong.). Likewise, the North Atlantic Treaty has been implemented by a series of acts, beginning with the Mutual Defense Assistance Act of 1949 (Public Law 329, 81st Cong.), which were initiated in the House of Representatives, in accordance with its traditional function of originating supply bills.

Further evidence of the increasing share of Congress in the development and execution of American foreign policy is seen in the evolution of our foreign aid program since World War II. Beginning with the Economic Cooperation Act of 1948 and continuing through successive aid legislation, Congress has spelled out in detail the conditions governing the administration and execution of our foreign policy in the field of economic aid. As a watchdog of the aid program the 1948 act set up a Joint Committee on Foreign Economic Cooperation consisting of three members each from the House Foreign Affairs and Senate Foreign Relations Committees and two from each of the Appropriations Committees. Moreover, since all the various forms of foreign aid cost money that must be appropriated annually and since all appropriation bills originate in the House of Representatives, its Committee on Appropriations has had a much stronger voice in the postwar conduct of our foreign relations than was traditionally true. The annual battle of the foreign aid budget on Capitol Hill has required the administration to submit our foreign aid programs to periodic "agonizing reappraisals" in order to maintain continued congressional support.

In a single postwar year, 1956, the State Department reported that the United States had concluded 260 treaties and other international agreements. Of these, only five were actually in the form of treaties that required the advice and consent of the Senate, while 95 percent of the agreements were entered into under legislative enactments that specified their terms.

Today, therefore, in the most important areas of our formal relations with foreign countries, the negotiations of those relations by the President are conducted in a framework provided by the Congress and governed by conditions spelled out in advance by Congress.[16]

The significance of these postwar developments is that, without any formal constitutional change, the role of the House in the foreign field has been greatly enhanced.

Recent years have thus witnessed a resurgence of legislative activity in the conduct of foreign affairs. The Fulbright and Connally resolutions placed both the Senate and the House of Representatives on record as favoring U.S. participation in an international peace organization. They were followed in 1945 by congressional approval of the United Nations Charter. Postwar programs of economic assistance for Europe, such as the British loan in 1946, the Greek-Turkish aid program in 1947, and the European recovery program in 1948–51 all had to be implemented by congressional appropriations.

Illustrations abound of congressional participation in the conduct of foreign affairs. Under its constitutional power to fix import duties Congress has shared since 1934 in the reciprocal trade-agreement programs. Through its power over immigration it has played a part in policy formulation on the entrance of displaced persons. By the National Security Act of 1947 it has prescribed the process of policy formulation and coordination with respect to the use of force in the conduct of foreign affairs. The 81st Congress alone enacted 18 major public laws relating to international affairs, including the continuance of the Marshall plan, extension of the reciprocal trade agreements, military aid to Western Europe and South Korea, and guarantees of private investments abroad under the point 4 program. Although the initiative remains largely with the President, the conduct of foreign affairs now calls for joint legislative-executive cooperation both in the determination of objectives and in the formulation and execution of policies.

The role of Congress in the conduct of our foreign affairs has received increased recognition in recent times from the executive branch. The Department of State held many informal conferences on foreign policy with members of the foreign affairs committees of Congress after the outbreak of hostilities in 1939. The President and the Secretary of State reported in person to Congress upon their conduct of our foreign relations after their return from international conferences at Yalta and Moscow. The State Department named one of its Assistant Secretaries to supervise the Department's liaison with Congress. Mr. Dean Acheson, who first functioned in this capacity, established a formal relationship with the Senate Committee on Foreign Relations and the House Committee on Foreign Affairs. And influential Members of both Houses of Congress participated by Presidential invitation in the actual negotiation of great international agreements at Bretton Woods, San Francisco, and London—a practice that won widespread congressional approval and greatly improved the climate of legislative opinion, as well as congressional understanding, of international political and economic problems.

---

[16] Walter S. Surrey, "The Legislative Process and International Law," *Proceedings* of the American Society of International Law, 1958, p. 13. Mr. Surrey was formerly Assistant Legal Adviser on Economic Affairs of the Department of State.

PROBLEM OF COORDINATION

There has been an enormous increase in the foreign affairs business of Congress over the past 35 years. In 1925 only 1 bill in 25 had any direct bearing on foreign relations, whereas 1 out of every 7 bills enacted in 1949 had some relationship to foreign affairs. Responsibility for handling this rising workload is scattered among 10 standing committees in each House of Congress and 3 joint committees: Atomic Energy, the Joint Economic Committee, and Immigration and Nationality Policy.[17]   A recent study by Holbert Carroll shows that in the decade after World War II—

10 committees of the House of Representatives pursued their sometimes inconsistent and usually uncoordinated philosophies in a fraction of 1 policy area, the area of international trade policy.[18]

Meanwhile, six House committees considered the subject of export control, and several committees were active in the field of shipping. The total picture is one of the widespread dispersal and uncoordinated control of interrelated foreign policy matters among many autonomous committees.[19]

Under these circumstances the need of coordination in the work of the House on foreign affairs has been generally conceded. But Members are skeptical of proposals to solve the problem of integrating congressional control of foreign policy.[20] Among possible coordinating devices the select committee, composed of Members drawn from interested standing committees of the House, has been used with considerable success in foreign affairs on three recent occasions: the Special Committee on Postwar Economic Policy and Planning (the Colmer committee), established early in 1944; the Select Committee to Investigate Soviet Seizure of the Baltic States (the Kersten committee), formed in the summer of 1953; and the Select Committee on Foreign Aid (the Herter committee), created in July 1947.[21]

COMMITTEE ON FOREIGN AFFAIRS

The Committee on Foreign Affairs and the Committee on Appropriations have been the two principal agents of the House in the international area. Created in 1822, the Foreign Affairs Committee has long had a broad jurisdiction over our foreign relations, including the primary duty of authorizing all appropriations for the conduct of foreign affairs by the Department of State, the International Cooperation Administration, and the U.S. Information Agency. Long regarded as a minor committee, Foreign Affairs has become in latter years one of the most popular committee assignments in the House. After World War II it was organized into several standing "consultative subcommittees" whose members have become specialists on particular geographical and problem areas. With the aid of a small professional staff this committee has been making a vital contribution to the development, implementation, and oversight of postwar foreign policy. The committee has kept itself and the House informed of international developments by means of frequent con-

---

[17] For a list of these 20 committees see L. Larry Leonard, *Elements of American Foreign Policy* (1953), p. 159.

[18] Holbert N. Carroll, *The House of Representatives and Foreign Affairs* (1958), p. 58.

[19] For the details of this picture see Carroll, *op. cit.*, ch. 5.

[20] See Carroll, *op. cit.*, ch. 11, for discussion of committee coordination.

[21] For a brief description of these select committees see Carroll, *op. cit.*, pp. 211–218.

ferences with top-level Government officials, both civil and military; by sending special study missions to various parts of the world; by setting up special legislative subcommittees to hold hearings and report on specific legislative proposals; by the participation of members of the committee in important international conferences; and by the representation of the committee, beginning in 1951, on the U.S. delegations to the General Assembly of the United Nations.

Holbert Carroll summarizes his intensive study of the Foreign Affairs Committee during the 12-year period, 1945-56, as follows:[22]

Like the nation, the foreign policy committee only gradually adjusted to the role of world leadership that fell to the United States. Like the nation, the committee matured slowly. * * * In the second half of 1947, the group developed fresh strength and moved into a more constructive phase of its history; it began to play a more responsible role in the control of foreign affairs. * * *

In testing and managing a large volume of bills and resolutions, however, the committee did not alter the fundamentals of American foreign policy. Rather, it modified the measures to harmonize with its views regarding the objectives of that policy and to anticipate the political realities of the lower chamber. The committee's control resembled erosion; the essentials remained but were shaped to suit the congressional temper. In molding legislation, moreover, the Committee on Foreign Affairs, in contrast to many other committees, generally succeeded in keeping the foreign policy objectives dominant and unfettered by the more unenlightened proposals of pressure and propaganda groups.

COMMITTEE ON APPROPRIATIONS

In the legislative process in Congress supply follows authorization to spend. The role of the House Committee on Appropriations is therefore a powerful one, all the more because the House tends to ratify its recommendations. Down to 1950 jurisdiction over the financing of international affairs was scattered among several appropriations subcommittees, so that it was not possible to obtain an integrated view of the foreign affairs budgets. But the creation of a Subcommittee on Foreign Operations in 1950 has enabled its members to specialize in the financing of foreign affairs and has tended to consolidate the consideration of our international expenditures.

Holbert Carroll's analysis of the role of the Committee on Appropriations in handling foreign affairs since the end of World War II shows that it has employed five major types of control: [23]

First, and most important, the committee determines how much money will be allowed for the foreign affairs purposes. Second, in the hearings it reviews policies and their administration. In the third place, it wields influence by the language employed in committee reports. Limitations and legislative provisions inserted in appropriation bills constitute a fourth type of control. Finally, the committee exercises year-around surveillance over the expenditure of funds.

The following figures show a few examples of the extent to which the House has trimmed the President's requests. For government and relief in the occupied areas the President asked Congress for a total of $4,970,876,000 for the fiscal years 1947 to 1952, inclusive, and the House approved a total of $4,110,500,000 for this period. For European recovery aid in 1950 the President requested $4,198,200,000 and the House granted $3,568,470,000. For the State Department and the U.S. Information Agency the estimates of the President ag-

---

[22] *Ibid.*, p. 137. The best full-length histories of the Committee on Foreign Affairs are those by Albert C. F. Westphal, *The House Committee on Foreign Affairs* (1942), for the period before World War II; and by Holbert N. Carroll, *The House of Representatives and Foreign Affairs* (1958), for the postwar period.
[23] Carroll, *op. cit.*, p. 154.

gregated $1,407,359,662 for the years 1951 to 1957, inclusive, while the House approved a total of $1,169,428,730 for this period.

SUMMARY AND CONCLUSIONS

Summarizing this chapter, we have seen that during most of the 19th century after the War of 1812 the House of Representatives, with intermittent foreign interruptions, was largely preoccupied with domestic issues; that down to World War II the House was distinctly a junior partner of the Senate in foreign affairs, but that it has become a coordinate member of the foreign policy team since the late war; that the foreign policy business of the House has greatly increased in recent decades and that responsibility for foreign affairs is divided among numerous standing committees which have jurisdiction over important aspects of the field, with a resulting lack of integration and perspective; that the House has met the problem of integrating congressional control of foreign affairs by improvised solutions such as the special Herter and Colmer committees and occasional joint hearings; that the Committee on Foreign Affairs, which experienced a rapid turnover among its chairmen and members during the 19th century, has now become one of the most eminent and sought-after committees in the House; that the enhanced role of the House in foreign affairs since World War II reflects both the emergence of the United States as the leading power of the free world and the dependence of the far-flung activities of the Department of State and the mutual security program upon the power of the purse for their implementation; that the House Committee on Appropriations has a major voice in the determination of our foreign policy through its control over funds for foreign expenditure; and that Congress also influences foreign policy through the passage of laws and resolutions like the Fulbright resolution, through congressional service on American delegations to international conferences and to the United Nations, and through frequent consultations with executive officials.

It may be added, in conclusion, that the House of Representatives performs a special role in the foreign field. Representing local interests as it does, it furnishes a sort of recurrent plebiscite on the foreign policy of the United States, acting as a mediator between the foreign policy specialists at Washington and the "public's" notions of what ought to be done. Moreover, the House interprets and transmits to the country information on complicated world problems. Thus Congress functions as a forum through which public opinion is brought to bear upon the Federal Government, and as a medium for gathering and disseminating information for the instruction and enlightenment of the people.

CHAPTER 13

THE ROLE OF THE REPRESENTATIVE

The modern system of political representation as we know it in the United States today is a product of the evolutionary development of the national state which dates back to 17th century England. The English Parliament had developed during the 14th century as a bicameral institution and had gradually acquired legislative power through its control over the purse, making its grant of funds to the King depend upon the redress of grievances. By the end of the 15th century the consent of both the House of Lords and the House of Commons was recognized as necessary in the enactment of legislation. The 17th century witnessed the classic English statements of the right of the people through their chosen representatives to control the form and policy of government.

ENGLISH IDEAS IN COLONIAL TIMES

By colonial times two ideas had developed in England regarding the proper role of the representative in relation to his constituents. One was the delegation theory, the idea that a Member of Parliament was an agent of his constituency that had elected him, bound to obey its wishes. This idea was held by the Levellers during the Commonwealth period (1640–60) and by the English Radicals in the late 18th century (1769–1800). It influenced the writings of political theorists like Harrington, Sydney, and Locke, and the policies of colonial political leaders such as William Penn and Roger Williams. One of the major items in the Radical program was the right of electors to instruct their Members of Parliament. A clear statement of this concept was made by Henry Cruger, a Radical who was elected with Edmund Burke to represent the city of Bristol in Parliament in 1774. He said: [1]

It has ever been my opinion that the electors have a right to instruct their members. For my part, I shall always think it my duty in Parliament to be guided by your counsels and instructions. I shall consider myself the servant of my constituents, not their master—subservient to their will, not superior to it. And let me add, I hold myself accountable to you for every action of my life which respects the public. By your upright judgment, I desire to stand or fall.

The other idea of political representation that developed in England during colonial times was the idea of virtual representation: the doctrine that the representative was a trustee for the entire nation, and was free to decide matters according to his own independent judgment. This idea had been expressed as early as 1745 by Sir William Yonge who, speaking of members of the House of Commons, said:

Every one knows that, by our Constitution, after a gentleman is chosen, he is the representative, or, if you please, the attorney of the people of England, and as such is at full freedom to act as he thinks best for the people of England in

---

[1] Quoted by P. T. Underdown in "Henry Cruger and Edmund Burke: Colleagues and Rivals at the Bristol Election of 1774," *William and Mary Quart.* January 1958, p. 31n.

general. He may receive, he may ask, he may even follow the advice of his particular constituents; but he is not obliged, nor ought he, to follow their advice, if
he thinks it inconsistent with the general interest of his country.

The classic statement of this position was contained in Burke's
address to the electors of Bristol in 1774 replying to Cruger's chal-
lenge. The representative, Burke said, owed his constituents not his
industry only, but also his judgment, and he betrayed instead of
serving them if he sacrificed it to their opinion. To deliver an opinion
was the right of all men, that of constituents was a weighty and re-
spectable opinion, which a representative ought always to rejoice to
hear, and which he ought most seriously to consider; but authoritative
instructions, mandates which the member was bound blindly and im-
plicitly to obey, to vote and to argue for, though contrary to the
clearest conviction of his judgment and conscience, were things utterly
unknown to the laws of the land, and arose from a fundamental mistake concerning the whole order and tenor of the Constitution. Parliament was not a congress of ambassadors from different and hostile
interests; it was a deliberative assembly of one nation with one interest, that of the whole, where not local purposes, not local prejudices
ought to guide, but the general good resulting from the general reason
of the whole. "You choose a member indeed, but when you have
chosen him, he is not a member for Bristol; he is a member of Parliament."

Despite occasional departures, this idea of virtual representation
was the prevailing theory and practice of members of Parliament
during 18th century England, especially after 1760 and at the time
of the American Revolution.

CONTINENTAL IDEAS

Meanwhile, on the Continent of Europe, theory and practice
differed as to the nature of the representative's responsibility to his
constituents. Writing in the later 18th century, Rousseau rejected
the representative principle which he considered inconsistent with
popular sovereignty. Whether the representatives sought to carry
out an imperative popular mandate or to exercise their own judgment
of the requirements of the general welfare, he felt that they would
reach decisions essentially different from what the people would
decide directly. The general will could be reliably expressed only in
primary assemblies.

In the Cortes of medieval Spain and in the Netherlands from the
15th century until 1814, representatives were bound by the instructions of their constituents. On the other hand, the French revolutionary assembly of 1789 proclaimed that its members, representing
the entire nation, could not be bound by instructions from their
particular constituencies; and a similar principle of free representation
was embodied in the mid-19th century constitutions of France,
Prussia, and Italy.[2]

REPRESENTATION IN COLONIAL ASSEMBLIES

Although the American colonists were deprived of the right of
electing members of the English Parliament, every colony had a legislative assembly whose members were chosen on the basis of a limited

[2] Article on "Representation" in the *Encyclopedia of the Social Sciences*, by Francis W. Coker and Carlton
O. Rodee.

popular suffrage. The colonial systems of representation were influenced by various factors. The colonial charters gave the colonists the full rights of English subjects, including the right to vote for representatives in the colonial assemblies. English customs and precedents exercised a controlling influence upon the qualifications of voters in the colonies. Tendencies toward direct democracy were seen in frequent elections of numerous officers, residence requirements, the decline of the real-property qualification for voting, and in the practice of instructions to representatives. McKinley gives an interesting example of an instruction in 1773 by the inhabitants of Orange County, N.C., to their delegates in the assembly:[3]

We have chosen you our Representatives at the next General Assembly and when we did so we expected and do still expect that you will speak our Sense in every case when we shall expressly declare it, or when you can by any other means discover it. In all other cases we suppose you left to your own discretion which is ever to be directed by the Good of our Country in general and of this County in particular. This is our notion of the Duty of Representatives, and the Rights of Electors.

"These practices all tended to reduce the representative to the delegate status, forcing the public servant to voice accurately and under pain of imminent defeat at the polls the sentiment of the majority of the constituency."[4] Over the long run, the trend in the colonies was thus away from the English idea of virtual representation, which the colonists strongly opposed, and toward the idea of direct representation, reminiscent of the Levellers of 17th century England. This trend was influenced, at least in New England, by Puritan theology with its theory of the social compact, its idea of an organic society, and its doctrine of magistracy. It was also modified somewhat by the idea of the representation of the prevailing material interests of the rising commercial classes which found expression during the revolutionary period.[5]

REVOLUTIONARY-CONSTITUTIONAL PERIOD

The years 1775-90 were marked by the growth of two basic ideas concerning the relationship of the representative and his constituents. One school of thought was composed of the direct democrats like Benjamin Franklin, Thomas Jefferson, Tom Paine, and James Wilson who stressed the social compact doctrine and the natural rights of man, including the right to control his representatives in the popular chamber. This group placed its faith in the common people, direct representation, and majority rule.

Representation to them was a simple matter of making governmental officials an exact working model of the mass of people in action. A representative ought to be immediately responsible to his constituents, he ought to follow instructions, elections ought to be frequent, the recall and referendum might be used, a constitution ought to restrict the powers of the representatives rather than the powers of the people, any office of power ought to be elective, and the sovereignty and will of the people, expressed through the just principle of the majority rule, had almost a magical quality.[6]

A second school of thought, of which Madison and Hamilton were leading exponents, saw society as composed of constantly shifting and

[3] Albert E. McKinley, *The Suffrage Franchise in the Thirteen English Colonies in America* (1905), p. 113.
[4] Alfred de Grazia, *Public and Republic* (1951), p. 56.
[5] On theories of representation in England, on the continent of Europe, and in America, see Robert Luce, *Legislative Principles* (1930), ch. XIX.
[6] De Grazia, *op. cit.*, pp. 242–243.

conflicting interests in an age of commercial expansion and they sought in the Constitution to create a system of representation in which these contending interests would check and balance each other. Representation was regarded by them as a means of accommodating and controlling interest groups. Reflecting the interests of the commercial and landed classes, this group reacted against the delegation theory of representation, which had prevailed in the formation of the State governments, and seemed to favor a kind of pluralistic scheme of representation that would safeguard the rights of minorities and check the excesses of direct democracy. It was this balancing-of-interests view of the conservatives that found expression finally in the structure of government established by the Constitution of 1787.

Madison with customary clarity voiced this view of society in No. 10 of the Federalist:

A landed interest, a manufacturing interest, a mercantile interest, a money interest, with many lesser interests, grow up of necessity in civilized nations, and divide them into different classes, actuated by different sentiments and views. The regulation of these various and interfering interests forms the principal task of modern legislation, and involves the spirit of party and faction in the necessary and ordinary operations of Government.

On the relations between a representative and his constituents, the authors of the Federalist papers also wrote that—

it is a sound and important principle that the representative ought to be acquainted with the interests and circumstances of his constituents. But this principle can extend no further than to those circumstances and interests to which the authority and care of the representative relate.[7]

Moreover—

if we consider the situation of the men on whom the free suffrages of their fellow-citizens may confer the representative trust, we shall find it involving every security which can be devised or desired for their fidelity to their constituents * * *. Duty, gratitude, interest, ambition itself, are the chords by which they will be bound to fidelity and sympathy with the great mass of the people.[8]

DEBATE IN FIRST CONGRESS

After the ratification of the Constitution, the First Congress debated a proposal to amend that document so as to permit constituents to instruct their representatives. Madison opposed this proposal and it was rejected by a vote of 41 to 10 after an extended debate in which 17 Members took part. The case for the amendments was presented by Mr. Page, of Virginia, and Mr. Gerry, of Massachusetts. Page thought that instruction and representation were inseparably connected in a republic.

I think, sir, [he said] to doubt the authority of the people to instruct their representatives, will give them just cause to be alarmed for their fate. I look upon it as a dangerous doctrine, subversive of the great end for which the United States have confederated. Every friend of mankind, every well-wisher of his country, will be desirous of obtaining the sense of the people on every occasion of magnitude; but how can this be so well expressed as in instructions to their representatives? * * * It is the sense of several of the [state] conventions that this amendment should take place; I think it is my duty to support it, and fear it will spread an alarm among our constituents if we decline to do it.

7 Federalist, No. 56.
8 Federalist, No. 57.

Gerry contended that instruction from the people would furnish an additional check against abuse which every government is subject to.

* * * to say the sovereignty vests in the people, and that they have not a right to instruct and control their representatives, [he said] is absurd to the last degree * * * the amendment * * * only declares the right of the people to send instructions; the representative will, if he thinks proper, communicate his instructions to the House, but how far they shall operate on his conduct, he will judge for himself * * * much good may result from a declaration in the Constitution that they possess this privilege; the people will be encouraged to come forward with their instructions, which will form a fund of useful information for the Legislature.

Much of this debate revolved around the question whether or not instructions from the people would be binding upon their representatives; but most of those who participated in the discussion opposed the amendment. Hartley of Pennsylvania considered Congress to be the best judge of proper measures and anticipated that instructions would never be resorted to but for party purposes, that they would embarrass the best and wisest men, and make it impossible to accommodate various viewpoints. Clymer, of Pennsylvania, believed that a constitutional right of instruction would be "a dangerous principle, utterly destructive of all ideas of an independent and deliberative body, which are essential requisites in the Legislatures of free Governments." Sherman, of Connecticut, thought that—

when the people have chosen a representative, it is his duty to meet others from the different parts of the Union, and consult, and agree with them to such acts as are for the general benefit of the whole community. If they were to be guided by instructions, there would be no use in deliberation; all that a man would have to do, would be to produce his instructions, and lay them on the table, and let them speak for him * * *. It is the duty of a good representative [said Sherman] to inquire what measures are most likely to promote the general welfare, and, after he has discovered them, to give them his support. Should his instructions, therefore, coincide with his ideas on any measure, they would be unnecessary; if they were contrary to the convictions of his own mind, he must be bound by every principle of justice to disregard them.

Sedgwick, of Massachusetts, wondered how the sense of a majority of the voters in a large State could be obtained and communicated. Lawrence, of New York, opposed the amendment because he thought that every Member ought to consider himself the representative of the whole Union and not of the particular district that had chosen him, whose interests might clash with those of the general good; unless instructions were to be considered as binding, they were superfluous. And Madison, of Virginia, did not believe that the inhabitants of any district could speak the voice of all the people. Far from it—

their ideas may contradict the sense of the whole people; hence the consequence that instructions are binding on the representative is of a doubtful, if not a dangerous nature.[9]

Evidently it was the preponderant opinion of the House in the First Congress, despite the inclusion of the principle of instructions in several of the State constitutions, that representatives were to be trustees for the whole Nation, not merely agents of their particular constituencies.

---

[9] *Annals of Congress*, vol. 1, pp. 733–748. Gales and Seaton edition (1834).

DEVELOPMENT OF DIRECT REPRESENTATION, 1800–1860

Thomas Jefferson's triumph over the Federalists in 1800 marked the opening of a new century and a change in the prevailing theory and practice of political representation. The ideas of Madison and Hamilton were eclipsed and faith in the common man and in the devices of direct democracy swept the country. The first decades of the 19th century witnessed the widening of the suffrage and the expansion of the electorate, a trend toward the direct election of officers, the dispersion of administrative functions, and widespread adoption of the practice of instructing representatives. The idea of direct representation now came into vogue, an idea which—

exalted the majority principle, brought social institutions as close to the individual as possible, challenged the division of labor between officers and public, and decried any failure of the representative to reflect immediately and faithfully the mathematical sum of his constituents' desires and characteristics.[10]

The nature of the relations that prevailed at this time between the Congressman and his constituents was reflected in the practice of instructions which were generally obeyed. Some conception of the role of the representative as it was then conceived may be had from the tenor of a resolution adopted by the Legislature of Virginia in 1812 when its Senators in Congress (Giles and Brent) had refused to follow legislative instructions. The resolution maintained that the instruction of representatives had been a legal practice in the English House of Commons since time immemorial, that it was "much more unquestionable in the United States, where the people are acknowledged to be the only legitimate source of all legislation," that the nature of representation required the right of instruction, and that the confidence and discretion with which a representative is endowed "is grounded on the supposition, that he is charged with the will, acquainted with the opinions, and devoted to the interests of his constituents." [11]

When Andrew Jackson was elected President in 1828, he received a letter of congratulation on his first annual message to Congress from the English philosopher, Jeremy Bentham, who had published a pamphlet on parliamentary reform in 1817. Bentham sent Jackson a set of documents entitled "Anti-Senatica" which attacked the unrepresentative character of the American Senate, but approved the representative quality of the House of Representatives in which he saw a "unity of interests and affections with the body of its constituents."[12]

President Jackson set forth his own concept of the role of a representative in his proclamation on the South Carolina secession movement in 1832 when, speaking of the Members of the House of Representatives, he declared:

However they may in practice, as it is their duty to do, consult and prefer the interests of their particular constituents when they come in conflict with any other particular or local interest, yet it is their first or highest duty, as representatives of the United States, to promote the general good.[13]

Not long after, Abraham Lincoln, then a young State legislator, expressed his own view upon the relation of a representative to his

---

[10] De Grazia, *op. cit.*, p. 246.
[11] *Ibid.*, pp. 126–127.
[12] *Ibid.*, p. 122.
[13] *Messages and Papers of the Presidents*, vol. II, p. 648. Quoted by De Grazia, *op. cit.*, p. 128.

constituency. When he was a candidate for reelection to the Illinois Legislature in 1836, he began his campaign by saying: [14]

If elected, I shall consider the whole people of Sangamon my constituents, as well those that oppose as those that support me. While acting as their representative I shall be governed by their will on all subjects upon which I have the means of knowing what their will is, and upon all others I shall do what my own judgment teaches me will best advance their interests.

Not all legislators of that period, however, felt the same way as Lincoln did. "Davy" Crockett, Congressman from Tennessee, is said to have sent to his constituents whose demands he was unwilling to obey this brusque message in 1836: "I am going to Texas, and you can go to Hell!" [15]

Writing in 1851, John C. Calhoun, who was concerned for the protection of States' rights and minority interests, developed an original theory of representation that rejected the principle of majority rule and called for the separate representation of classes and interests, each of which should possess a veto over the acts of the others. Before any law of general application could be valid, he argued, it must receive the assent of each interest, in which event it has been enacted by a "concurrent majority." Otherwise, legislation is null and void in States that have rejected it. Calhoun's theory was liquidated by the Civil War, but echoes of it are still heard in the land. [16]

POST-CIVIL WAR TRENDS

The century since the Civil War has seen conflicting forces at work in the theory and practice of political representation in America. The psychological reaction of the Southern States to their defeat in the war, the emergence of many new economic groups with the postwar expansion of industry and agriculture and the growth of trade unions, the changes in the ethnic composition of the population as millions of European immigrants entered our gates, and the slow enfranchisement of the Negroes in recent decades, all combined to effect far-reaching changes in the ideas and tactics of representation.

The proponents of direct democracy and direct representation sought to democratize the political parties by substituting direct primaries for controlled conventions. They furnished much of the drive for the woman suffrage movement, for the direct election of judges, and for the popular election of U.S. Senators. They advocated the initiative, referendum, and recall: a movement for the popular control of government that reached its crest in the late 19th and early 20th centuries. Twenty States had adopted the initiative and referendum by 1938. The development of public opinion polls after World War I was seen as another manifestation of the democratic surge and as a device for inducing the representative to comply with the expressed desires of his constituents. The third-party movements of the 1890's, of 1912, and 1924, all sought reforms in representation and political institutions that would strengthen the "people" as against the "interests" in the Halls of Congress, in the executive departments, and on the Federal bench. [17]

[14] Nicolay and Hay, *Abraham Lincoln*, vol. I, p. 129.
[15] George H. Haynes, *The United States Senate* (1938), vol. 2, p. 1030n.
[16] John C. Calhoun, *Disquisition on Government* and *Discourse on the Constitution and Government of the United States*.
[17] For a full discussion of these developments, see De Grazia, *op. cit.*, ch. VI.

Meanwhile, with the growing complexity of American society and the increasingly mixed character of many constituencies, the legislator tended to become a broker among competing interests in the political marketplace rather than a direct representative of the people. The development of powerful lobbies in Washington, described as "a third house of Congress," exposed Members to the pressures of organized interest groups and converted the task of the representative into an effort to compromise their differences. As Representative T. V. Smith of Illinois expressed it: [18]

Legislatures are the readiest exemplars of the process of compromise. This is a humble but honorable view of the democratic process * * *. Legislation is * * * a business in which you do something, then wait to see who hollers, and then relieve the hollering as best you can to see who else hollers.

In recent times the role of the Representative has become increasingly that of broker for a Member's constituency in its individual and collective dealings with the Federal Government. Legislative intervention in the life of the Federal executive has become "more complex, more subtle, and more detailed" than ever before. Constituents expect their Congressman to intercede on their behalf with agencies to obtain a contract from the Navy or secure a favorable decision from a regulatory agency or what not. Congressional intervention in administration is apparently greater in programs involving loans, subsidies, contracts, franchises, and permits of various kinds. Marver Bernstein remarks that many Members of Congress would be relieved of an awkward and time-consuming burden if they were forbidden to intervene in matters of formal adjudication in an agency. But almost all of them regard such services to constituents as a necessary and proper part of their representative function.[19]

Paradoxically, the same basic developments that have brought an ever-increasing mass of constituent requests and claims and pressures have at the same time made the Representative in some respects more and more a free agent in making his decisions. Interest group organization and means of influence have been perfected, mass education, growing interest in public affairs, and greater ease of communication have all resulted in more and more demands on the Member, but the increased diversity of interests in most constituencies makes it more difficult for any segment of the district or any particular interest to dominate. The Member's increased "freedom" does not, of course, make his job easier, but it does help to explain why the mounting mass of constituent claims does not result in his functioning more and more in accordance with the Jeffersonian-Jacksonian theories.

Many Members have regarded themselves and have behaved as free agents, enjoying a large range of discretion, guided by their own best judgment, their convictions, and the dictates of conscience. Other Members have acted as delegates of their districts, bound to follow instructions received from or pledges given to their constituents, even when they have conflicted with their own judgment or principles. In actual practice most Representatives have combined both roles with changing circumstances, acting at times as free agents in making decisions on matters on which they were uninstructed, and at other times as delegates with a mandate to follow the wishes of the folks

[18] T. V. Smith, *The Legislative Way of Life* (1940), p. 71. On the legislator as broker, politician, parliamentarian, and party member, see Herman Finer, *The Theory and Practice of Modern Government* (1949), pp. 379–384.
[19] Marver H. Bernstein, *The Job of the Federal Executive* (1958), p. 101.

back home.   At still other times they have acted as brokers seeking compromises between conflicting interests in a system of checks and balances.   In any session of Congress Members have had to make scores of voting decisions both in committee and on the floor.   In so doing they have been influenced, in varying degrees, by the wishes of their constituencies, by their political parties, by the pressures of special interests, and by their own views of the general welfare.   Constituent instructions, personal pledges, party policies, interest group pressures, individual convictions, conceptions of the general welfare: all of these factors have entered in varying proportions into the countless decisions made by Representatives in Congress since 1789.[20]

A recent analysis of the role of the Representative distinguishes between the focus of representation and the style of representation. In undertaking his legislative task the Representative may be guided by the view that legislation should benefit a geographical unit (district, State or Nation), or carry out his party's campaign promises, or favor some special interest group, or support an administrative organization. Each of these "publics" is a possible focus of orientation for the Representative.   As regards his style of representation, he may take either the role of free agent, following his own convictions, or the role of delegate, bound by the instructions of his constituents.[21]

The same analysis identifies three major role types of representatives: the "trustee" who is a free agent and follows his own convictions, principles, judgment, or conscience; the "delegate" who is inclined to consult and follow the instructions of his constituents; and the "politico" who expresses both orientations either simultaneously or serially.[22]   The writers think that, under modern conditions, the legislature has become "an agency for the coordination and integration of diverse social, economic, and political interests" and that "the Representative has become less and less a Delegate and more and more a trustee as the business of government has become more and more intricate and technical." [23]

CONGRESSIONAL VIEWS OF REPRESENTATIVE FUNCTION

The congressional concept of the representative function is reflected in the views expressed by Members themselves down through the years.   In response to criticisms from some of his constituents, Representative Garfield in an open letter set forth his theory of the relations of a Representative to his district.

I believe—

he wrote in 1865—

a representative should get all the light on every matter of public importance that his position enables him to and then speak and vote in such a manner as will, in his judgment, enhance the best interests of his constituents and the whole country.   If the constituency, in reviewing the action of their representative, find him deficient in ability, judgment or integrity they have always the remedy of choosing another in his place.   But while he is in office his course should be guided by his own judgments, based upon the suggestions of his constituents and

    [20] Cf.   Ernest S. Griffith, The American System of Government (1953), ch. 6, "How Congress Makes up its Mind."
    [21] Heinz Eulau et al., "The Role of the Representative," American Political Science Review, September 1959, pp. 742–756.
    [22] Ibid., pp. 749–750.
    [23] Ibid., pp. 750–751.

all other obtainable information.　On no other ground could I have accepted the office I now hold, on no other ground could I continue to hold it.[24]

Seven years later he confided to his diary:

It is a terrible thing to live in fear of their constituents to the extent which many members do.　I would rather be defeated every day in the year than suffer such fear.[25]

Representative Robert Luce of Massachusetts, who sat in the House for 20 years, voiced his mature view of the role of the Representative in 1926 as follows: [26]

The lawmaker is not to be purely an agent, vainly trying to decide what the majority of his principals desire.　He is not to be purely a trustee, making wholly independent decisions, self-conceived and self-sustained.　He is to be both agent and trustee as far as may be.　He is to feel it as much his duty to try to modify in others opinions with which he disagrees, as to try to let his own opinions be modified by the advice of others.　He is to deal fairly both by his constituents and by himself.　Such a man deems it necessary to break with constituency or with party only on those very rare occasions when Judgment must step aside and let Conscience rule.　The great mass of legislation is matter of expediency. Not once in a thousand times is it matter of what is usually thought of as right and wrong.　Only when right and wrong are at stake may the legislator refuse to concede, to compromise, or to yield.

During the 1945 hearings of the La Follette-Monroney committee many members discussed their relations with their constituents.　The general theme was that the people had come to look upon a Congressman not as their representative in Congress but as their errand-boy in Washington.　Some members defended errand-running on the ground that it won friends at home and helped to humanize relations between the people and the Washington bureaucracy.　Other members complained that errand-running left them little time for their primary legislative duties.　They offered a variety of remedies for the problem, of which perhaps the most original was the suggestion of Representative Ramspeck of Georgia that the job be divided in two parts: the legislative part to be handled by elected representatives in Congress, the service function by elected agents before the executive branch of the Government.

After a decade in the House of Representatives, Representative Jerry Voorhis of California disputed the view that Congress should merely echo the voice of the people.

The truly valid conception of "representative government"—

he said—

holds that the people elect their representatives because they expect from those representatives better, more farsighted action than the people as a whole, with their limited access to all the facts, can provide.[27]

Recently Mrs. Coya Knutson of Minnesota responded to a questionnaire on the job, responsibility, and principles of representatives in Congress in part as follows: [28]

Congressmen are elected on the basis of their party and personal principles. These principles govern our judgment and our actions.　It would be impossible to let the various shadings of constituent opinion guide our actions.　We would be stuck on dead center of every issue.　It would be unrealistic to base actions on a numerical average of opinion-letters on various measures.　These do not neces-

[24] Theodore C. Smith, *Life and Letters of James A. Garfield*, vol. I, p. 382.
[25] James A. Garfield, *Diary*, Feb. 19, 1872, in Manuscript Division, Library of Congress.
[26] Robert Luce, *Congress: An Explanation* (1926), pp. 52-53.
[27] Jerry Voorhis, "A Call to Congress To Lead, Not Follow," *New York Times Magazine*, Jan. 25, 1948, p. 12.
[28] *Congressional Record*, June 28, 1958, p. A5889, daily edition.

sarily reflect cross-section opinion as there are many people who never write letters to their Representatives.

There are always times when compromise is necessary—but never compromise with principles. We were elected by the people of our districts. They had to have confidence in us, else we would not have been elected, nor would we continue in office. They have given us the responsibility for making their laws and representing them to our best ability. Exchange of opinion between Congressman and constituent is fundamental to our democratic way of life, but the final decisions have to be ours.

Whether or not a Member should compromise his principles in order to keep his seat in the House is a dilemma that sooner or later faces every politician. Former Senator William Benton of Connecticut put this question to some of his former colleagues and summarized their replies in an article in the *New York Times*. One of the replies came from Representative John Vorys of Ohio, then ranking Republican member of the Foreign Affairs Committee, who said:

I am extremely cautious about calling political decisions moral issues. On the other hand, I think that Congressmen and Senators are expendable rather than indispensable, and no Congressman or Senator should cast a vote he knows is wrong in order to be reelected. It makes no difference whether the wrongness is on a moral, legal, economic, or other issue.[29]

Another reply was that of Representative John W. McCormack of Massachusetts, majority leader of the House, who wrote:

I never place myself mentally in the position of compromising principle and conscience. But there are times when I might harmonize differences in order to make progress, or maintain unity, and then start the journey from there. The extent of "compromise" or "harmonization" depends upon the circumstances of each case, the atmosphere, the strength of the opposition, as well as the support for a measure, and other factors. But sometimes there can be no "compromise" or "harmonization," such as the extension of the Selective Service Act in 1941, three months before Pearl Harbor.[30]

In the course of participating in a reciprocal trade study conducted under the auspices of the Center for International Studies of the Massachusetts Institute of Technology, Lewis A. Dexter interviewed several members of Congress. Subsequently he wrote an article based upon these congressional interviews in which he reached the following conclusions on the ways Congressmen today view representation.[31]

The congressman represents his image of the district or of his constituents, or he fails to do so * * *. In large measure, their personalities, careers, and public images make them choose what they hear and how they interpret it.

The first difference between some congressmen and others is how (consciously or unconsciously) they define their responsibilities * * * their conception of "their professional obligation". A few made explicit and many apparently hold implicit theories of representation * * * derived not from philosophical or academic sources, but from practical experience.

Some members expressed themselves in terms of their obligation to select the right course, regardless of the views of their constituents. * * * Another member said: "My first duty is to get reelected. I'm here to represent my district * * *. This is part of my actual belief as to the function of a congressman. * * *" Another member would see his responsibility on some issues as being almost

    [29] William Benton, "The Big Dilemma: Conscience or Votes," *New York Times Magazine*, Apr. 26, 1959.
    [30] *Ibid.* For two recent senatorial statements on the representative function, see Wayne Morse, "What Do the American People Want From Their Politicians?", James Lecture on Government, University of Illinois, 1951; and Richard L. Neuberger, "Are the People Ahead of Their 'Leaders'?" *New York Times Magazine*, Aug. 23, 1959.
    [31] Lewis Anthony Dexter, "The Representative and His District," *Human Organization*, spring 1957, pp. 2–13.

exclusively to the district. On other issues he would be strongly inclined to emphasize national interest in some form as against district concern.

Congressmen tend to see their obligations as being either to the nation or to their constituency * * *. The congressman'. definition of national interest and responsibility on a particular issue depends in large measure upon his understanding of the facts of a particular issue * * *.

A congressman's conception of his district confirms itself, to a considerable extent, and may constitute a sort of self-fulfilling prophecy * * *. A congressman hears most often from those who agree with him. Some men automatically interpret what they hear to support their own viewpoints * * *.

In more general terms, what congressmen hear and how they interpret what they hear depends on who they are * * *. A congressman's reputation among those who might want to influence him determines in large measure what actually is said to him.

The author cited important instances when congressmen were changed by their districts and concluded that:

It should never be forgotten that most congressmen * * * respect the right of petition. They have a general feeling that everyone should have a right to talk or write to them about any public issues—that's what they're there for. But they aren't as worried about each communication as college professors might expect. They generally feel they have an equal right to disregard the petitioner's point, once it has been courteously received and acknowledged * * *.

CHAPTER 14

RELATIONS WITH THE SENATE

There is a legend that Thomas Jefferson, after his return from France, once asked Washington at breakfast why he had agreed to a second Chamber in Congress. According to the story, Washington asked him: "Why did you pour that tea into your saucer?" "To cool it," Jefferson replied. "Just so," said Washington, "we pour House legislation into the senatorial saucer to cool it."

This anecdote may be apocryphal, but it reflects the expectation of the framers of the Constitution that the actions of the House of Representatives—the direct representatives of the people—might be more "emotional" than those of the Senate whose Members were indirectly elected. The founders intended that the Senate should serve as a council of revision in relation to measures passed by the House, and as a forum where the States would be equally represented. Madison wrote during the Convention that—

I am fully of the opinion that the numerous and immediate representatives of the people composing the House will decidedly predominate in the Government—

and Hamilton said that—

the most popular branch of every government, by being generally the favorite of the people, will be generally a full match, if not an over-match, for every other member of the Government.[1]

Proposals were made in the Federal Convention, both in the Randolph plan and in Pinckney's plan, that the Members of the second branch of the National Legislature be elected by those of the first branch; but they were not adopted.[2] Another suggestion was that of Mr. Wilson who moved that the advice and consent of the House, as well as that of the Senate, be required in the making of treaties. As treaties, he said, were to have the operation of laws, they ought to have the sanction of laws also. But his motion was rejected.[3]

In the Constitution as it was finally adopted and ratified the two branches were linked together in several important respects. They were to share in all legislative powers "herein granted." The House was to have the sole power of impeachment and the Senate the sole power to try all impeachments. All bills for raising revenue were to originate in the House of Representatives, but the Senate might propose or concur with amendments as on other bills. The House claims the exclusive right to originate all general appropriation bills, and does so in practice, but the approval of both Houses is required for appropriation bills to become law. Neither House during a session should adjourn for more than 3 days, nor to any other place, without the consent of the other. Under the 12th amendment (1804) the electoral count takes place at a joint session of the two Houses on

---

1 George H. Haynes, *The Senate of the United States* (1938), vol. 11, p. 999.
2 Madison's *Journal of the Federal Convention* (1893), pp. 61, 65.
3 *Ibid.*, p. 680.

the 6th day of January following every meeting of the electors. The President of the United States is not elected directly by the people, but by electors in the several States who meet on a prescribed day and cast their votes for President and Vice President, respectively, in the manner directed by the Constitution. Certificates of the votes cast are forwarded by registered mail to the President of the Senate in Washington.

Representatives and Senators stand on an equal footing under the Constitution in that they receive compensation for their services which, in practice, has been the same for both groups; are bound by oath or affirmation to support the Constitution; are privileged from arrest during their attendance at sessions of their respective Chambers, and in going to and returning from the same, except in case of treason, felony, or breach of the peace; and may not be questioned in any other place for any speech or debate in either House. They are also subject to the same prohibitions against holding any office under the United States or being appointed to any civil office which has been created or whose emoluments have been increased during their terms or serving as a presidential elector or engaging in insurrection or rebellion against the United States or giving aid or comfort to its enemies.

INTERCAMERAL COMITY

Except for joint and conference committees, the passage of bills and joint and concurrent resolutions, and joint sessions for special occasions, the two Houses of Congress generally operate independently of each other. Comity, courtesy, and mutual deference customarily characterize their relations. Jefferson in his *Manual* early laid down the rule that debate and proceedings in one House are not to be noticed in the other:

It is a breach of order in debate to notice what has been said on the same subject in the other House, or the particular votes or majorities on it there; because the opinion of each House should be left to its own independency, not to be influenced by the proceedings of the other; and the quoting them might beget reflections leading to a misunderstanding between the two Houses.[4]

This rule of parliamentary law, when invoked, is usually followed in the House of Representatives. Reference to debates or votes on the same subject in the Senate, or to the action or probable action of the Senate, or to its methods of procedure, as bearing on the course to be taken on a pending matter has always been held a breach of order in the House. It is, however, permissible to refer to proceedings in the other House generally, provided the reference does not contravene the principles of the rule. But a Member may not in House debate read the record of speeches and votes of Senators in such a way as might be expected to lead to recriminations.

Although the Senate may be referred to properly in debate, discussion of its functions, criticism of its acts, reference to a Senator in terms of personal criticism, even anonymously or complimentarily, or reading a paper making such criticism is out of order in the House. This inhibition extends to comment on actions outside the Senate. After examination by a committee a speech reflecting on the character of the Senate was ordered stricken from the *Record* on the ground that it tended to create "unfriendly conditions between the two bodies

---

[4] Jefferson's *Manual of Parliamentary Practice*, sec. XVII.

* * * obstructive of wise legislation and little short of a public calamity."[5] But where a Representative has been assailed in the Senate, he has been permitted to explain his own conduct and motives, without bringing the whole controversy into discussion or assailing a Senator. Resolutions relating to breaches of these principles are entertained in the House as questions of privilege.[6]

Jefferson's *Manual* also prescribes that—

neither House can exercise any authority over a Member or officer of the other, but should complain to the House of which he is, and leave the punishment to them.

In a notable instance in which a Member of the House had assaulted a Senator in the Senate Chamber for words spoken in debate, the Senate examined the breach of privilege and transmitted its report to the House, which punished the Member. But where certain Members of the House, in a published letter, sought to influence the vote of a Senator in an impeachment trial, the House declined to consider the matter as a breach of privilege.

According to Jefferson, preventing expressions offensive to the other House is the duty of the Speaker:

Where the complaint is of words disrespectfully spoken by a Member of another House, it is difficult to obtain punishment, because of the rules supposed necessary to be observed (as to the immediate noting down of words) for the security of Members. Therefore it is the duty of the House, and more particularly of the Speaker, to interfere immediately, and not to permit expressions to go unnoticed which may give a ground of complaint to the other House, and introduce proceedings and mutual accusations between the two Houses, which can hardly be terminated without difficulty and disorder.

In the House of Representatives this rule of parliamentary law is considered as binding on the Chair.

CONTRASTS IN POLITICAL CONTROL

The relations between the two branches of Congress down through the decades have also been affected by their political complexion. During the 19th century, when Senators were elected by the State legislatures, there were numerous occasions when opposing political parties controlled the two Houses: a situation that tended to make for legislative deadlocks. Between 1854 and 1916 there were 10 Congresses in which one party controlled the House of Representatives and the other party controlled the Senate. For example, in 1854, the Democratic percent of the two-party membership of the House was 43.5, and of the Senate 73.7. In 1890 the situation was reversed when the Democrats had 72.4 percent of the two-party membership of the House and 45.3 percent of the Senate. Since 1913, however, when Senators have been directly elected by the people of the several States, the same political party has controlled both Houses of every Congress except the 72d, and there has been a much closer correspondence in the measure of their majority in the two Chambers than was normally the case before 1913.[7]

Behind the nominal control of Congress by the same political party in recent decades, however, have been internal cleavages in both

---

[5] *Hinds' Precedents of the House of Representatives* 5129.

[6] *Rules and Manual of the House of Representatives* (1951), secs. 371–372. See also *Congressional Record*, Sept. 27, 1951, pp. 12516–12517, and 8 *Cannon's Precedents of the House of Representatives* 2516.

[7] For party divisions of the Senate and House of Representatives from 1855 (34th Cong.) to 1947–49 (80th Cong.), see Louis H. Bean, *How to Predict Elections* (1948), p. 189, table 10.

parties and the frequent control of the legislative process by bi-partisan coalitions in both Houses.   Fundamental divisions between liberals and conservatives have characterized both congressional parties for many years and have produced situations in which the balance of power in both Chambers has been in the hands of moderate Republican-Southern Democratic coalitions that have largely domi-nated the National Legislature during the past quarter century. Many major measures of the Roosevelt, Truman, and Eisenhower administrations have depended for their passage upon coalition support.   The relations between the House and the Senate in recent times have thus been marked by the collaboration of conservative coalitions in both Chambers.   Bipartisan combinations in Congress have often supported the foreign policy and moderate domestic pro-grams of the President and offset the hazards implicit in periods of divided Government.

The irregular movement of political tides has not only produced political contrasts between the House and the Senate in days gone by, but also within State delegations.   It has frequently happened in the course of congressional history that one political party has dominated the House delegation from a particular State whose Senators belonged to the opposite party.   In the 86th Congress, for example, seven of the eight Representatives from Kentucky were Democrats, but both Senators—John Sherman Cooper and Thruston B. Morton—were Republicans.   Another example from the same Congress was the Maryland delegation both of whose Senators were Republicans and all of whose Representatives were Democrats.

JOINT MACHINERY

Under a bicameral legislative system like ours the process of law-making is a dual one in that all bills must run the gauntlet of both Houses and win the approval of each.   In view of the differences between the two Chambers in their politics, tenure, and membership, the possibility of their arriving independently at identical conclusions on legislative measures is quite remote.   Obviously, therefore, some machinery and methods of cooperation had to be devised to avoid deadlock and impasse in the performance of congressional functions.

Several devices and procedures have been developed over the years to facilitate joint action.   The principal mechanisms for the meshing of the legislative gears have been the joint committee and the con-ference committee.   Congress has also made more or less use of joint hearings and joint staffs, of joint and concurrent resolutions, of joint rules and joint sessions.   The introduction of "companion bills" has also facilitated joint action.

JOINT COMMITTEES

Joint committees have been used at intervals from the earliest days of the Republic, mainly for ceremonial and routine administra-tive purposes and for the conduct of investigations.   The 1st Congress set up select joint committees to prepare conference rules, choose chaplains, and arrange for the inauguration of President Washington, for the assignment of space in the Capitol building, and for fixing a time for adjournment.   Henry Clay used a joint committee in 1821 to consummate the Missouri Compromise. Joint committees flourished during the Civil War and Reconstruction period when they were formed to investigate the conduct of the war, emancipation and reconstruction, retrenchment and southern outrages, and the condition of the Indian tribes. During the 54th Congress the subjects of charities in the District of Columbia and free alcohol in the arts were referred to joint committees. More recent examples of their use have been on revision of the laws (1907), on the Ballinger-Pinchot controversy (1910), to investigate short-term rural credits (1920), veterans' benefits (1932), governmental reorganization (1937), Federal expenditures (1941—), the organization of Congress (1945–1946), the economic report (1946—), atomic energy (1947—), and defense production (1950—). And Congress has long used joint standing committees on enrolled bills (1789), the library (1806), printing (1846), and the disposition of executive papers (1889).

Since 1945 there has been a noteworthy increase in the use of joint committees for purposes of study, investigation, and oversight. Eight such committees have been created in recent years. The Atomic Energy Act of 1946 established a joint committee of 18 Members to "make continuing studies of the activities of the Atomic Energy Commission and of problems relating to the development, use, and control of atomic energy." The Employment Act of 1946 set up a joint committee of 14 Members to prepare an annual report "containing its findings and recommendations with respect to each of the main recommendations made by the President in the Economic Report * * *." The Labor-Management Relations Act of 1947 charged a joint committee of 14 Members to investigate the entire field of labor-management relations. The Economic Cooperation Act of 1948 created a joint "watchdog" committee of 10 Members "to make a continuous study of the programs of the United States economic assistance to foreign countries, and to review the progress achieved in the execution and administration of such programs." The Defense Production Act of 1950 directed a joint committee of 10 Members "to make a continuous study of the programs authorized by the * * * Act * * *, and to review the progress achieved in the execution and administration of such programs." A Joint Committee on Indian Administration was set up in 1950, another on Immigration and Nationality was established in 1952, and a Joint Committee on the District of Columbia metropolitan problems was created in 1959.

Most of these committees were assigned monumental tasks and were granted ample funds; they employed competent expert staffs and engaged in a wide variety of important activities; they published valuable reports and achieved substantial results. Only the Joint Committee on Atomic Energy was given legislative authority. The Joint Committee on Foreign Economic Cooperation was terminated on August 31, 1950, after a varied career. The Joint Committee on Labor-Management Relations functioned only during the 80th Congress, but its work was continued in a limited fashion by a subcommittee of the Senate Committee on Labor and Public Welfare. Eleven joint committees were in existence during the 86th Congress and had a combined membership of 110.

Each of these joint committees was composed of an equal number of Members from the two Houses, except that the Joint Committee on Federal Expenditures included the Secretary of the Treasury and the Director of the Budget. Some of the new joint committees are popularly known as "watchdog committees," because they have been set up to supervise administrative developments in such fields as atomic energy and defense production. Others are research and study groups in their respective fields. They have highly competent staffs and have provided many valuable and informative reports. The Joint Committees on Atomic Energy and the Economic Report have been especially successful as joint ventures, perhaps because they have paid special attention to their House Members by holding committee meetings on the House side, rotating their chairmanships, and sometimes selecting Representatives as chairmen of their subcommittees.

The postwar achievements of joint congressional committees have led to suggestions for even greater use of this device as a means of intercameral cooperation, to minimize the use of conference committees, and as "watchdogs" of the administration. Greater use of joint committees was the most favored proposal in replies by Members of Congress to a 1950 questionnaire on congressional reorganization.[8] Representative Monroney of Oklahoma thought that a good case could be made for the establishment of the joint statutory committees on atomic energy, the Economic Report, and the European recovery program. But he felt that the most rigid tests should be applied to the creation of any more joint groups beyond those three. "Otherwise," he said, "the committee structure of the House and Senate will be badly confused again with duplicating and overlapping statutory joint committees." [9]

Joint committees have some obvious advantages. With the rising burden of the public business, they are more economical of the time and energy of busy legislators and administrators, substituting a single inquiry for two separate investigations. Moreover, they accelerate the legislative process—an important consideration in periods of national emergency. The joint committee device also helps to maintain coordinate equality with the executive branch by preventing it from playing one House off against the other. Furthermore, when measures are matured by joint action in this way, differences between the Houses are not so likely to arise and require subsequent adjustment in conference. For these reasons joint committees are widely and successfully used by American State legislatures and have been commended in recent times for more frequent use by Congress as well.

In actual practice, however, the House and Senate seldom cooperate in this manner on major matters of public policy, so jealous are the two Houses of their independence and prerogatives. The question of which House shall supply the chairman was usually answered in favor of the Senate, with the lower House naming a vice chairman. However, the Joint Standing Committee on Internal Revenue Taxation customarily elects a chairman and vice chairman annually, alternating these offices between the chairman of the House Ways and Means Committee and the chairman of the Senate Finance Committee—a happy solution of this question and an example recently followed by the Joint Committees on Atomic Energy, the Economic Report, and Defense Production.

[8] Hearings on the Organization and Operation of Congress, June 1951, p. 7.
[9] Hearings on Evaluation of Legislative Reorganization Act of 1946, February 1948, p. 82.

CONFERENCE COMMITTEES

One of the most important pieces of congressional machinery is the conference committee. As noted above, it is used to adjust differences between the Senate and the House of Representatives that arise when a bill or resolution does not pass both Houses in identical form, and neither House is willing to yield to the other. Growing out of early English parliamentary practice, the conference committee system is an evolutionary product whose principal threads were woven on the loom of congressional practice into a unified pattern by the middle of the 19th century.

By 1852—

wrote Ada McCown—

the customs of presenting identical reports from the committees of conference in both Houses, of granting high privilege to these conference reports, of voting upon the conference report as a whole and permitting no amendment of it, of keeping secret the discussions carried on in the meetings of the conference committee, had become established in American parliamentary practice.[10]

Conference committees are composed of the senior members of the committees or subcommittees in charge of bills that the Houses have disagreed upon, appointed by the presiding officers of House and Senate (with the latter's approval) for the purpose of adjusting differences between bills they have passed. They vary in size from three to nine members from each House, but do not necessarily have an equal number of Senators and Representatives. The Senator first named usually serves as chairman; both parties are represented, with the majority party having the larger number; the members from each House vote separately on all questions; and a majority from each House must sign the conference report. Their proceedings are secret and unrecorded, affording protection from both external and internal pressures; and their jurisdiction is limited to the differences in the forms in which the same bill has passed both Houses. Conferees are not authorized to delete matter agreed to by both Houses or to include new matter. However, section 135 of the Legislative Reorganization Act provided that—

(a) In any case in which a disagreement to an amendment in the nature of a substitute has been referred to conferees, it shall be in order for the conferees to report a substitute on the same subject matter; but they may not include in the report matter not committed to them by either House. They may, however, include in their report in any such case matter which is a germane modification of subjects in disagreement.

(b) In any case in which the conferees violate subsection (a), the conference report shall be subject to a point of order.

This device has been used by every Congress since 1789. Most important legislation goes through the conference closet and is there revised, sometimes beyond recognition, by the all-powerful conferees or "managers," as they are styled. Of the 217 public laws enacted by the 2d session of the 82d Congress, for example, 90 went through conference; of these, 13 were appropriation bills.

A large body of law and practice has developed over the years governing conference procedure and reports, which operate under the limitations of a code of rules that occupies 16 pages of the Senate

---

[10] Ada C. McCown, *The Congressional Conference Committee* (1927), pp. 254-255.

Manual, 14 pages of the House *Manual,* and 22 pages of *Cannon's Procedure.*

From the outset the conference committee has been a medium of continuous struggle for legislative supremacy between the House of Representatives and the Senate. Here behind the legislative scenes many decisive battles of congressional history have been waged, lasting from a few hours to many weeks. Appropriation bills, for example, have always been sent to conference where the practice has long been to settle for sums somewhere between the upper and lower grants proposed by the two Houses. Intercameral conflicts have customarily been compromised in conference, sometimes after protracted deadlocks. During the 79th Congress, for example, the conferees on the "full employment" bill locked horns for 2 weeks. In the 81st Congress the Army civil functions supply bill was tied up in conference for 4 months. Occasionally one House has sought to secure the compliance of the other in a certain course of action by attaching legislative "riders" to supply bills, a procedure long outlawed by the rules of the House except for legislative provisions tending to reduce expenditures under the "Holman rule."

JOINT HEARINGS

The authors of the Legislative Reorganization Act of 1946 hoped that the correlation of the committee systems of the House and Senate, for which it provided, would facilitate joint action by the parallel committees. To this end the reorganization bill as it passed the Senate authorized—

the standing committees of the two houses to hold joint hearings with respect to subject matter within their respective jurisdiction.

Although this permissive provision was deleted from the bill on the House side, there have been some instances of joint action by congressional committees in recent years. The foreign affairs committees have held joint meetings on several occasions for consultation purposes with the Secretary of State; their subcommittees have met jointly; and they have also held a few joint hearings on foreign aid and on the mutual defense assistance programs. The Foreign Relations and Armed Services Committees of the Senate held extended joint hearings on Far Eastern policy during 1951. The special small business committees of the two Houses have also held several joint hearings on matters of mutual interest.

Congressional sentiment in favor of joint hearings has mounted with the growing pressure of committee business. A dozen witnesses who testified on the subject at hearings before the Senate Expenditures Committee in June 1951 strongly advocated joint hearings on identical or similar bills as a means of saving the time of witnesses, printing costs, and the repetition of testimony. Joint hearings followed by separate committee action, it was urged, would not trespass upon committee prerogatives.

I think we could save a tremendous amount of time, a lot of money, and a lot of wear and tear on the heads of various departments—

said Representative Multer, of New York—

if we had joint hearings. I would make it mandatory to hold public hearings hearings jointly so that * * * they would be held jointly by the twin committees of both Houses with the right on the part of either House or either committee to require additional public hearings, conditioned only upon their giving notice to the other * * *.[11]

Similar views were expressed by Representatives Holifield, of California, and Furcolo, of Massachusetts.

On the other hand, some Members are dubious of the practicability of joint action by the parallel committees of Congress. Their doubts were well expressed by Dr. Francis Wilcox, former chief of staff of the Senate Committee on Foreign Relations, who spoke out of much practical experience. He said:

> One of the main difficulties with joint hearings is that our calendars simply do not coincide. Take this session, for example, the Senate committee has been busy with the troops-for-Europe issue, and with the issues that have stemmed from the recall of General MacArthur. The House committee has not seen fit to launch a study of either one of those major problems. As a result, it would have been difficult for us to cooperate because they have been busy on other matters. Moreover, I am not sure that joint meetings would save much time, because if you add 25 members to 13 members, you come up with a total of 38 and that increases the questioning period time. I am not sure that joint sessions under such circumstances will in the long run save time. Furthermore, our committee members do not seem to like it and to my mind that is probably the most conclusive argument that I can put forward.[12]

JOINT STAFFS

Congress has also had some experience with joint staffing through the staffs of its joint committees. The most noteworthy current examples of such joint staffs are those serving the Joint Committees on Taxation, Atomic Energy, and the Economic Report. The Joint Committee on Internal Revenue Taxation functions in large part through its staff of 25 economists, statisticians, attorneys, and clerks under the direction of Colin F. Stam, chief of staff. Created by statute in 1926 and appointed on merit, this joint staff has rendered invaluable service to the members of the Senate Finance Committee and the House Committee on Ways and Means. Its success has inspired proposals to equip the Committees on Appropriations with a similar joint staff.

Aside from joint staffing, there has been some joint action through the collaboration of the staffs of the corresponding committees of the two houses. To a limited extent they consult with each other individually and collectively and exchange information and memorandums. But it is difficult for them to engage in joint research on the same problems or to collaborate in the preparation of studies and reports because of the varying agenda of their committees, surviving disparities in their jurisdiction, and differing methods of operation and perspective among their members. With parallel committees in the two chambers considering the same problems at different times, it is difficult for their staffs to work together simultaneously on the same schedule or to integrate their research.

---

[11] Hearings on the Organization and Operation of Congress, June 1951, p. 507.
[12] *Ibid.*, pp. 72-73.

PROCEDURAL LINKS

In addition to the joint mechanisms described in the foregoing pages, the House and Senate have also been linked together by joint and concurrent resolutions, joint rules, joint sessions, and joint attendance at impeachment trials.

A *joint resolution* is a bill so far as the legislative process is concerned. All joint resolutions except those proposing constitutional amendments are sent to the President for approval and have the full force of law. They are used for incidental, unusual, or interior legislative purposes such as extending the thanks of the Nation to individuals, the invitation to Lafayette to visit America, the welcome to Kossuth, and notice to a foreign government of the abrogation of a treaty. Joint resolutions have also been used to declare our intervention in Cuba, to correct an error in an existing law, to elect managers for the national Soldiers' Home, and to make special appropriations for minor and incidental purposes.

Congress has developed the *concurrent resolution* as a means of expressing facts, principles, opinions, and the purposes of the two houses. Joint committees are authorized by this form of resolution which is binding on neither house until agreed to by both, and which is not sent to the President for approval. It was a concurrent resolution, for example, which early in 1945 launched the joint La Follette-Monroney inquiry into the defects and improvement of our National Legislature.

The two Houses of Congress early adopted *joint rules* to govern their procedure in matters requiring concurrent action, but they were abrogated in 1876 after a continuous existence of 87 years. Their most useful provisions continue to be observed, however, in practice.

Finally, *joint sessions* of Congress are held in the Hall of the House from time to time to hear the President deliver a message in person or for memorial or ceremonial purposes. Occasionally the House of Representatives or its managers have attended impeachment trials in the Senate Chamber. It did not attend at all in the trials of Blount, Swayne, and Archbald; and after attending at the answer of Secretary of War Belknap, the House decided that it would be represented for the remainder of the trial by its managers alone. At the trial of President Andrew Johnson the House, in Committee of the Whole, attended throughout the trial, but this was exceptional.

We may conclude this description of the joint machinery of Congress by saying that, by and large, there has been little formal cooperation between the House and Senate in the early formulative stages of the legislative process; but very considerable collaboration via conference committees in the concluding stages. Behind the scenes over the long years, however, there has been much friendly and informal intercourse between their members and staffs, and among the members of State delegations in the two Chambers, as well as a spirit of mutual respect and comity, which have belied superficial signs of separatism.

APPENDIXES

APPENDIX A
Speakers of the House of Representatives

Congress	Speaker	State	Congress	Speaker	State
1st	Frederick A. C. Muhlenberg.	Pennsylvania.	44th	Milton Saylor	Ohio (pro tempore).
2d	Jonathan Trumbull	Connecticut.		Samuel J. Randall	Pennsylvania.
3d	Frederick A. C. Muhlenberg.	Pennsylvania.	45th	----do	Do.
			46th	----do	Do.
4th	Jonathan Dayton	New Jersey.	47th	J. Warren Keifer	Ohio.
5th	----do	Do.	48th	John G. Carlisle	Kentucky.
	George Dent	Maryland.	49th	----do	Do.
6th	Theodore Sedgwick	Massachusetts.	50th	----do	Do.
7th	Nathaniel Macon	North Carolina.	51st	Thomas B. Reed	Maine.
			52d	Charles F. Crisp	Georgia.
8th	----do	Do.	53d	----do	Do.
9th	----do	Do.	54th	Thomas B. Reed	Maine.
10th	Joseph B. Varnum	Massachusetts.	55th	----do	Do.
11th	----do	Do.	56th	David B. Henderson	Iowa.
12th	Henry Clay	Kentucky.	57th	----do	Do.
13th	----do	Do.	58th	Joseph G. Cannon	Illinois.
	Langdon Cheves	South Carolina.	59th	----do	Do.
			60th	----do	Do.
14th	Henry Clay	Kentucky.	61st	----do	Do.
15th	----do	Do.	62d	Champ Clark	Missouri.
16th	----do	Do.	63d	----do	Do.
	John W. Taylor	New York.	64th	----do	Do.
17th	Philip P. Barbour	Virginia.	65th	----do	Do.
18th	Henry Clay	Kentucky.	66th	Frederick H. Gillett	Massachusetts.
19th	John W. Taylor	New York.			
20th	Andrew Stevenson	Virginia.	67th	----do	Do.
21st	----do	Do.	68th	----do	Do.
22d	----do	Do.	69th	Nicholas Longworth	Ohio.
23d	----do	Do.	70th	----do	Do.
	John Bell	Tennessee.	71st	----do	Do.
24th	James K. Polk	Do.	72d	John N. Garner	Texas.
25th	----do	Do.	73d	Henry T. Rainey	Illinois.
26th	Robert M. T. Hunter	Virginia.	74th	Joseph W. Byrns	Tennessee.
27th	John White	Kentucky.		William B. Bankhead	Alabama.
28th	John W. Jones	Virginia.	75th	----do	Do.
29th	John W. Davis	Indiana.	76th	----do	Do.
30th	Robert C. Winthrop	Massachusetts.		Sam Rayburn	Texas.
31st	Howell Cobb	Georgia.	77th	----do	Do.
32d	Linn Boyd	Kentucky.	78th	----do	Do.
33d	----do	Do.	79th	----do	Do.
34th	Nathaniel P. Banks	Massachusetts.	80th	Joseph W. Martin, Jr	Massachusetts.
35th	James L. Orr	South Carolina.	81st	Sam Rayburn	Texas.
36th	William Pennington	New Jersey.	82d	----do	Do.
37th	Galusha A. Grow	Pennsylvania.	83d	Joseph W. Martin, Jr	Massachusetts.
38th	Schuyler Colfax	Indiana.			
39th	----do	Do.	84th	Sam Rayburn	Texas.
40th	----do	Do.	85th	----do	Do.
	Theodore M. Pomeroy	New York.	86th	----do	Do.
41st	James G. Blaine	Maine.	87th	----do	Do.
42d	----do	Do.		John W. McCormack	Massachusetts.
43d	----do	Do.			
44th	Michael C. Kerr	Indiana.	88th	----do	Do.
	Samuel S. Cox	New York (pro tempore).	89th	----do	Do.

APPENDIX B
Parliamentarians of the House of Representatives

Congress	Year	Parliamentarian	Congress	Year	Parliamentarian
70th [1]	1927	Lehr Fess.	80th	1947	Lewis Deschler
71st	1929	Lewis Deschler.	81st	1949	Do.
72d	1931	Do.	82d	1951	Do.
73d	1933	Do.	83d	1953	Do.
74th	1935	Do.	84th	1955	Do.
75th	1937	Do.	85th	1957	Do.
76th	1939	Do.	86th	1959	Do.
77th	1941	Do.	87th	1961	Do.
78th	1943	Do.	88th	1963	Do.
79th	1945	Do.	89th	1965	Do.

[1] Prior to the 70th Congress duties of the Parliamentarian were performed by the "Clerk at the Speaker's Table."

Source: Congressional Directory, 70th-89th Congresses.

APPENDIX C

Chaplains of the House of Representatives of the United States

Chaplains	Denomination	Date service began [1]
Rev. William Lynn	Presbyterian	Mar. 4, 1789
Rev. Samuel Blair	----do	Jan. 4, 1790
Rev. Ashbel Green	----do	Nov. 5, 1792
Rev. Thomas Lyell	Methodist	Nov. 17, 1800
Rev. W. Parkinson	Baptist	Dec. 7, 1801
Rev. James Laurie	Presbyterian	Nov. 5, 1804
Rev. P. Elliott	----do	Dec. 1, 1806
Rev. O. B. Brown	Baptist	Oct. 26, 1807
Rev. Jesse Lee	Methodist	May 22, 1809
Rev. N. Sneathen	----do	Nov. 4, 1811
Rev. Jesse Lee	----do	Nov. 2, 1812
Rev. O. B. Brown	Baptist	Sept. 19, 1814
Rev. S. H. Cone	----do	Dec. 4, 1815
Rev. B. Allison	----do	Dec. 2, 1816
Rev. J. N. Campbell	Presbyterian	Nov. 18, 1820
Rev. Jared Sparks	Unitarian	Dec. 3, 1821
Rev. J. Breckenridge	Presbyterian	Dec. 2, 1822
Rev. H. B. Bascom	Methodist	Dec. 1, 1823
Rev. Reuben Post	Presbyterian	Dec. 6, 1824
Rev. Ralph Gurley	----do	Dec. 6, 1830
Rev. Reuben Post	----do	Dec. 5, 1831
Rev. William Hammett	Methodist	Dec. 3, 1832
Rev. Thomas H. Stockton	----do	Dec. 2, 1833
Rev. Edward Dunlap Smith	Presbyterian	Dec. 1, 1834
Rev. Thomas H. Stockton	Methodist	Dec. 7, 1835
Rev. Oliver C. Comstock	Baptist	Dec. 5, 1836
Rev. Septimus Tustan	Presbyterian	Sept. 4, 1837
Rev. Levi R. Reese	Methodist	Dec. 4, 1837
Rev. Joshua Bates	Congregationalist	Dec. 2, 1839
Rev. T. W. Braxton	Baptist	Dec. 7, 1840
Rev. J. W. French	Episcopalian	May 31, 1841
Rev. John N. Maffit	Methodist	Dec. 6, 1841
Rev. J. S. Tiffany	Episcopalian	Dec. 5, 1842
Rev. J. S. Tinsley	Baptist	Dec. 4, 1843
Rev. William M. Daily	Methodist	Dec. 4, 1844
Rev. William H. Milburn	----do	Dec. 1, 1845
Rev. W. S. S. Sprole	Presbyterian	Dec. 7, 1846
Rev. R. R. Gurley	----do	Dec. 6, 1847
Rev. L. F. Morgan	Methodist	Dec. 1, 1851
Rev. James Gallagher	Presbyterian	Dec. 6, 1852
Rev. W. H. Milburn	Methodist	Dec. 5, 1853
Rev. T. H. Stockton	Methodist	July 4, 1861
Rev. W. H. Channing	Unitarian	Dec. 7, 1863
Rev. Charles B. Boynton	Congregationalist	Dec. 4, 1865
Rev. J. G. Butler	Presbyterian	Mar. 4, 1869
Rev. S. L. Townsend	Episcopalian	Dec. 6, 1875
Rev. John Poise	Methodist	Oct. 15, 1877
Rev. W. P. Harrison	----do	Dec. 3, 1877
Rev. Frederick D. Power	Christian	Dec. 5, 1881
Rev. John S. Lindsay	Episcopalian	Dec. 3, 1883
Rev. W. H. Milburn	Methodist	Dec. 7, 1885
Rev. Samuel W. Haddaway	----do	Aug. 7, 1893
Rev. Edward B. Bagby	Christian	Dec. 4, 1893
Rev. Henry N. Couden	Universalist	Dec. 2, 1895
Rev. James Shera Montgomery	Methodist	Apr. 11, 1921
Rev. Bernard Braskamp	Presbyterian	Jan. 3, 1950

[1] Date of beginning of session of Congress in which each Chaplain first served; not necessarily the date of his appointment.

NOTE.—From 1855 until 1861 the House of Representatives did not elect regular Chaplains. Instead, the different members of the District of Columbia clergy took turns in opening each daily session with a prayer and in preaching on Sundays. The 37th Congress, meeting in 1861, returned to former practice of choosing a Chaplain.

Source: Congressional Record, Aug. 14, 1957 (A6672–6673).

APPENDIX D

Floor leaders of the House of Representatives, 1901–65 [1]

Congress	Dates	Majority leader	Minority leader
57th	1901–3	Sereno E. Payne, [2] New York (Republican).	James D. Richardson, [3] Tennessee (Democrat).
58th	1903–5	....do [3]	John Sharp Williams, [4] Mississippi (Democrat).
59th	1905–7	....do [3]	Do. [3]
60th	1907–9	....do [3]	John Sharp Williams, [3] Mississippi (Democrat); Champ Clark, [5] Missouri (Democrat).
61st	1909–11	....do [3]	Champ Clark, Missouri (Democrat).
62d	1911–13	Oscar W. Underwood, Alabama (Democrat).	James R. Mann, Illinois (Republican).
63d	1913–15	....do	Do.
64th	1915–17	Claude Kitchin, North Carolina (Democrat).	Do.
65th	1917–19	....do	Do.
66th	1919–21	Franklin W. Mondell, Wyoming (Republican).	Champ Clark, Missouri (Democrat).
67th	1921–23	....do	Claude Kitchin, North Carolina (Democrat).
68th	1923–25	Nicholas Longworth, Ohio (Republican).	Finis J. Garrett, Tennessee (Democrat).
69th	1925–27	John Q. Tilson, Connecticut (Republican).	Do.
70th	1927–29	....do	Do.
71st	1929–31	....do	John N. Garner, Texas (Democrat).
72d	1931–33	Henry T. Rainey, Illinois (Democrat)	Bertrand H. Snell, New York (Republican).
73d	1933–35	Joseph W. Byrns, Tennessee (Democrat).	Do.
74th	1935–37	William B. Bankhead, Alabama (Democrat).	Do.
75th	1937–39	Sam Rayburn, Texas (Democrat)	Do.
76th	1939–41	Sam Rayburn, Texas (Democrat); John W. McCormack, [6] Massachusetts (Democrat).	Joseph W. Martin, Jr., Massachusetts, (Republican).
77th	1941–43	John W. McCormack, Massachusetts (Democrat).	Do.
78th	1943–45	....do	Do.
79th	1945–47	....do	Do.
80th	1947–49	Charles A. Halleck, Indiana (Republican).	Sam Rayburn, Texas (Democrat).
81st	1949–51	John W. McCormack, Massachusetts (Democrat).	Joseph W. Martin, Jr., Massachusetts (Republican).
82d	1951–53	....do	Do.
83d	1953–55	Charles A. Halleck, Indiana (Republican).	Sam Rayburn, Texas (Democrat).
84th	1955–57	John W. McCormack, Massachusetts (Democrat).	Joseph W. Martin, Jr., Massachusetts (Republican).
85th	1957–59	....do	Do.
86th	1959–61	....do	Charles A. Halleck, Indiana (Republican).
87th	1961	....do	Do.
	1962–	Carl Albert, Oklahoma (Democrat)	
88th	1963–64	....do	Do.
89th	1965–	....do	Gerald R. Ford, Michigan (Republican).

[1] Fragmentary party records have not permitted the compilation of a complete list of the floor leaders of the House during the 19th century.

[2] Sereno E. Payne was first appointed majority floor leader in the 56th Congress by Speaker Henderson. The Speaker made few changes in his appointments in the 57th Congress, and the bulk of evidence indicates that Congressman Payne continued in this post under Speaker Cannon through the 61st Congress. De Alva Stanwood Alexander, *History and Procedure of the House of Representatives*, 1916, pp. 110, 127. Brown, George R., *The Leadership of Congress*, 1922, pp. 158, 168. Clark, Champ, *My Quarter Century of American Politics*, 1920, vol. 2, p. 339.

[3] Clark, Champ, *My Quarter Century of American Politics*, 1920, vol. 2, p. 271. Stealey, O. O., *Twenty Years in the Press Gallery*, 1906, p. 419.

[4] Gwinn, William R., *Uncle Joe Cannon, Archfoe of Insurgency*, 1957, p. 97.

[5] Champ Clark was elected to fill out the uncompleted term of John S. Williams as minority leader, when Williams was nominated for Senator from Mississippi in 1908. Clark, Champ, *My Quarter Century of American Politics*, 1920, vol. 2, pp. 27–28.

[6] John W. McCormack was elected majority leader on Sept. 16, 1940, to succeed Sam Rayburn.

Source: *Biographical Directory of the American Congress*, 1774–1949, Washington, U.S. Government Printing Office, 1950; *Congressional Directory*, 67th–89th Congresses.

APPENDIX E

Clerks of the House of Representatives, 1789–1965

Congress	Year	Clerk	State
1st	1789	John Beckley	Virginia.
2d	1791	----do	Do.
3d	1793	----do	Do.
4th	1795	----do	Do.
5th	1797	Jonathan W. Condy	Pennsylvania.
6th	1799	John Holt	Do.
7th	1801	John Beckley	Virginia.
8th	1803	----do	Do.
9th	1805	----do	Do.
10th	1807	Patrick Magruder	Maryland.
11th	1809	----do	Do.
12th	1811	----do	Do.
13th	1813	----do	Do.
14th	1815	Thomas Dougherty	Kentucky.
15th	1817	----do	Do.
16th	1819	----do	Do.
17th	1821	Matthew St. Clair Clarke	Pennsylvania.
18th	1823	----do	Do.
19th	1825	----do	Do.
20th	1827	----do	Do.
21st	1829	----do	Do.
22d	1831	----do	Do.
23d	1833	Walter S. Franklin	Do.
24th	1835	----do	Do.
	1837	----do	Do.
25th	1837	Hugh A. Garland (3rd ses.)	Virginia.
26th	1839	----do	Do.
27th	1841	Matthew St. Clair Clarke	Pennsylvania.
28th	1843	Benjamin B. French	New Hampshire.
29th	1845	----do	Do.
30th	1847	Thomas J. Campbell	Tennessee.
31st	1849	Richard M. Young	Illinois.
32d	1851	John W. Forney	Pennsylvania.
33d	1853	----do	Do.
34th	1855	William Cullom	Tennessee.
35th	1857	James C. Allen	Illinois.
36th	1859	John W. Forney	Pennsylvania.
37th	1861	Emerson Etheridge	Tennessee.
38th	1863	Edward McPherson	Pennsylvania.
39th	1865	----do	Do.
40th	1867	----do	Do.
41st	1869	----do	Do.
42d	1871	----do	Do.
43d	1873	----do	Do.
44th	1875	George M. Adams	Kentucky.
45th	1877	----do	Do.
46th	1879	----do	Do.
47th	1881	Edward McPherson	Pennsylvania.
48th	1883	John B. Clark, Jr	Missouri.
49th	1885	----do	Do.
50th	1887	----do	Do.
51st	1889	Edward McPherson	Pennsylvania.
52d	1891	James Kerr	Do.
53d	1893	----do	Do.
54th	1895	Alexander McDowell	Do.
55th	1897	----do	Do.
56th	1899	----do	Do.
57th	1901	----do	Do.
58th	1903	----do	Do.
59th	1905	----do	Do.
60th	1907	----do	Do.
61st	1909	----do	Do.
62d	1911	South Trimble	Kentucky.
63d	1913	----do	Do.
64th	1915	----do	Do.
65th	1917	----do	Do.
66th	1919	William Tyler Page	Maryland.
67th	1921	----do	Do.
68th	1923	----do	Do.
69th	1925	----do	Do.
70th	1927	----do	Do.
71st	1929	----do	Do.
72d	1931	South Trimble	Kentucky.
73d	1933	----do	Do.
74th	1935	----do	Do.
75th	1937	----do	Do.
76th	1939	----do	Do.
77th	1941	----do	Do.
78th	1943	----do	Do.
79th	1945	----do	Do.

APPENDIX E—Continued

Clerks of the House of Representatives, 1789-1965—Continued

Congress	Year	Clerk	State
80th	1947	John Andrews	Massachusetts.
81st	1949	Ralph R. Roberts	Indiana.
82d	1951	____do	Do.
83d	1953	Lyle O. Snader	Illinois.
84th	1955	Ralph R. Roberts	Indiana.
85th	1957	____do	Do.
86th	1959	____do	Do.
87th	1961	____do	Do.
88th	1963	____do	Do.
89th	1965	____do	Do.

Source: Alexander, De Alva Stanwood, "History and Procedure of the House of Representatives," Cambridge, Houghton Mifflin, 1916. Annals of Congress, 1st–18th Congresses. Congressional Globe, 23d–42d Congresses. Congressional Record, 43d–87th Congresses. Congressional Directory, 21st–89th Congresses.

APPENDIX F

Sergeants at Arms of the House of Representatives

Congress	Year	Sergeant at Arms	Congress	Year	Sergeant at Arms
1st	1789	Joseph Wheaton.	45th	1877	John G. Thompson, Ohio.
2d	1791	Do.	46th	1879	Do.
3d	1793	Do.	47th	1881	George W. Hooker, Vermont.
4th	1795	Do.	48th	1883	John P. Leedom, Ohio.
5th	1797	Do.	49th	1885	Do.
6th	1799	Do.	50th	1887	Do.
7th	1801	Do.	51st	1889	Adoniram J. Holmes, Iowa.
8th	1803	Do.	52d	1891	Samuel S. Yoder, Ohio.
9th	1805	Do.	53d	1893	Herman W. Snow, Illinois.
10th	1807	Thomas Dunn, Maryland.	54th	1895	Benjamin F. Russell, Missouri.
11th	1809	Do.	55th	1897	Do.
12th	1811	Do.	56th	1899	Henry Casson, Wisconsin.
13th	1813	Do.	57th	1901	Do.
14th	1815	Do.	58th	1903	Do.
15th	1817	Do.	59th	1905	Do.
16th	1819	Do.	60th	1907	Do.
17th	1821	Do.	61st	1909	Do.
18th	1823	Do.	62d	1911	U. Stokes Jackson, Indiana.
19th	1825	John Oswald Dunn, District of Columbia.	63d	1913	R. B. Gordon, Ohio.
			64th	1915	Do.
20th	1827	Do.	65th	1917	Do.
21st	1829	Do.	66th	1919	J. G. Rodgers, Pennsylvania.
22d	1831	Do.	67th	1921	·Do.
23d	1833	Thomas B. Randolph, Virginia.	68th	1923	Do.
24th	1835	Roderick Dorsey, Maryland.	69th	1925	Do.
25th	1837	Do.	70th	1927	Do.
26th	1839	Do.	71st	1929	Do.
27th	1841	Eleazor M. Townsend, Connecticut.	72d	1931	Kenneth Romney, Montana.
			73d	1933	Do.
28th	1843	Newton Lane, Kentucky.	74th	1935	Do.
29th	1845	Do.	75th	1937	Do.
30th	1847	Nathan Sargeant, Vermont.	76th	1939	Do.
31st	1849	Adam J. Glossbrenner, Pennsylvania.	77th	1941	Do.
32d	1851	Do.	78th	1943	Do.
			79th	1945	Do.
33d	1853	Do.	80th	1947	William F. Russell, Pennsylvania.
34th	1855	Do.			
35th	1857	Do.	81st	1949	Joseph H. Callahan, Kentucky.
36th	1859	Henry W. Hoffman, Maryland.	82d	1951	Do.
37th	1861	Edward Ball, Virginia.	83d	1953	William R. Bonsell, Pennsylvania.
38th	1863	Nathaniel G. Ordway, New Hampshire.	84th	1955	Zeake W. Johnson, Jr., Tennessee.
39th	1865	Do.			
40th	1867	Do.	85th	1957	Do.
41st	1869	Do.	86th	1959	Do.
42d	1871	Do.	87th	1961	Do.
43d	1873	Do.	88th	1963	Do.
44th	1875	John G. Thompson, Ohio.	89th	1965	Do.

Source: Alexander, De Alva Stanwood, "History and Procedure of the House of Representatives," Cambridge, Houghton Mifflin, 1916. Annals of Congress, 1st–18th Congresses. Congressional Globe, 23d–42d Congresses, Congressional Directory, 21st–89th Congresses.

Appendix G

Doorkeepers of the House of Representatives

Congress	Year	Doorkeeper	Congress	Year	Doorkeeper
1st	1789	Gifford Dalley.	45th	1877	John W. Polk.
2d	1791	Do.	46th	1879	Charles W. Field.
3d	1793	Do.	47th	1881	W. P. Brownlow.
4th	1795	Thomas Claxton.	48th	1883	James G. Wintersmith.
5th	1797	Do.	49th	1885	Do.
6th	1799	Do.	50th	1887	A. B. Hurt.
7th	1801	Do.	51st	1889	Charles W. Adams.
8th	1803	Do.	52d	1891	Do.
9th	1805	Do.	53d	1893	A. B. Hurt.
10th	1807	Do.	54th	1895	W. J. Glenn.
11th	1809	Do.	55th	1897	Do.
12th	1811	Do.	56th	1899	Do.
13th	1813	Do.	57th	1901	Do.
14th	1815	Do.	58th	1903	F. B. Lyon.
15th	1817	Do.	59th	1905	Do.
16th	1819	Do.	60th	1907	Do.
17th	1821	Benjamin Burch.	61st	1909	Do.
18th	1823	Do.	62d	1911	J. J. Sinnott.
19th	1825	Do.	63d	1913	Do.
20th	1827	Do.	64th	1915	Do.
21st	1829	Do.	65th	1917	Do.
22d	1831	Overton Carr.	66th	1919	Bert W. Kennedy.
23d	1833	Do.	67th	1921	Do.
24th	1835	Do.	68th	1923	Do.
25th	1837	Do.	69th	1925	Do.
26th	1839	Joseph Follansbee.	70th	1927	Do.
27th	1841	Do.	71st	1929	Do.
28th	1843	Jesse E. Dow.	72d	1931	Do.
29th	1845	C. S. Whitney.	73d	1933	Joseph J. Sinnott.
30th	1847	Robert E. Horner.	74th	1935	Do.
31st	1849	Do.	75th	1937	Do.
32d	1851	Z. W. McKnew.	76th	1939	Do.
33d	1853	Do.	77th	1941	Do.
34th	1855	Nathan Darling.	78th	1943	Do.
35th	1857	Robert B. Hackney.	79th	1945	Ralph R. Roberts.
36th	1859	George Marston.	80th	1947	M. L. Meletio.
37th	1861	Ira Goodnow.	81st	1949	William M. Miller.
38th	1863	Do.	82d	1951	Do.
39th	1865	Do.	83d	1953	Tom Kennamer.
40th	1867	Charles E. Lippincott.	84th	1955	William M. Miller.
	1868	Otis S. Buxton (3d sess.).	85th	1957	Do.
41st	1869	Do.	86th	1959	Do.
42d	1871	Do.	87th	1961	Do.
43d	1873	Do.	88th	1963	Do.
44th	1875	Lafayette H. Fitzhugh.	89th	1965	Do.

Source: Annals of Congress, 1st–18th Congresses. Congressional Globe, 23d–42d Congresses. Congressional Record, 43d–87th Congresses. Congressional Directory, 21st–89th Congresses.

APPENDIX H

Postmasters of the House of Representatives

Congress	Year	Postmaster	Congress	Year	Postmaster
21st [1]	1829	William J. McCormick.	56th	1899	Joseph C. McElroy.
22d	1831	Do.	57th	1901	Do.
23d	1833	Do.	58th	1903	Do.
24th	1935	Do.	59th	1905	Do.
25th	1837	Do.	60th	1907	Samuel A. Langum.
26th	1939	Do.	61st	1909	Do.
27th	1841	Do.	62d	1911	William M. Dunbar.
28th	1843	Do.	63d	1913	Do.
29th	1845	John Morgan Johnson.	64th	1915	Do.
30th	1847	Do.	65th	1917	Do.
31st	1849	Do.	66th	1919	Frank W. Collier.
32d	1851	Do.	67th	1921	Do.
33d	1853	Do.	68th	1923	Do.
34th	1855	Robert Morris.	69th	1925	Do.
35th	1857	Michael W. Cluskey.	70th	1927	Do.
36th	1859	Josiah M. Lucas.	71th	1929	Do.
37th	1861	William S. King.	72d	1931	Do.
38th	1863	Do.	73d	1933	Finis E. Scott.
39th	1865	Josiah Given.	74th	1935	Do.
40th	1867	William S. King.	75th	1937	Do.
41st	1869	Do.	76th	1939	Do.
42d	1871	Do.	77th	1941	Do.
43d	1873	Henry Sherwood.	78th	1943	Do.
44th	1875	James M. Stuart.	79th	1945	Do.
45th	1877	Do.	80th	1947	Frank W. Collier.
46th	1879	Do.	81st	1949	Finis E. Scott.
47th	1881	Henry Sherwood.	82d	1951	Do.
48th	1883	Lycurgus Dalton.	83d	1953	Beecher Hess.
49th	1885	Do.	84th	1955	H. H. Morris.
50th	1887	Do.	85th	1957	Do.
51st	1889	James L. Wheat.	86th	1959	Do.
52d	1891	J. W. Hathaway.	87th	1961	Do.
53d	1893	Lycurgus Dalton.	88th	1963	Do.
54th	1895	Joseph C. McElroy.	89th	1965	Do.
55th	1897	Do.			

[1] First Congress in which a Postmaster was listed as an officer of the House.

Source: Congressional Globe, 23d–42d Congs.; Congressional Record, 43d–89th Congs.; Congressional Directory, 21st–89th Congresses.

APPENDIX I

Political divisions of the House of Representatives [1]

Congress	Number of Representatives	Delegates	Federalists	Whigs	Republicans	Democrats	Others	Vacant
1st	65		53			12		
2d	69		55			14		
3d	105	1	51			54		
4th	105		46			50		
5th	105		51			54		
6th	105	1	57			48		
7th	105		34			71		
8th	141	1	38			103		
9th	141		29			112		
10th	141	3	31			110		
11th	141	3	46			95		
12th	141	4	36			105		
13th	182	4	67			115		
14th	183	4	61			122		
15th	185	3	57			128		
16th	187	3	42			145		
17th	187	3	58			129		
18th	213	3	72			141		
19th	213	3	79			134		
20th	213	3	85			128		
21st	213	3			71	142		
22d	213	3			83	130		
23d	240	3			93	147		
24th	242	2			98	144		
25th	242	3			115	117	10	
26th	242	3			132	103	6	1
27th	242	3			132	103	6	1
28th	223	3			81	142		
29th	225	2			78	141	6	

See footnote at end of table, p. 216.

APPENDIX I—Continued

Political divisions of the House of Representatives [1]—Continued

Congress	Number of Representatives	Delegates	Federalists	Whigs	Republicans	Democrats	Others	Vacant
30th	227	1		115		108	4	
31st	227	2		111		116		
32d	233	4		88		140	5	
33d	234	6		71		159	4	
34th	234	7			108	83	43	
35th	237	7			92	131	14	
36th	237	5			113	101	23	
37th	178	8			106	42	28	2
38th	183	9			103	80		
39th	191	9			145	46		
40th	193	8			143	49		1
41st	243	9			170	73		
42d	243	10			139	104		
43d	293	10			203	88		2
44th	293	8			107	181	3	2
45th	293	8			137	156		
46th	293	8			128	150	14	1
47th	293	8			152	130	11	
48th	325	8			119	200	6	
49th	325	8			140	182	2	1
50th	325	8			151	170	4	
51st	330	4			173	156	1	
52d	333	4			88	231	14	
53d	357	4			126	220	8	
54th	357	4			246	104	7	
55th	357	3			206	134	16	1
56th	357	3			185	163	9	
57th	357	*5			198	153	5	1
58th	386	*5			207	178		1
59th	386	*5			250	136		
60th	386	*5			222	164		
61st	391	*5			219	172		
62d	391	*5			162	228	1	
63d	435	*3			127	290	18	
64th	435	*3			193	231	8	3
65th	435	*3			216	210	9	
66th	435	*3			237	191	7	
67th	435	*3			300	132	1	2
68th	435	*3			225	207	3	
69th	435	*3			247	183	5	
70th	435	*3			237	195	3	
71st	435	*3			267	163	1	4
72d	435	*3			218	216	1	
73d	435	*3			117	313	5	
74th	435	*3			103	322	10	
75th	435	*3			89	333	13	
76th	435	*3			169	262	4	
77th	435	*3			162	267	6	
78th	435	*3			209	222	4	
79th	435	*3			190	243	2	
80th	435	*3			246	188	1	
81st	435	*3			171	263	1	
82d	435	*3			199	234	2	
83d	435	*3			221	213	1	
84th	435	*3			203	232		
85th	435	*3			201	234		
86th	437	**1			153	283		
87th	437	**1			175	262		
88th	435	**1			176	258		1
89th	435	**1			140	295		

[1] Source: DeAlva S. Alexander, History and Procedure of the House of Representatives (1916), pp. 411–12; Factual Campaign Information, Office of the Secretary of the U.S. Senate (1960), p. 18.
*Including Resident Commissioner from Puerto Rico.
**Resident Commissioner from Puerto Rico.